The New Global Oil Market

UNDERSTANDING ENERGY ISSUES IN THE WORLD ECONOMY

EDITED BY Siamack Shojai

PRAEGER

Westport, Connecticut
London

Library of Congress Cataloging-in-Publication Data

The new global oil market : understanding energy issues in the world
  economy / edited by Siamack Shojai.
       p.   cm.
    Includes bibliographical references and index.
    ISBN 0–275–94583–9 (alk. paper)
       1. Petroleum industry and trade.   2. Petroleum products—Prices.
    3. Energy policy—Economic aspects.   I. Shojai, Siamack.
    HD9560.5.N465   1995
    338.2'7282—dc20   94–25960

British Library Cataloguing in Publication Data is available.

Library of Congress Catalog Card Number: 94–25960
ISBN: 0–275–94583–9

First published in 1995

Praeger Publishers, 88 Post Road West, Westport, CT 06881
An imprint of Greenwood Publishing Group, Inc.

Printed in the United States of America

The paper used in this book complies with the
Permanent Paper Standard issued by the National
Information Standards Organization (Z39.48–1984).

10 9 8 7 6 5 4 3 2 1

To
My Uncle Dr. Ezatollah M. Shojai and
My Aunt Margaret Rutonno Shojai

Contents

Part IV   Energy, National Security, and Public Policy Debate

Preface

The end of the Cold War has culminated in the idea of globalization of business, including the oil markets. Rivalry between the superpowers in the last 50 years led to many political and military confrontations that affected the economics of oil markets in an unprecedented way. For example, the Arab-Israeli conflicts in the 1960s led to an oil embargo imposed by Arabic countries that changed the politics as well as the economics of oil markets. In no time, oil became a strategic commodity in the eyes of producers and consumers. In an emerging post-Cold War new world order, the economics and politics of the oil industry will be quite different than what it was earlier. Already, new approaches and mechanisms are under way that will deal with new challenges and old difficulties such as environmental imperatives and the uncertainty of oil prices and availability.

This volume deals with these new challenges facing global oil markets and attempts to provide an authoritative and comprehensive view of the changing global oil markets. Part I provides an informative discussion of global oil reserves, production, and consumption trends. It also presents the latest developments in the areas of oil pricing, futures markets, oil marketing, and refining. Part II deals with the political economy of global oil markets. The historical role of international oil cartels and agencies is also discussed. Global environmental concerns are dealt with in Part III. A thorough discussion of alternative sources of energy and their impact on the environment is presented. Finally, Part IV addresses issues related to energy and national security as well as public policy choices available domestically and internationally.

The views presented in this volume are those of the authors and do not represent the official views of their affiliated organizations. No attempt was made to accept or reject a submitted manuscript based on its orientation or conclusions.

I would like to thank Eileen Casey for her dedication and assistance in the preparation of the manuscript. Erika Pomako and Lauren Mehnert, my research assistants, deserve recognition for their dedication and efforts in this project. Margaret Rotunno has my deepest gratitude for her invaluable editorial assistance. Also, Professor John Mahoney, Professor Kudret Topyan, and three other anonymous professors deserve special thanks for agreeing to serve on the board of referees for this volume. Preparation of this book has been supported by a generous grant from the Capalbo Grant Fund of the School of Business of Manhattan College. Louis F. Capalbo and his family deserve my gratitude for the support they have provided to the project and a previous volume on oil markets.

Introduction

Siamack Shojai

As a student of oil markets since the 1970s, I have been overwhelmed by the abundance of material published about oil. However, the joy of having access to ample resources has been tainted by the dispersion of the material. To address this need, I have edited this comprehensive, succinct, and authoritative volume on global oil markets.

This volume includes chapters on technical features, pricing and marketing, political economy, environmental issues, national security, and public policy choices and debates in global oil markets. A major and diverse undertaking such as this was felt to require the expertise and experience of a diverse group of scholars to come to a successful conclusion. I have been fortunate and honored to have over 25 experts in the field join me to accomplish this task. We believe that the contents of this book are of compelling interest to both the professional and the academic community.

In Chapter 1, Frank W. Millerd examines proven global oil reserves. He provides a thorough discussion of the meaning of proven reserves, methods of estimating reserves, the geographical distribution of global oil reserves, unconventional oil reserves, and reasons for revising reserve estimates. He concludes that concerns about oil scarcity are not warranted.

An informing overview of current, past, and possible future global and regional oil production is presented by Dr. Millerd in Chapter 2. He highlights the significance of Organization of Petroleum Exporting Countries (OPEC), especially the Middle Eastern oil producers, in global oil markets.

In Chapter 3, Edward T. Dowling and Francis G. Hilton analyze how the rise and retreat of self-sufficiency imperatives affected the demand for oil in the past and how future global energy consumption could be restructured by environmental imperatives.

Chapter 4 presents oil extraction models and empirical evidence regarding pricing tendencies. Author J. Cale Case also investigates the impact of four market failures—the common property resources, divergence between private and social rates of discounts, noncompetitive market structures, and externalities—on petroleum prices. The roles of uncertainty and political factors are also discussed.

Robert A. Biolsi, in Chapter 5, examines economic functions of oil futures contracts and demonstrates how producers and consumers can hedge their positions by utilizing oil futures. Oil options and their differences and similarities to oil futures contracts are discussed. In addition, he mentions exotic oil options such as Asian, Crack spread, Lockback, Knockout, and Down and Out.

Marketing aspects of oil and oil products in the United States are discussed in Chapter 6 by Carolyn E. Predmore.

In Chapter 7, John T. Boepple studies the linkage between refined prices and refining processes. He demonstrates that refined product prices are affected by the cost structure and yield pattern for a refinery configuration. He also explains types of refinery margins and factors that affect refined product differentials.

Massood V. Samii, in Chapter 8, studies the behavior of OPEC since its inception in 1960. He argues that OPEC has never acted as a revenue-maximizing cartel; rather, each member determines its optimum output and price based on its own social benefit maximization, which is highly influenced by political as well as financial and economic factors. He suggests that OPEC conferences provide a forum to promote individuals positions, and that OPEC's ability to fix oil prices in the future will be impossible or marginal at best.

Siamack Shojai studies the International Energy Agency and its effectiveness in achieving its stated goals and objectives in Chapter 9.

In Chapter 10, Lowell S. Feld studies four of the thirteen oil crises that the world has witnessed during the past 40 years: the 1973 Arab oil embargo, the Iranian revolution of 1979, the Iran-Iraq War, and the Iraqi invasion of Kuwait. He analyzes the differences in the reaction of the oil market to these crises and concludes that the Iranian revolution and the Iran-Iraq War did not lead to a major increase in oil prices because of Saudi Arabia's role, the OECD oil stockpiles, and coordinated efforts among consuming countries.

In Chapter 11, Dominick Salvatore provides a narrative description of statistics on energy use and energy efficiency in the G-7 countries as a group and individually. He concludes that the share of oil in total energy use has risen since the 1970s in all of these countries.

In Chapter 12, Salah El Serafy examines the impact of oil revenues on the economies of oil exporting countries since 1973. He argues that most oil exporting developing countries have not utilized their oil revenues for productive purposes. A combination of high defense spending, imports of consumer goods, irresponsible fiscal expansion, and artificially high exchange rates has led to mismanagement of their economies and missed historical opportunity to develop their economies.

Carlos G. Elías, in Chapter 13, analyzes the positive and adverse sociopolitical impacts of the oil industry on oil exporting countries in general and on Vene-zuela in particular.

The fuel cycle (from production to consumption) of oil and ten other sources of energy, and the factors that affect their environmental impact, are discussed in Chapter 14 by Asbjorn Torvanger. He also studies the environmental impacts of extraction, conversion, distribution, and consumption of energy.

In Chapter 15, Clive L. Spash and Andrew Young provide an elaborate study of social costs of fossil fuel and suggest that renewable sources of energy are falsely priced and seen more expensive than fossil fuels because their external benefits are ignored. The authors present an excellent study of the environmental impacts of alternative sources of energy based on land use, physical changes, air pollution, aesthetics, and health and safety considerations.

Following the excellent discussions of the environment energy markets in the previous two chapters, in Chapter 16, Kusum W. Ketkar studies the trend of global oil spills since 1973 and their environmental impacts. She also analyzes the potential global and domestic effects of the Oil Pollution Act of 1990 on oil and marine transport industries.

In Chapter 17, Diana Denison, Thomas D. Crocker, and Genevieve Briand analyze the impact of voluntary and mandatory environmental protection actions on the time pattern and volume of petroleum exploration, development, and extraction. The authors employ a sequential optimization framework to assess the time pattern and volume of production consequences of fixed and variable compliance costs. International trade effects of environmental controls are also discussed.

In Chapter 18, Wallace E. Tyner studies the key determinants of the use of ethanol as a fuel or oxygenate. Among the issues discussed in this chapter are federal and state subsidies for ethanol production and use, environmental pro-tection regulations, market competition, prices of substitutes, and export poten-tials. He concludes that it is likely that ethanol production as well as corn production and prices will increase substantially in the future.

An excellent examination of sources of externalities associated with the quan-tity of oil imports and the volatility of oil prices is provided in Chapter 19, by Douglas R. Bohi and Michael A. Toman. They conclude that there are limited and quantitatively insignificant externalities in the oil market that require gov-ernment action. Also, import tariffs and quotas are not wise options to use in addressing externalities related to OPEC market power.

In Chapter 20, Robert R. Copaken provides a brief historical survey of oil as an element of national power and explores the strategic role of oil in modern-age political and military conflicts.

David L. Weimer, in Chapter 21, focuses on the energy security of the United States and provides a framework for analyzing the costs of oil price shocks and the advantages as well as the shortcomings of oil import fees and oil stockpiling. He concludes that oil stockpiles are preferred to oil import fees for increasing energy security.

Finally, Harry E. Welsh and John C. Gormley provide an authoritative source of information on the oil industry.

In conclusion, oil has become a global commodity. The globalization of oil markets indicates that oil will play a major role in international political and economic scenes in ways that have not been imagined during the Cold War era. The contributors to this volume seem to agree that the world has plenty of oil reserves and the uncertainty about oil prices and availability are diminished through the development of futures markets and the globalization of the oil industry. OPEC seems to have lost its historical market power and future oil prices are more likely to be determined in competitive global oil markets. It is observed that oil has been a mixed blessing for many oil exporting developing countries. Many OPEC nations missed the historical opportunity to attain self-sustaining economic development through wise investment of their oil revenues.

Global environmental imperatives will affect exploration, extraction, transportation, and marketing of oil and the development of oil substitutes. Finally, oil will be a pivotal source of energy and will continue to dominate public policy debates regarding sources of energy and national security. Renewed efforts in research and development of renewable sources of energy and reliance on market forces can lead to energy security and protection of the environment in the twenty-first century.

PART I

GLOBAL OIL RESOURCES, PRICES, AND MARKETING ACTIVITIES

Chapter 1

Global Oil Reserves

Frank W. Millerd

DEFINITION OF RESERVES

Proved or proven reserves are those resources known, with a high degree of certainty, to be present and that can be produced at current prices and with available technology. Reserves are a proportion of resources delineated by increasing degrees of both geological assurance and economic feasibility. A more comprehensive definition is that used by the U.S. Department of Energy:

Reservoirs [of oil] are considered proved if economic producibility is supported by actual production or conclusive formation test, or if economic producibility is supported by core analysis, electric, or log interpretations. The area of a reservoir considered to be proved includes (1) that portion delineated by drilling and defined by gas-oil and/or oil-water contacts, if any: and (2) the immediately adjoining portions not yet drilled, but which can be reasonably judged as economically productive on the basis of available geological and engineering data. Reserves of crude oil which can be produced economically through application of improved recovery techniques, such as fluid injection, are included in this "proved" classification under certain circumstances. It is not necessary that production, gathering, or transportation facilities be installed or operative for a reservoir to be considered proved (Barnes 1993).

As this definition suggests, proved reserves are a fraction of both the total resources and the total reserves available. Ion (1980) lists a hierarchy of resource classifications, beginning with the broadest and moving to the most specific. The resource base is the total amount of the resource occurring in recognizable form; resources are the proportion of the resource base estimated to be recoverable in useful form; reserves are the proportion of the resources economically and technically feasible to recover; possible reserves are those with limited geological information on costs and recoverability, their extent is a matter of individual judgment; probable reserves are those likely to be currently recoverable with only a small increase in economic and geological information; and proved reserves are those about which it is reasonably certain they can be recovered under current economic and technical conditions. As Peter Odell (1992) notes, there is a qualitative difference between resources and reserves. Resources exist as part of the environment while reserves are generated through investment in exploration and development.

The data used here on reserves are published proved reserves, "generally taken to be the volume of oil remaining in the ground which geological and engineering information indicate with reasonable certainty to be recoverable in the future from known reservoirs under existing economic and operating conditions" (*BP Statistical Review*).[1] Several qualifications to this data should be mentioned. Data for the former USSR are "explored reserves," which include proved, probable, and some possible (*Oil and Gas Journal* 1991). "The estimates for some countries, for example China, are from necessity, based on what appear to be broad guesses presumably related to very old or restricted field data" (Barnes 1993). Barnes also mentions that the estimates usually include condensates and exclude natural gas liquids, but there is some inconsistency on this.[2]

Publication of specific data on proved reserves may give the impression that the level of reserves is known with certainty and that a clear distinction can be made between resources and reserves. Richard Gilbert (1981) suggests that reserves should be viewed as those resources with a high probability of existence and low extraction cost. The amount of a resource is inversely related to the probability of presence and positively related to extraction cost. The lower the probability of existence and/or the higher the extraction cost, the greater the amount of the resource. Reserves are then defined as resources with a probability of existence greater than a given value and an extraction cost lower than the current market price. The line between resources and reserves is indistinct, a more appropriate way, suggests Gilbert, of representing the actual situation.

These point estimates of reserves, of course, provide no indication of the cost of additional reserves or the level of geological assurance associated with additional reserves. The full picture of reserves depends on the probability of added volumes in known fields, the probability of fields other than those included in current reserves, and the costs of producing from these fields. Nor is there any indication of the possibilities of technical change lowering costs and increasing recovery rates, thus adding to reserves. In the long run it is the shape of the supply curve beyond the current position that is important (Bradley 1987).

ESTIMATING RESERVES

Reserve estimates are initially made from a combination of exploratory drilling and seismic or other geophysical and geographical data. When an exploratory well enters an oil-bearing zone or reservoir, information on flows and thickness along with other measurements provide the basis for an initial estimate of the reservoir size. Additional wells, further measurements, and production increase the reliability of reserve estimates. As production from a field progresses, the reserve estimates may change due to depletion and the availability of further information on the field. Country or area reserve estimates, at any point in time, will consist of estimates from fields in various periods of their productive life, leading to diverse changes in reserve estimates, a matter discussed further below.

An estimate of the amount of oil in a field depends on the recovery factor: the proportion of oil in a field that can be removed. Eden et al. (1981) report recovery factors to average between 25 and 30 percent, but with a wide variance. For a particular reservoir the recovery factor depends on the conditions in the reservoir; the composition of the oil, particularly its specific gravity; and the particular drive mechanism by which the oil will be extracted. The oil may be naturally driven or forced out by gas or water or both. Enhanced recovery methods, such as pumping water into the reservoir, reinjecting gas, hot water injection, solvent injection, and steam injection may be possible to further increase recovery.

DISTRIBUTION OF RESERVES

Table 1.1 presents an estimate of oil reserves, by area and country, as of January 1, 1993. These are published proved reserves as previously discussed. The most striking feature of the distribution, of course, is the large proportion of world oil reserves held by Middle Eastern countries and by the members of the Organization of Petroleum Exporting Countries.[3] Almost two-thirds of reserves are in the Middle East and over three-quarters of world reserves are held by OPEC members.

It is highly likely that Middle East reserves are much larger than reported but, with already-published plentiful supplies for most Middle Eastern countries and OPEC's wish to control prices, there is little incentive to reveal additional reserves or search for oil. Revealing additional discoveries would make OPEC's attempts to control prices more difficult (Adelman 1986).

The ratio of current reserves to current production (R/P ratio) is sometimes referred to as the reserves life index. It represents the years that the current level of reserves would last if production continued at the present level. It is only a crude measure of future reserve availability and should not be used as an indication of when oil reserves will be exhausted. If reserves do not change and production continues at the current level, then scarcity will occur and oil prices will increase, causing reductions in demand and increases in supply, both of which will increase the R/P ratio. Also, the R/P ratio at any time is not necessarily an equilibrium ratio. Both reserves and production could be changing and be subject to future change. Despite that it is worthwhile noting the contrast between the high R/P ratios for the Middle East and the lower ratios for most

Table 1.1
Oil Reserves, by Area and Country, Beginning of 1993

Area and Country		Reserves (tonnes x 10^9)	Share of Total	R/P Ratio
North America	USA	4.1	3.2%	9.8
	Canada	0.9	0.8%	9.6
	Total	5.0	4.0%	9.8
Latin America	Mexico	7.2	5.1%	46.2
	Venezuela	9.0	6.2%	69.7
	Other	1.3	1.0%	11.2
	Total	17.5	12.4%	43.7
OECD Europe	Norway	1.2	0.9%	10.8
	United Kingdom	0.6	0.4%	5.9
	Other	0.4	0.3%	13.7
	Total	2.2	1.6%	9.2
Non-OECD Europe and former USSR	Russia	6.6	4.8%	16.7
	Kazakhstan	0.7	0.5%	26.5
	Other	0.8	0.5%	20.2
	Total	8.1	5.9%	17.5
Middle East	Abu Dhabi	12.1	9.2%	*
	Dubai & N. Emirates	0.8	0.6%	36.6
	Iran	12.7	9.2%	73.6
	Iraq	13.4	9.9%	*
	Kuwait	12.9	9.3%	*
	Neutral Zone	0.7	0.5%	42.0
	Oman	0.6	0.4%	17.1
	Saudi Arabia	35.1	25.6%	82.0
	Other	1.2	1.0%	20.3
	Total	89.5	65.7%	99.6
Africa	Algeria	1.2	0.9%	21.0
	Egypt	0.9	0.6%	18.6
	Libya	3.0	2.3%	41.2
	Nigeria	2.4	1.8%	26.6
	Other	0.8	0.6%	12.3
	Total	8.3	6.2%	24.9
Asia and Australasia	China	3.2	2.4%	22.2
	India	0.8	0.6%	28.1
	Indonesia	0.8	0.6%	10.5
	Other	1.1	0.9%	12.8
	Total	5.9	4.5%	17.9
Total OPEC		104.9	76.7%	81.8
World		136.5	100.0%	43.1

* Over 100 years

Source: BP Statistical Review of World Energy, June 1993, from Oil and Gas Journal, December 29, 1992.

Note: Shale oil and tar sands reserves not included. North American data include an estimate of natural gas liquids.

Table 1.2
Net Change in World Oil Reserves, 1970–93

Year	Proven reserves at beginning of year	Production	Gross addition to reserves	Net change in reserves	R/P Ratio
		(tonnes x 10^9)			(years)
1970	73.2	2.0	12.9	+10.9	42.1
1971	84.1	2.0	4.9	+2.9	43.5
1972	87.0	2.2	6.1	+3.9	41.3
1973	90.9	2.4	-2.5	-4.9	35.8
1974	86.0	2.3	14.0	+11.7	42.5
1975	97.7	2.1	-5.2	-7.3	43.0
1976	90.4	2.3	0.2	-2.1	38.4
1977	88.3	2.4	2.7	+0.3	36.9
1978	88.6	2.4	1.9	-0.5	36.7
1979	88.1	2.5	2.4	-0.1	35.2
1980	88.0	2.4	3.3	+0.9	37.0
1981	88.9	2.9	3.2	+0.3	31.8
1982	92.1	2.8	2.7	-0.1	32.9
1983	92.0	2.8	2.8	0.0	32.9
1984	92.0	2.8	6.9	+4.1	34.3
1985	96.1	2.8	2.5	-0.3	34.2
1986	95.8	2.9	2.3	-0.6	32.8
1987	95.2	2.9	28.9	+26.0	41.8
1988	121.2	3.0	5.6	+2.6	41.3
1989	123.8	3.1	16.1	+13.0	44.1
1990	136.8	3.2	2.9	-0.3	42.7
1991	136.5	3.1	2.0	-1.1	43.7
1992	135.4	3.2	4.3	+1.1	42.7
1993	136.5				

Source: For proven reserves at beginning of year: BP Statistical Reviews.

Notes: 1. Net change in reserves = reserves at beginning of year - reserves at end of year.

2. Gross addition to reserves = production + net change in reserves

3. R/P ratio = Reserves/Production ratio = reserves at end of year ÷ production in that year.

of the rest of the world. Middle East reserves are being exploited at a lower rate than elsewhere. Net changes in world oil reserves from 1970 to 1993 are presented in Table 1.2. The annual net change in reserves is estimated by subtracting reserves at the end of the year from reserves at the beginning of the year. The annual gross addition to reserves is the production in that year plus the net change in reserves, and the R/P ratio for a year is calculated by dividing

Table 1.3
Oil Reserves, by Area, 1970–93

Area or Country	1970	1975	Reserves at beginning of 1980	1985	1990	1993	Change 1970-1993 tonnes x 10⁹	Percent
			(in tonnes x 10^9)					
U.S.A.	4.8	5.3	4.2	4.4	4.3	4.1	-0.7	-14.6%
Canada	1.4	1.1	1.1	1.1	1.0	0.9	-0.5	-35.7%
Latin America	4.1	5.7	7.9	11.7	17.6	17.5	+13.4	+326.8%
Western Europe	0.3	3.5	3.2	3.3	2.4	2.2	+1.9	+633.3%
Middle East	45.4	55.0	49.2	54.2	89.3	89.5	+44.1	+49.3%
Africa	7.2	9.1	7.6	7.5	7.8	8.3	+1.1	+15.3%
Former U.S.S.R.	7.9	11.4	9.1	8.6	8.0	7.8	-0.1	-1.3%
Eastern Europe	0.3	0.4	0.4	0.2	0.2	0.3	0	0%
China	**	3.4	2.7	2.6	3.2	3.2	-0.2	-5.9%
Other eastern hemisphere	1.8	2.8	2.6	2.5	3.0	2.7	+0.9	+50.0%
World	73.2	97.7	88.0	96.1	136.8	136.5	+63.3	+86.5%

*   change from 1975 to 1993
** no data available

Source: BP Statistical Review of the World Oil Industry and BP Statistical Review of
         World Energy (various issues) and World Oil.

Note: Shale oil and tar sands reserves not included. North American data include
         an estimate of natural gas liquids.

the reserves at the end of the year by the production that year. The significant
increases in reserves for several years in the 1980s were primarily due to revisions to Middle East reserves. Kuwaiti reserves were revised upward by 3.5
billion tonnes in 1984; in 1997 published oil reserves increased by 27 percent
due to major revisions by OPEC members—Venezuela, Abu Dhabi, Iraq, and
Iran; and in 1989 Saudi Arabia announced an increase of 11 billion tonnes in
its reserves.

Despite the 23 years of production covered here, published proved reserves
have increased by over 80 percent between 1970 and 1993. The average annual
change in net reserves was 2.75 percent. It is difficult to say the world is running
out of oil. It should be kept in mind, however, that the increase in world reserves
has been significantly affected by reevaluations of existing reserves in the Middle East. Generally, R/P ratios declined until the early 1980s and increased since
then.[4]

Changes in reserves from 1970 to 1993, by area of the world, are presented
in Table 1.3. Published proven reserves declined in the United States and Canada

while large increases occurred in Latin America and, especially, the Middle East. The Middle East proportion of world reserves increased from 62.0 percent in 1970 to 65.7 percent in 1993. Despite the recent drop in the reserves of the former USSR and central Europe, there is the hope in Russia that assistance from the West in the form of technology, management, and finance can reverse the decline (World Energy Council 1992).

UNCONVENTIONAL OIL

All of the above data are for conventional crude oil and closely related commodities such as heavy oil may also be produced from the unconventional sources of oil shale and natural bitumen. Oil shale is sedimentary rock with a high percentage of organic matter; natural bitumen is very high viscosity oil, higher than heavy crude oil and requiring dilution or upgrading before refining (World Energy Council 1992). The potential of both oil shale and natural bitumen is very large but neither is generally economically feasible at present. Higher real prices and technological improvements are necessary for widespread production. Table 1.4 offers estimates of world supplies. With world conventional crude reserves at 136 billion tonnes, oil shale and natural bitumen are potential significant future sources of oil.

REVISION OF RESERVE ESTIMATES

Published proved reserve estimates are continually revised, for several reasons. Reserve additions may occur due to the discovery of new oil fields or pools; reserves appreciation may occur as more information on established reserve is acquired; changes may occur in the assumptions about reserve estimates; and there may be political strategic, and economic reasons to revise published estimates of reserves.

Even with current relatively low oil prices, exploration and discovery continues. Many wish to find sources in countries that are not members of OPEC, oil companies wish to maintain their inventory, and there are some who believe oil prices will increase (Oxley 1988). Research on enhancing oil recovery also continues, which will lead to increases in reserves through increased recovery rates and the use of unconventional sources.

Proved reserve estimates at a given time are usually underestimates of the amount of oil that can be recovered from a field or a country. This is most true for recently discovered oil. Few wells may have been drilled in a newly discovered field and thus there is limited information on the field. In some cases all that can be reported is the amount of oil that can be produced from the discovery well (Odell and Rosing 1980). The expansion of information on the field and usually the increase in the estimates of the reserves available have to wait until further work is done in the field.

The normally expected and projected production profile of a new oil field has

The New Global Oil Market

Table 1.4
Oil Shale and Natural Bitumen, Major Reported Reserves, Beginning of 1991

Country	Oil Shale		Natural Bitumen	
	Proved Recoverable Reserves	Estimated Additional Reserves	Proved Recoverable Reserves	Estimated Additional Reserves
	(tonnes x 10^9 of oil)			
Australia	3.6	32.3		
Brazil	.4	8.9		
Canada			0.5	11.5
China		1.3	.3	
Israel	.7			
Jordan	4.0	20.0		
Morocco	1.6	7.4		
U.S.A.		217.0		8.7
Former U.S.S.R.	2.0	35.0		19.0
Venezuela			1.5	14.4

Source: World Energy Council, 1992 Survey of Energy Resources.

Notes: 1. Proved recoverable reserves is that amount, in tonnes of oil, that "has been both carefully measured and has also been assessed as exploitable under present and expected local economic conditions with existing available technology" (World Energy Council).

2. Estimated additional reserves is that amount, in tonnes of oil, "additional to proved reserves that are of foreseeable economic interest". Estimates are based on reasonable confidence, not speculation (World Energy Council).

three phases. The first is the rapid increase in production as the operating company attempts to earn back its initial investment. The second phase is a longer plateau of production sufficient to be economically viable. The third is a gradual winding down of production as the oil field moves toward economic exhaustion. For major fields, however, the profile of production is different, due to increasing knowledge of the field as production progresses and the use of new technology. The second phase plateau is replaced by a series of further increases as new wells are brought into operation and the full extent of the field becomes known. Also, the third winding-down phase is postponed through the use of various procedures to enhance production. These include pumping; drilling further wells; stimulation flows by water, steam, gas, and/or solvent injection; fracturing, flooding or heating; and directional and lateral drilling. Economizing on the use of already-built pipelines and processing facilities is a further production-prolonging factor in many fields. After a field has produced for a time, the capital costs have been depreciated and the level of production will depend on operating costs alone.

The World Energy Council reports that the ultimately recoverable level of reserve in most fields is usually much higher than that first estimated and reported. It is only after four or five years of production that the estimated reserves in a field may be fairly close to the final value (Barnes 1993). If production from a field does not start immediately after discovery, then it may be many more years after discovery before the full size of a field is known.

Barnes reports that, according to Shell International, increased estimates of recovery from producing fields comprise more than three-quarters of the annual revisions to reserves, while the discovery of new fields only adds one-quarter of annual additions to reserves. For the United States, according to the Department of Energy, 88 percent of the average addition to crude oil reserves is due to revised estimates for already-discovered fields.

As well, both the economic and technical assumptions on which reserve projections were made can change. Increasing prices of oil will increase reserve estimates as will decreases in the costs of discovery, production, and transportation. Changes in discovery, drilling, production, and transportation technology will, by increasing discoveries, lowering costs, and increasing extraction rates, tend to increase reserve estimates. Since technical and managerial expertise is required for discovery and production, its availability will also influence the size of estimated reserves. A related consideration is raised by Peter Odell and Kenneth Rosing (1980), who mention that recovery rates of new fields should improve as they can be developed with more advanced and productive primary, secondary, and tertiary recovery methods.

Since these published estimates give some indication of future availability and possible producer strategies, there may be economic, political, and strategic reasons for not publishing full information on reserves. This is particularly true when one group, such as OPEC, controls a significant proportion of the reserves and information on the reserves. Changes in strategic and political considerations can lead to changes in published reserves.

Oil price increases since 1973 have often precipitated concerns about oil scarcity. The data on reserve, however, indicate that more oil has been added to reserves in that period than has been produced from reserves. Oil is not getting scarcer, if anything it is becoming more plentiful.

An increasing stock of oil, however, does not necessarily mean an increasing flow, and it is flows that determine prices. Market prices are largely determined by the relationship between demand and supply flows. In the world oil market, as Morris Adelman (1988) points out, demand stems from the decision of millions of individual firms and households, while supply decisions are made by few, specifically a few governments and the OPEC cartel. The result is an oligopolistic market for oil, supply is limited by a cartel to raise prices, and even non-OPEC countries do not always respond in an easily predictable way. For most OPEC producers, the marginal cost of production, both now and in the future, is a fraction of price, further indicating that world oil prices are not indicators of world oil scarcity (Adelman and Shani 1989).

This leads to the view that reserves should be regarded as a form of semifinished inventory.[5] They are partially ready for the production process since further development (drilling, production, and collection) must take place before they are usable. Oil producers have accumulated these inventories in anticipation of future production.

Short-run and long-run effects should be kept separate. In the short run the real costs of finding oil may increase along with the real price of oil. As Brown (1984) points out, this is not necessarily due to long-run increases in the cost of oil but to the inelastic short-run supply of those resources specific to discovering and developing oil. In the long run the supply elasticity for these resources would increase, leading to reduced costs of finding and developing oil.

UNDISCOVERED OIL

There is little doubt that further oil will be discovered, both in existing and new fields. Barnes provides a global supply profile based on current views on the total amount of oil available. The most optimistic case is an ultimately recoverable resource base of 435 billion tonnes allowing production of almost 4.5 million tonnes a year until 2050.[6] This estimate includes proven reserves, current reserve extensions, and undiscovered reserves. Most of this oil is assumed to be available at costs below US$30 per barrel. Unconventional oil is not included.

Any estimate of this type should be regarded only in the most general way. Changes in technology, efficiency, substitutes, and the rate of discoveries can all alter these estimates. Also, if scarcity does occur and prices increase, then production will decline and supplies will last much longer.

SUMMARY AND CONCLUSIONS

The information presented suggests that world oil reserves are increasing rather than decreasing, despite high levels of production for the last 23 years. The major source of reserves and reserve additions is the Middle East, a situation with both negative and positive implications. A relatively small area of the world, somewhat politically unstable, controls a large proportion of reserves. The positive aspect of this situation is that the Middle East is a low-cost producer. While this does not mean lower prices in the future, it also does not necessarily mean higher prices.

The data presented here are for published proven reserves, reserves known with a high degree of geological assurance and that can be produced at current prices and with currently available technology. This is the data that has been made available by the countries, companies, and other organizations responsible

Tables and Figure

for preparing it. Reserve data are continually subject to revision as new fields are discovered, production continues in current fields, economic and technical conditions change, and strategies with respect to releasing data change.

NOTES

1. The major data sources used here are various issues of the *BP Statistical Review of the World Oil Industry* and the *BP Statistical Review of World Energy*. The BP data are from the generally accepted estimates published in the *Oil and Gas Journal*, which in turn, obtains information from governments, industry associations, oil companies, and consultants. Metric measurements are used, one metric tonne is equal to 2,205 pounds or approximately 7.33 barrels of oil.

2. Alternative sources of reserve data are American Petroleum Institute (1993), Degolyer and MacNaughton (1990), and World Energy Council publications. The World Energy Council provides extensive information on definitions and sources.

3. OPEC members in 1992 were Algeria, Ecuador, Gabon, Indonesia, Iran, Iraq, Kuwait, Libya, Nigeria, Qatar, Saudi Arabia, United Arab Emirates, and Venezuela.

4. See Odell (1992) for another estimate of net changes in reserves for this period.

5. This view, originally attributable to Adelman, is discussed in Kregel (1985).

6. Current annual production is approximately 71 percent of this level.

REFERENCES

Adelman, Morris A. "Scarcity and World Oil Prices." *Review of Economics and Statistics* 68(3) (1986): 387–397.

————. "Modelling World Oil Supply." *Energy Journal* 14(1) (1988): 1–32.

Adelman, Morris A. and Manoj Shani. "Oil Development-Operation Cost Estimates." *Energy Economics* 11(1) (1989): 2–10.

American Petroleum Institute. *Basic Petroleum Data Book*, vol. 13, no. 2. Washington, DC: API, May 1993.

Barnes, Philip. "The Oil Supply Mountain: Is the Summit in Sight?" Oxford Institute for Energy Studies, 1993.

Bradley, Paul G. "Cost and Output Analysis in Mineral and Petroleum Production." In Richard L. Gordon, Henry D. Jacoby, and Martin Zimmerman (eds.), *Energy: Markets and Regulation*. London: MIT Press, 1987, 281–303.

British Petroleum Company Limited. *BP Statistical Review of the World Oil Industry*. London: BP Ltd., various years.

British Petroleum Company plc. *BP Statistical Review of World Energy*. London: BP plc., various years.

Brown, Keith C. "Reserves and Reserve Production Ratios in Imperfect Markets." *Energy Journal* 10(2) (1984): 177–186.

Clark, John B. *The Political Economy of World Energy*. New York: Harvester Sheatsheaf, 1990.

Degolyer and MacNaughton Consulting Company. *Twentieth Century Petroleum Statistics*. Dallas, December 1992.

Eden, Richard, Michael Posner, Richard Bending, Edmond Crouch, and Joe Stanislaw. *Energy Economics*. Cambridge: Cambridge University Press, 1981.

Gilbert, Richard J. "The Social and Private Value of Exploration Information." In James B. Ramsey (ed.), *The Economics of Exploration for Energy Resources*. London: JAI Press, 1981, 173–216.

Ion, D.C. *Availability of World Energy Sources*. London: Graham and Trotman, 1980.

Kaufman, Gordon M. "Oil and Gas Resource and Supply Assessment." In Richard L. Gordon, Henry D. Jacoby, and Martin Zimmerman (eds.), *Energy: Markets and Regulation*. London: MIT Press, 1987, 259–280.

Kregel, Jan A. (ed.). *The International Oil Market*. London: Macmillan, 1985.

Odell, Peter R. "Global and Regional Energy Supplies, Recent Fictions and Facts Revisited." *Energy Policy* 20(4) (1992): 284–296.

Odell, Peter R. and Kenneth E. Rosing. *The Future of Oil*. London: Kogan Page, 1980.

Oil and Gas Journal. "Worldwide Look at Reserves and Production." December 18, 1992.

Oxley, Philip. "An Exploration-Production View of Oil." *Energy Policy* 16(1) (1988): 3–5.

Reinsch, Anthony E. and Jennifer E. Considine. *After the Crisis: World Oil Market Projections 1991–2006*. Calgary: Canadian Energy Research Institute, 1992.

World Energy Council. *1992 Survey of Energy Resources*. London: World Energy Council, 1992.

Chapter 2

Global Oil Production

Frank W. Millerd

This chapter discusses the current, past, and possible future patterns of world oil production, emphasizing the location of production. Exports and imports are examined because the distribution of production does not coincide with the distribution of demand, leading to extensive international trade in crude oil and oil products. Because it is a major feature of world oil production, the past, present, and potential future roles of OPEC are specifically addressed.

CURRENT GLOBAL OIL PRODUCTION

Oil production for 1992, by area and country, is presented in Table 2.1.[1] The top five producers, in order, are Saudi Arabia, the United States, Russia, Iran, and Mexico. Perhaps surprisingly, the United States produced almost as much oil as Saudi Arabia in 1992. Not surprisingly, the Middle East was the area with the largest production. Kuwait and Iraq outputs in 1992 were well below their pre-1990 or pre-Gulf crisis peaks.[2] Members of OPEC accounted for slightly over 40 percent of production.[3]

The current distribution of production is considerably different than the distribution of published proven reserves. The most significant differences are for North America, which contributed 16.2 percent of world production but had only 4.0 percent of reserves; Western Europe with 7.2 percent of production and 1.6 percent of reserves; and the Middle East with the reverse situation of 28.4 percent of production but 65.7 percent of reserves.[4] This is reflected in the total reserves to annual production ratios for these areas; less than 10 for North America and Western Europe, almost 100 for the Middle East.[5]

Table 2.1
Oil Production, by Area and Country, 1992

Area and Country		Production (tonnes x 10^6)	Share of Total
North America	USA	416.6	13.1%
	Canada	98.2	3.1%
	Total	514.8	16.2%
Latin America	Mexico	154.9	4.9%
	Venezuela	129.0	4.1%
	Other	116.1	3.7%
	Total	400.0	12.6%
OECD Europe	Norway	106.6	3.4%
	United Kingdom	94.2	3.0%
	Other	29.2	0.9%
	Total	229.9	7.2%
Non-OECD Europe	Russia	396.0	12.5%
and former USSR	Kazakhstan	26.7	0.8%
	Other	39.5	1.2%
	Total	462.2	14.6%
Middle East	Abu Dhabi	96.7	3.1%
	Dubai & N. Emirates	21.8	0.7%
	Iran	172.2	5.4%
	Iraq	23.6	0.7%
	Kuwait	45.6	1.4%
	Neutral Zone	17.0	0.5%
	Oman	36.1	1.1%
	Qatar	22.6	0.7%
	Saudi Arabia	427.9	13.5%
	Syria	25.2	0.7%
	Other	11.0	0.3%
	Total	899.7	28.4%
Africa	Algeria	57.0	1.8%
	Angola	27.0	0.9%
	Egypt	46.1	1.5%
	Libya	73.0	2.3%
	Nigeria	91.6	2.9%
	Other	37.6	1.2%
	Total	332.4	10.5%
Asia and Australasia	China	142.0	4.5%
	India	28.7	0.9%
	Indonesia	74.3	2.3%
	Malaysia	32.6	1.0%
	Australasia	26.9	0.9%
	Other	26.3	0.9%
	Total	330.7	10.4%
Total OPEC		1,283.7	40.5%
World		3,169.7	100.0%

Source: BP Statistical Review of World Energy, June 1993.

Note: Includes crude oil, shale oil, oil sands, and natural gas liquids.

Table 2.2
World Oil Production and OPEC Share, 1970–92

Year	World Production (tonnes x 10^6)	Change from previous year	OPEC Share
1970	2,362.5	+9.6%	49.6%
1971	2,494.9	+5.6%	50.8%
1972	2,633.8	+5.6%	51.5%
1973	2,871.6	+9.0%	53.9%
1974	2,879.3	+0.3%	53.4%
1975	2,733.1	-5.1%	49.8%
1976	2,954.3	+8.1%	52.1%
1977	3,066.7	+3.8%	51.0%
1978	3,094.1	+0.9%	48.3%
1979	3,226.6	+4.3%	48.1%
1980	3,083.5	-4.4%	44.1%
1981	2,910.4	-5.6%	39.5%
1982	2,795.2	-4.0%	35.0%
1983	2,775.6	-0.7%	32.5%
1984	2,840.7	+2.3%	31.8%
1985	2,801.8	-1.4%	30.1%
1986	2,933.2	+4.7%	32.5%
1987	2,928.2	-0.2%	31.7%
1988	3,047.6	+4.1%	33.9%
1989	3,109.0	+2.0%	36.7%
1990	3,157.6	+1.6%	38.2%
1991	3,132.5	-0.8%	38.6%
1992	3,169.7	+1.2%	40.5%

Source: BP Statistical Reviews.

Note: Production includes crude oil, shale oil, oil sands and natural gas liquids.

PAST OIL PRODUCTION

Table 2.2 shows world oil production, the annual percent change, and OPEC's share from 1970 to 1992. Over this period world oil production increased by 34.2 percent, an average annual increase of 1.35 percent.[6] Most of this increase was between 1970 and 1980, when production increased by 30.5 percent. The period of most rapid growth was the early 1970s; growth abruptly slowed by the oil price increases of 1973 and 1974.[7] In contrast, production increased only by a total of 2.89 percent between 1980 and 1992. Higher prices, slower economic growth, increased efficiency in oil use, and expanded use of substitutes all eased the demand for petroleum in the last 12 years.

Further historical data are presented in Table 2.3.[8] Production of crude oil in total and by area from 1920 to 1991 is shown. Obviously, there has been a tremendous increase in production over this period but growth, by decade, has been uneven. Production more than doubled in the 1920s, 1950s, and 1960s but

Table 2.3
Oil Production, by Area, 1920–91

Area	Production for (in tonnes x 10^6)										
	1920	1930	1940	1950	1960	1970	1975	1980	1985	1990	1991
North America	60.5	122.7	185.8	273.3	377.2	543.1	488.0	501.4	521.2	445.5	447.4
Latin America	22.4	31.2	42.7	97.7	186.3	261.2	218.7	278.1	315.1	341.5	365.0
Western Europe	0.1	0.2	1.5	3.3	13.7	16.0	23.8	121.1	185.8	198.9	213.6
Eastern Europe	5.3	23.7	37.3	42.8	162.3	369.0	502.8	593.4	580.6	548.9	517.2
Middle East	1.7	6.4	14	87.4	262.4	695.0	976.9	921.4	515.2	827.0	809.9
Africa	0.1	0.3	0.9	2.3	14.4	302.2	249.1	305.7	267.2	323.6	336.9
Far East	4.0	7.8	11.2	12.0	30.7	88.5	184.2	241.6	286.9	321.1	331.3
World	94.0	192.4	293.3	518.8	1,046.9	2,275.1	2,643.6	2,962.7	2,672.1	3,006.5	3,021.4

Source: DeGolyer and MacNaughton

Notes: 1. North America is the United States and Canada. Mexico is included with Latin America.

2. Data are for the production of crude oil only.

3. Eastern Europe includes the former USSR.

increased only by 50 percent in the 1930s, by 30 percent in the 1970s, and minimally in the 1980s.

All areas have large overall increases in production over this period but there are significant changes in the distribution of world production. Until 1950 North America, predominantly the United States, produced over half of the world's oil; 64.4 percent in 1920 falling to 52.7 percent in 1950. By 1990 the North American proportion had fallen to 14.8 percent and, after 1970, its absolute level of production had also fallen. Contrast this with the Middle East, which produced only 1.8 percent of world production in 1920 but 37.0 percent in 1975, although falling to 27.5 percent in 1990. While Latin American production increased considerably over this period, its share of world production actually declined, from 23.8 percent in 1920 to 11.4 percent in 1990.

OPEC OIL PRODUCTION

OPEC's share of world oil production has varied considerably between 1970 and the present. An increase in OPEC's proportion in the early 1970s was followed by a decline until the mid-1980s and then an increase; currently it is approximately 40 percent. The highest proportion of world production for OPEC was 53.9 percent in 1973 and the lowest, 30.1 percent in 1985.

There is a considerable difference between OPEC's average share of production and its share of marginal production. OPEC's share of both annual increases and decreases in world production is usually much higher than its share of total production. Two periods illustrate this: when world production increased rapidly in the early 1970s, OPEC's share of the increase was between 65 and 80 percent while its share of total output was between 50 and 54 percent; when world production decreased in the early 1980s, OPEC's production decreased each year by more than the decrease in world production. Most recently, between 1991 and 1992, OPEC's increase in production was almost twice the world increase in production. OPEC is often referred to as the "swing" producer, absorbing the greatest impact of changes in production.

INTERNATIONAL TRADE IN OIL

Due to the mismatch between the distributions of world production and demand, world trade in oil and products is considerable. Data for selected countries and areas are presented in Table 2.4. A total of 1613.2 tonnes of crude oil and product were traded between the areas listed in 1992, slightly over 50 percent of the total tonnage of crude oil produced. This data includes only trade between the areas or countries listed and not trade within the areas, such as trade within Latin America. The Middle East is by far the largest exporter, exporting 743.6 million tonnes of crude oil and product per year, 82 percent of its production. Other significant exporters are Latin America and North Africa. Major importers

Table 2.4
Crude Oil and Product Imports and Exports, 1992

Country or Area	Crude Oil			Product		
	Imports	Exports	Net Imports	Imports	Exports	NetImports
			(tonnes x 10^6)			
U.S.A.	302.3	1.6	300.7	85.9	44.0	41.9
Canada	25.4	39.7	-14.3	8.4	14.1	-5.7
Latin America	35.4	134.3	-98.9	9.0	46.0	-37
OECD Europe	425.8	34.8	391.0	82.0	34.2	47.8
Middle East	1.1	675.8	-674.7	2.2	67.8	-65.6
North Africa	5.7	103.7	-98.0	2.3	33.7	-31.4
West Africa	1.5	118.9	-117.4	4.3	2.5	1.8
East & Southern Africa	21.5	0	21.5	6.1	0	6.1
South Asia	35.7	0.3	35.4	11.2	1.2	10.0
Other Asia	147.7	48.3	99.4	53.1	27.2	25.9
Japan	215.6	0	215.6	46.7	5.8	40.9
Australia	16.6	7.7	8.9	2.0	3.6	-1.6
Non-OECD Europe & China	32.2	80.2	-48.0	15.6	39.7	-24.1
Unidentified	2.4	23.6	-21.2	15.5	24.5	-9.0
World	1,268.9	1,268.9	0	344.3	344.3	0

Source: BP Statistical Review of World Energy, June 1993.

Note: Net imports computed from published data, negative value indicates a net export.

are Western Europe, the United States, and Japan, using this geographical break-down.

The extent of oil market regionalization is important because, if markets are regional, then importers may not always have access to oil. This has been ex-amined by Robert Weiner (1991). Hypothesizing that the market is regionalized if prices across regions are not closely correlated, Weiner finds a high degree of regionalization, although, as he states, this could be due to price discrimi-nation on the part of crude oil sellers. This finding is rejected by Adelman (1992), who believes the world oil market is "one great pool" and that access to crude oil is not a concern.

Table 2.5
Interarea Crude Oil and Product Movements, 1970, 1980, and 1992

FROM		U.S.A	Canada	Latin America	Western Europe	Africa	USSR, E.Europe Other E. Hem.	Destination not known	TOTAL EXPORTS
		(tonnes x 10^6)							
U.S.A.	1970		1.3	1.2	3.3	-	7.3	-	13.0
	1980	-	5.2	14.8	8.2	0.3	0.6	-	29.1
	1992	-	3.4	6.3	11.4	0.4	15.7	8.4	45.6
Canada	1970	34.3	-	-	-	-	-	1.3	35.5
	1980	18.6	-	-	1.5	-	1.0	1.2	22.3
	1992	51.9	-	0.2	0.7	-	1.0	-	53.8
Latin America	1970	106.3	25.3	13	26.5	1.0	2.3	-	164.3
	1980	105.4	10.7	13.8	31.1	2.5	15.9	17.3	196.7
	1992	131.4	5.2	-	33.8	0.1	9.8	-	180.3
Western Europe	1970	10.5	0.3	1.5	-	4.0	0.5	14.2	31.0
	1980	18.1	0.2	-	-	4.2	0.7	-	23.2
	1992	23.3	16.4	1.0	-	5.4	15.5	7.4	69.0
Middle East	1970	8.8	7.5	12.0	309	20.8	251.3	22.3	631.5
	1980	77.2	14.8	80.4	362.3	22	307.6	5.0	869.3
	1992	88.3	5.1	23.5	197.4	28.5	400.2	-	743.6
Africa	1970	6.3	1.8	10.5	264.8	0.2	5.0	-	288.5
	1980	97.6	0.5	27.5	120.2	3.8	11.6	-	261.2
	1992	11.4	0.2	0.9	84.6	1.0	136.0	2.1	236.2
USSR, E. Europe, Other E. Hemis.	1970	4.0	-	5.3	40.0	1.8	38.3	-	89.4
	1980	20.1	-	10.2	65.6	1.2	89.3	-	186.4
	1992	11.4	0.2	0.9	84.6	1.0	136.0	2.1	236.2
TOTAL IMPORTS	1970	170.0	36.0	43.5	643.6	27.8	304.7	37.8	
	1980	337	31.4	146.7	588.9	34.0	426.7	23.5	
	1992	388.2	33.8	44.4	507.8	41.4	601.9	17.9	

Source: BP Statistical Reviews, 1970, 1980, 1993.

Note: 1992 Import totals include some unidentified shipments.

Table 2.5 is an examination of interarea trade in crude oil and products for 1970, 1980, and 1991.[9] Over this period Latin America has been the major supplier to the United States but increasing amounts have been imported from the Middle East and Africa. Western Europe's major suppliers are the Middle East, Africa, and other Eastern Hemisphere countries. In 1992 the countries of the former USSR were the major other Eastern Hemisphere exporters to Western

Europe. The amounts imported from the Middle East and Africa have generally declined as Western Europe increased its own production. The Middle East also exports large volumes to other Eastern Hemisphere, primarily Asian, countries such that Asian countries other than China depend on the Middle East for 73.4 percent of their imports. Much of the world remains dependent on Middle East production, as everyone was reminded during the 1990–91 Gulf crisis (International Energy Agency 1992).

FUTURE OIL PRODUCTION

Further total world production will, no doubt, be a function of the same determinants as in the past: price, the rate of economic growth, the availability and relative price of substitutes, technological change in production and transportation, efficiency in use, and public policies. As Chapter 1 discusses, there are certainly sufficient world supplies to sustain high levels of production for a considerable period, but the distribution of reserves strongly favors OPEC members. Thus the future role of OPEC and the implication of this role are major questions.

OPEC's dilemma is not in finding oil but in deciding how much to produce now and what production facilities to plan for the future. Too much restriction of production either now or in the future may result in oil price increases harmful to OPEC by reducing demand and encouraging substitutes. Conversely, increasing production, resulting in lower prices, could similarly be harmful by reducing total revenues. Similar conditions apply to the planning of future production capacity.[10] Failure to increase future capacity could result in higher prices, while adding capacity could result in, from OPEC's viewpoint, overproduction (Centre for Global Energy Studies 1993).

The past actions of non-OPEC countries may have strengthened the future position of OPEC. John Clark (1990) believes the distribution of production that has occurred since the mid-1970s has left Western countries in an awkward situation with respect to future supplies of oil. Between the mid-1970s and the mid-1980s Middle East producers, mostly members of OPEC, reduced production. Although Middle East production has recently increased, it is still not back to the levels of the mid-1970s. The decline in Middle East production was partly offset by increases in other, mostly non-OPEC, areas such as Western Europe and Latin America. In Clark's view the West's safest sources of oil have been depleted while the West has remained heavily dependent on oil.

In determining the future role of Middle East and OPEC producers the critical element appears to be the rate of growth of the demand for oil, with non-OPEC production, energy efficiency, conservation, and substitutes also important. George Kowalski (1992) forecasts that, if governments take no action to restrain demand growth and even if crude oil prices rise in real terms, world oil demand will grow by 1.7 percent per year until 2005. With a decline in OECD oil production, this will mean that the Middle East will supply an increasing proportion of world oil. Georgiou (1993) also suggests OPEC control will grow with the core group of Middle East OPEC countries becoming a more powerful cartel than in the mid-1970s. Kowalski suggests, however, that the increasing dominance of Middle East producers would be avoided if countries act, because of the greenhouse effect, to reduce carbon dioxide emissions, resulting in a reduction in the demand for oil.[11]

Peter Odell (1992), however, predicts annual average growth rates for oil demand of less than 1 percent from 1990 to 2020, based on increased efficiency of oil use and production, more substitutions for oil, a shift to less-energy-intensive activities, and the introduction of policies to reduce carbon dioxide emissions and thus reduce the use of oil, particularly for transportation. Odell also suggests increases in supply may be expected from the countries now comprising the former USSR and from non-OPEC developing countries. With the forecast that increases in the demand for oil will be moderate and at least partly offset by increased non-OPEC supplies, Odell does not see a return to OPEC dominance of the world oil market.

Several reasons why non-OPEC production may stay at relatively high levels are added by Philip Oxley (1988): exploration and development technology is constantly improving; research and development continue to increase the proportion of oil recovered from existing wells; countries will wish to increase oil production revenues and thus will improve their terms for exploration, discovery, and development; and some exploration and development will be motivated by some people's expectation of an increase in oil prices. No estimate is presented of the impact of these activities.

A rise in the promotion of world oil produced by OPEC members or any other group, however, does not necessarily mean detrimental cartel behavior, but it does increase its likelihood. Market control and higher prices are not the result of world oil scarcity but of oligopsony or a few producers controlling a large proportion of output.

SUMMARY AND CONCLUSIONS

Past, present, and possible future world oil production patterns are examined here. Present production is characterized by the major role of OPEC members, particularly those in the Middle East. Major contributions to world oil output also come from North America and Eastern Europe. There have been significant changes in production over time; rapid growth occurred before 1980 but very slow growth after 1980; North America was the major producer until 1950, but has been replaced by the Middle East; and significant production increases have come from Eastern Europe, Western Europe, and Asia in recent years.

The distribution of production does not coincide with the distribution of demand, leading to extensive international trade in oil. Nor does the distribution of production coincide with the distribution of reserves, leading to uneven rates of depletion and concerns about the future position of OPEC.

NOTES

1. Metric measurements are used here. One metric tonne is equal to 2,205 pounds or approximately 7.33 barrels of oil. Alternate sources of data are the publications listed from the American Petroleum Institute, OPEC, and the World Energy Council.

2. Maximum production was in 1989 with 81.1 million tonnes produced by Kuwait and 138.6 million tonnes by Iraq.

3. OPEC members in 1992 were Algeria, Ecuador, Gabon, Indonesia, Iran, Iraq, Kuwait, Libya, Nigeria, Qatar, Saudi Arabia, United Arab Emirates, and Venezuela.

4. See Chapter 1 on reserves for full data on world oil reserves and their distribution.

5. The European members of the Organization for Economic Cooperation and Development (OECD) are Austria, Belgium, Denmark, Finland, France, Germany, Greece, Iceland, Ireland, Italy, Netherlands, Norway, Portugal, Spain, Sweden, Switzerland, Turkey, and the United Kingdom. "Western Europe" may also be used to describe these countries.

6. Over the same period the average annual net increase in published proven reserves was 2.75 percent.

7. In 1973–74 the spot price of Middle East crude oil increased by approximately 270 percent.

8. Table 2.3 data are for crude oil production, Tables 2.1 and 2.2 data include crude oil, shale oil, oil sands, and natural gas liquids.

9. Construction of this historical series has necessitated more grouping of countries than would otherwise be desirable.

10. As Adelman (1988) states, proper modeling or understanding of OPEC requires focusing on investment and capacity.

11. A carbon tax has been suggested as a policy to reduce carbon dioxide emissions.

REFERENCES

Adelman, Morris A. "Scarcity and World Prices." *Review of Economics and Statistics* 68(3) (1986): 387–397.

———. "Modeling World Oil Supply." *Energy Journal* 14(1) (1988): 1–32.

———. "World Oil Market 'One Great Pool?' Comment." *Energy Journal* 13(1) (1992): 157–158.

American Petroleum Institute. Basic Petroleum Data Book, vol. 13, no. 1 (May 1993). Washington, DC: API.

British Petroleum Company Limited. *BP Statistical Review of the World Oil Industry.* London: BP Ltd., various years.

British Petroleum Company plc. *BP Statistical Review of World Energy.* London: BP plc, various years.

Centre for Global Energy Studies. *Global Oil Report* 4(2) (March–April 1993).

Clark, John B. *The Political Economy of World Energy.* New York: Harvester Wheatsheaf, 1990.

Degolyer and MacNaughton Consulting Company. *Twentieth Century Petroleum Statistics.* Dallas, December 1992.

Georgiou, George. "US Energy Security and Policy Options for the 1990s." *Energy Policy* 21(8) (1993): 831–839.

International Energy Agency. *Energy Policies of IEA Countries, 1991 Review.* Paris: OECD/IEA, 1992.

Kohl, Wilfrid L. (ed.)). After the Oil Price Collapse: OPEC, the United States, and the World Oil Market. London: Johns Hopkins University Press, 1991.

Kowalski, George. "World Oil and Energy Demand Outlook to 2005." *Energy Policy* 20(10) (1992): 921–929.

Kregel, Jan A. (ed.). *The International Oil Market.* London: Macmillan, 1985.

Odell, Peter R. "Prospects for Non-OPEC Oil Supply." *Energy Policy* 20(10) (1992): 931–941.

Oil and Gas Journal. "Worldwide Look at Reserves and Production." December 28, 1992.

Organization of Petroleum Exporting Countries. *Annual Statistical Bulletin.* Vienna: OPEC, 1991.

Oxley, Philip. "An Exploration-Production View of Oil." *Energy Policy* 16(1) (1988): 3–5.

Weiner, Robert J. "Is the World Oil Market One Great Pool?" *Energy Journal* 12(3) (1991): 95–107.

World Energy Council. *1992 Survey of Energy Resources.* London: World Energy Council, 1992.

Chapter 3

The Changing Determinants of Global Energy Consumption

Edward T. Dowling and Francis G. Hilton

Twenty years have passed since the 1973 oil crisis pummeled the global economy. That oil crisis quadrupled oil prices, eliminated economic growth, doubled inflation rates, and launched many nations into urgent pursuit of energy self-sufficiency. The 1979–80 oil crisis—a result of Iran's revolution, the Iraq/Iran War, and the West's panicked response to both events—tripled oil prices, dragged economic growth to yet another halt, reignited inflation rates, and underscored again the need for energy self-sufficiency. The 1986 crash in oil prices exerted an opposite effect. The very forces that collapsed oil prices—the fall in worldwide oil demand and the increase in non-OPEC production—suggested that there was no reason to pursue greater self-sufficiency. The 1990–91 Gulf conflict subsequently demonstrated greater cooperation between oil producers and consumers and further persuaded nations to slow the pursuit of energy independence. The fall of the self-sufficiency imperative, like its rise, reshaped the world's energy consumption patterns.

The retreat of security concerns has allowed other issues—financial, diplomatic, and regulatory—to influence worldwide energy demand. The environmental imperative, more than any of the other issues and imperatives, promises to exert the greatest impact on global energy use. This chapter examines how the rise and retreat of the self-sufficiency imperative changed demand patterns. It then considers some of the probable ways in which the environmental imperative could further restructure worldwide energy consumption.

THE RISE AND RETREAT OF THE SELF-SUFFICIENCY IMPERATIVE

The two oil shocks traumatized the global economy and drove most nations to pursue greater energy self-sufficiency. Market forces and ambitious government policies forced entire nations to undertake unprecedented and sometimes painful measures to achieve greater energy self-reliance. The 24 members of the Organization for Economic Cooperation and Development, the world's leading industrialized economies, made particularly strong efforts in this regard. Between 1973 and 1979, OECD's energy self-sufficiency rating (measured by the ratio of energy production to energy requirements) increased modestly from 63.2 percent to 65.4 percent. Stimulated by the second oil crisis, the ratio jumped to 68.8 percent in 1980 and then increased steadily, to an all-time high of 75.8 percent in 1985. OECD's energy self-sufficiency then went into a decline, bottoming out at 72.6 percent in 1989—its lowest level since 1981 (International Energy Agency 1991: 58; and earlier editions). The self-sufficiency imperative evidently peaked in 1985.

Although strategies differed from country to country, nearly every nation emphasized conservation, enhanced energy efficiency, domestic energy production, and fuel diversification as the most effective tactics for improving energy self-sufficiency. Each of these efforts, like the overall quest for energy security, made significant progress before 1986, but then faltered. Both in their rise and in their decline, these strategies shaped the demand for fossil fuels and nuclear power. For ease of exposition, enhanced energy efficiency will henceforth be considered under the broad umbrella of conservation.

CONSERVATION

A close look at key indicators, such as growth in worldwide primary energy consumption and improvements in energy efficiency, suggests that the security imperative produced a successful conservation effort prior to 1985, but that the effort lost momentum after 1985. The world's total primary energy consumption expanded from 4,780 million tonnes of oil equivalent (mtoe) in 1970 to 7,053 mtoe in 1985 (Cambridge Energy Research Associates 1993: 16). This increase translates into a healthy 2.6 percent annual growth rate. However, that robust overall growth rate conceals important reductions that occurred within the period. While global energy demand increased at an annual average rate of 3.2 percent throughout the 1970s, that growth rate dropped to 1.4 percent for the period 1980–85, which was less than half of what it had been in the preceding decade. This demand slowdown reveals that when given enough time to make long-term adjustments, many nations engineered major conservation gains. If they had not made these adjustments and had allowed energy demand to increase during the 1980s as it had in the 1970s, the world's total primary energy demand in 1990 would have been over 9,000 mtoe instead of 7,800 mtoe. The same numbers indicate that the conservation effort lost steam in the late 1980s. Between 1985 and 1989 the world's total primary energy consumption climbed from 7,053 mtoe to 7,895 mtoe. This late-1980 annual growth rate of 2.8 percent was double what it had been in the early 1980s. The oil price collapse marked the end of substantial conservation gains.

Economic recession can explain some, but not all, of the changes in demand growth. Energy-to-GDP ratios, which net out the impact of economic fluctuations, tell a similar story: worldwide conservation efforts, especially in the industrialized countries, realized great success prior to 1986. Whereas in 1970 the world's industrialized countries consumed 0.55 tonnes of oil equivalent of primary energy (toe) in the process of generating $1,000 GDP in 1985 dollars and exchange rates, by 1980 they required only 0.49 toe to achieve the same end (CERA 1993: 20). Thus, between 1970 and 1980, OECD energy efficiency improved by roughly 1.2 percent a year. That pace of annual improvement then leapt to 2.6 percent for the period 1980–85. The efficiency improvements slacked off after 1985. The OECD's overall energy-to-GDP ratio dropped from 0.43 in 1985 to 0.42 in 1986, but did not drop again until 1989, when it improved only marginally, to 0.41. The ratio declined slightly to 0.40 in 1990 but showed no improvement in 1991. This reduction in efficiency improvements, from 2.6 percent per year in the early 1980s to only 1.2 percent during the latter part of the decade, reveals that the conservation effort stumbled severely after the 1985 crash in oil prices.

The energy-to-GDP ratios for individual countries also warrant attention. Whereas in 1970 the United States needed 0.59 toe in primary energy to produce $1,000 GDP in 1985 prices, it needed only 0.45 toe in 1985, an annual reduction over 15 years in the energy-to-GDP ratio of 1.8 percent. Over the same 15 years Japan slashed its energy-to-GDP ratio from 0.38 to 0.27, an annual reduction of 2.3 percent; the United Kingdom went from 0.62 to 0.45, a drop of 2.1 percent; West Germany, from 0.53 to 0.42 (2.2 percent); and Italy from 0.43 to 0.33 (1.8 percent). Reflecting earlier patterns, the rate of reduction in individual countries slowed markedly after 1985. Between 1985 and 1990 the energy-to-GDP ratio in the United States moved from 0.45 to 0.42, a yearly drop of 1.3 percent, only to rise again in 1991; in Japan, it went from 0.27 to 0.26, a decrease of less than 1 percent.

With most countries making significant improvements in energy efficiency from 1973 to 1985 and slowing but not reversing the trend thereafter, the data clearly show that, by the end of 1990, Japan with its high degree of import-dependence was most efficient in its use of energy, requiring only 0.26 toe per $1,000 GDP. Italy required 0.32; France, 0.37; West Germany, 0.38; and the United Kingdom, 0.40. Despite major strides the United States, which started with one of the highest ratios (0.59) and failed to cut as deeply as others, still remained one of the most inefficient major users of energy, consuming 0.42 toe per $1,000 GDP, approximately 65 percent more than Japan (0.26) and 13 percent more than West Germany (0.38), its two strongest competitors (CERA, 1993: 20; and earlier editions).

In 1990, with only 4.6 percent of the world's population, the United States consumed 24.6 percent of the total energy used worldwide, a staggering proportion but down considerably from the 1970 figure of 32.8 percent. Japan, with 2.3 percent of the world's population, consumed only 5.4 percent of the energy.

Germany, with 1.5 percent of the total population, consumed 4.3 percent. Re-lating energy consumption to the relative size of the economy, the United States used 24.6 percent of the world's energy to produce 29.8 percent of the world's GDP; Japan, 5.4 percent of the energy to supply 16.6 percent of the global GDP; and Germany, 4.3 percent of energy to produce 7.2 percent of the GDP (United Nations 1992: 202, 205). To highlight the contrasts and bring them into perspective, with slightly less than half the population of the United States and slightly more than half the American GDP, Japan used only 22 percent of the energy expended by the United States in 1990. Germany, with roughly one-third the population and one-fourth the GDP of the United States, consumed less than one-fifth the energy (17.4%) used by the United States. Put in monetary terms, while the United States spends roughly 11 percent of its GNP on energy, Japan spends only 5 percent. This relative inefficiency is estimated to cost the United States $220 billion a year and to give the Japanese a 5 percent economic edge for all they sell on the world market.

DOMESTIC ENERGY PRODUCTION

Energy self-sufficiency ratings rise and fall with the level of domestic energy production. Steady production increases assisted the 1973–85 gains in OECD self-sufficiency. During that 12-year period between the first oil crisis and the oil-price collapse, OECD energy production (measured in million tonnes oil equivalent) grew at an annual average rate of 2.1 percent. The growth in OECD energy output tumbled in the years after the oil-price crash, to an average annual rate of only 1.2 percent for the remainder of the decade—40 percent less than previously.

Of the three OECD regions—North America, Europe, and the Pacific—North America has typically maintained the highest level of energy production and the highest level of energy self-sufficiency. At the outbreak of the first oil crisis, North America produced 1,637 mtoe of fossil fuels, far in excess of OECD Europe's 415 mtoe or OECD Pacific's 101 mtoe. Its energy self-sufficiency rating of 87 percent also dwarfed the ratings of 36 percent and 26 percent in Europe and the Pacific, respectively. At the end of the 1980s, North America was still producing more than twice as much energy as Europe and nearly nine times as much as the Pacific region (IEA 1991: 116). Were it not for major increases in coal production in the United States, however, North America's energy production would not have fared so well. Coal production accounted for only 25 percent of fossil fuel output in the United States in 1973, but by 1980 it was responsible for 30 percent, and by 1990 it accounted for 40 percent. On balance, from 1973 to 1990, U.S. coal output (measured in energy content, not in total tons) grew by more than 60 percent while oil and gas production each fell by nearly 20 percent. This shift toward coal reflects the structure of Amer-ica's energy reserves. The United States, which in 1991 possessed less than 4 percent of the world's oil and gas reserves, contained 23 percent of the world's coal reserves. U.S. coal reserves will last, at the current rate of production, for more than two centuries. Its oil and gas reserves, by comparison, will last for only ten years (British Petroleum 1992: 2, 26).

Like the overall pursuit of energy self-sufficiency, the growth in U.S. coal production dropped off sharply after 1985. Between 1973 and 1985, American coal miners increased yearly tonnage at an average annual rate of 3.4 percent. Between 1985 and 1989, coal production increased by only 2.4 percent annually. The evidence clearly suggests that 1985 marks a transition in the U.S. coal industry. That same year also marks the onset of the great decline in oil production in the United States. American oil output had climbed from 8.4 million barrels per day (mbd) in 1975 to 8.6 mbd in 1980 and then to nearly 9.0 mbd in 1985. Alaska's oil provided a good portion of this growth. The price crash then drove many high-cost producers out of the industry and restrained domestic exploration activity. Oil output in the United States has declined in every year since the price collapse. Rising oil output and rapid coal expansion produced the pre-1985 energy production increases. Falling oil output and lower rates of coal growth caused the post-1985 stagnation in North American output.

Neither in its energy production nor in its energy self-sufficiency ratio has Europe ever approached North America. Europe has, however, far outpaced North America in terms of improvement rates. Between 1973 and 1989, Europe's fossil fuel production increased by over 90 percent, far more than North America's 15 percent gain. In that same period, its energy self-sufficiency rating soared from 36 to 60 percent, while North America's held steady at 87 percent. Nearly all of Europe's production and self-sufficiency increases resulted from growth in North Sea oil, especially before 1985. The first oil crisis greatly intensified the search for North Sea oil and helped raise Britain's and Norway's combined reserve estimates from less than 1 billion barrels (bbl) in 1970 to nearly 20 bbl in 1975. Britain and Norway's total production levels grew with the reserve estimates, from nothing in 1970 to 3.32 million barrels per day (bpd) in 1985 (CERA 1993: 28). Between 1985 and 1990, however, the United Kingdom's reserve estimates fell from 9.5 bbl to 8.8 bbl and its output slipped from 2.5 million bpd to 1.8 million bpd. Norway, by comparison, enjoyed a major upturn in reserve estimates, from 8.3 to 11.3 bbl, and its production climbed from 0.5 million bpd to 1.6 million bpd. Norway's oil production offers the best hope for Europe's faltering energy production and self-sufficiency. Increases in nuclear power production, mostly in France and Germany, helped improve Europe's self-sufficiency rating, especially in the early 1980s. Europe's nuclear power production grew at an average annual rate of 20 percent from 1980 to 1985, but only 5 percent from 1985 to 1990.

Fossil fuel production increased even more rapidly in OECD Pacific than it did in OECD Europe. The region's energy production climbed from 101 mtoe in 1973 to 237 mtoe in 1990, as oil production increased by 50 percent, coal production doubled, and natural gas output quadrupled. The increases in domestic production helped lift the area's fossil fuel self-sufficiency rating from

26 percent in 1973 to 44 percent in 1990. Japan's energy imports, especially its oil imports, have historically limited the OECD Pacific's energy self-sufficiency. Energy production in Australia and New Zealand, the other two Pacific members of OECD, has boosted the region's energy independence. Australia's coal production has contributed enormously to the region's energy supply. That production grew at the exceptional rate of 10 percent annually between 1980 and 1985 and then declined to a less stellar pace of only 2 percent for the remainder of the decade. Australia's oil output, which never exceeded 1 percent of global output, followed a similar pattern. It increased at an average annual rate of 8 percent between 1970 and 1985 and then went into a slump—not until 1990 did Australia recover its 1985 production level, and then only for one year.

In sum, 1985 clearly marks the end of OECD's concerted effort to increase domestic energy production. According to a wide variety of indicators, OECD's energy production went into a slump after the 1985 collapse in oil prices. While it lasted, the efforts to raise energy production enabled many nations to diversify their energy use.

DIVERSIFICATION

The two oil shocks convinced most nations, especially the industrialized ones, that the time had come to diversify their energy consumption. The diversification mandate implied two goals: to become less oil-dependent, and to use less imported oil to satisfy remaining oil requirements. Like conservation, the diversification movement made its greatest gains before 1985. Oil's share of world primary energy consumption, which rose marginally from 48 percent in 1970 to 49 percent in 1975, declined slightly to 47 percent in 1980 and then dropped dramatically, to 41 percent in 1985. After edging down to 40 percent in 1988, the proportion remained unchanged in each of the following four years (CERA 1993: 18). The remarkable gains made in the early 1980s dwarf those of the later 1980s.

Oil's share of the energy market declined because cutbacks in the growth of oil consumption during this period far outstripped the reductions in energy demand. Several reasons explain the disparity. There are more relatively close substitutes for oil than for energy in general. Fears of supply uncertainties lingering from the continued volatility of the Middle East political situation enhanced the value and reduced the relative cost of the more reliable alternate fuels. Environmental concerns over air pollution and acid rain encouraged the use of noncarbon fuels and cleaner-burning carbon fuels such as natural gas. Technological advances in the automotive industry increased fuel efficiency dramatically, doubling average mileage per gallon in even the most recalcitrant American market. And many industries and utilities invested in fuel-switching capabilities that allow easy operational changeovers from oil to natural gas in response to relative fuel prices.

Two forces in particular, however, warrant special attention in explaining the radical, pre-1985 drop in oil's share of total primary energy consumption. First, between 1980 and 1985, world oil consumption actually declined from 62.7 to 60.1 mbd. This major reduction in fuel oil consumption—used primarily as boiler fuel in industrial furnaces and electric utilities—explains most of the 1980–85 decrease in oil dependence. Japan, Western Europe, and the United States cut their combined use of fuel oil from 8.2 mbd in 1980 to 4.6 mbd in 1985 (CERA 1993: 14). This 3.6 mbd reduction actually exceeds the net decline in worldwide oil demand. Utilities in the United States exemplify the oil-saving adjustments made during these years. Responding to price and policy developments, they slashed the portion of electricity generated by oil, which fell from 17 percent in 1977, to 11 percent in 1980, and then to 4 percent in 1985. In keeping with the post-1985 demise of the diversification effort, the share of electricity in the United States produced by oil increased to nearly 6 percent in 1989 (CERA 1992a: 26).

A second factor—the comparatively rapid rise in demand for other energy sources—also explains the marked drop in worldwide oil dependence between 1980 and 1985. As demand for other fuels increased more quickly than the demand for oil, oil's share of total primary energy consumption became significantly smaller. During this period, when worldwide oil use declined at an average annual rate of 1.3 percent, use of other fossil fuels increased impressively. Consumption of natural gas grew at an annual average rate of 2.5 percent and coal consumption increased by nearly 2.3 percent annually. Concurrently, global use of nuclear power rose 15 percent per year and the demand for hydropower increased at an average annual rate of 2.8. Thus, while oil lost nearly 6 percent of the world's energy market, gas gained 1.2 percent of it, coal picked up 1.5 percent, nuclear acquired an additional 2.3 percent, and hydro captured 0.5 percent more of the market (BP 1992: 32; and earlier editions). The gap between oil-demand growth and demand growth for other fuels narrowed significantly after 1985. Between 1985 and 1990 oil use actually grew more quickly than either coal use or hydropower.

The pre-1985 diversification effort would have achieved even greater success if it had been able to reduce transportation fuel use by the same proportion that it reduced stationary oil use. But the transportation sector, especially in the United States, proved intractable. Motorists in the United States consume 40 percent of all the petroleum used in the country and nearly 15 percent of all the oil used in the world. A variety of forces encourage such liberal use. First, the United States maintains the world's largest network of roads and superhighways. Its transportation system is designed mainly for automobiles and trucks. The average American motorist drives nearly 8,000 miles each year, more than twice as far as European drivers and three times as far as drivers in Japan. Second, Americans have maintained their preference for comparatively large, heavy cars. Automobiles in the United States average 26 miles per gallon (mpg), compared to 40 to 50 mpg in Europe and Japan. Third, tax policies in the United States do little to discourage gasoline consumption. During the late 1980s, when American drivers paid an average gasoline tax of 14 cents/gallon, comparable taxes registered $1.84 in Japan; $2.75 in Germany; and $3.16 in Italy. The conditions that encourage Americans to use transportation fuel have consistently thwarted the diversification effort. Even between 1980 and 1985, when world oil consumption fell by over 2.6 mbd, gasoline consumption in the United States remained completely unchanged. Transportation fuels in other industrialized nations also resisted reduction, falling by a total of less than 1 percent.

The 1980s diversification effort would also have proved more effective if natural gas had been able to claim an unimpeded share of the world energy market. But restrictive forces prevented the expansion of gas markets in both the United States and Europe. The leaders of Europe's industrialized economies planned in the early 1980s for a massive increase in gas imports from the Soviet Union. In the Cold War atmosphere, however, the United States opposed the move and maneuvered with considerable success to bar Europe from using American equipment to transport Soviet gas to European markets. The effort alienated Western Europe but it managed to keep Soviet gas out of Europe for a number of years. It also restricted gas consumption and impeded Europe's diversification effort. Concurrent U.S. policy likewise stymied the expansion of its domestic gas markets. The Powerplant and Industrial Fuel Use Act of 1979, which was intended to preserve domestic gas resources, limited industry's consumption of natural gas, banned the construction of new gas boilers, and forced some utilities to switch to coal. Gas consumption in industrial and electric utility sectors tumbled from 10.9 trillion cubic feet (tcf) in 1980 to 8.2 tcf in 1986 (CERA 1992b: 42). Some of this decline in demand reflects an unusually sharp drop in gas-powered industrial activity. Much of it, however, stems from the policies that restricted gas consumption.

The diversification effort's second goal—to reduce the portion of imported oil used to satisfy unavoidable oil requirements—met with great success in the early 1980s, and then faltered. The United States used imported oil to satisfy 21 percent of its total oil needs in 1970. That peaked at 46 percent in 1977 and edged down to 43 percent in 1979. Then, in the aftermath of the second oil crisis, U.S. import-dependence dropped to 26 percent in 1985. The trend reversed direction after the 1985 price collapse. U.S. reliance on imported oil increased in each year between 1985 and 1990 (CERA 1993: 36). The United States experienced particularly good results in its effort to reduce the portion of OPEC oil used to satisfy its total oil requirements, slashing that dependency rating from 30 percent in 1979 to 11 percent in 1985. Like its overall import-dependence, the U.S. OPEC dependence rebounded after 1985, climbing to 25 percent in 1990. Similar patterns prevailed all around the world. Western Europe imported all the oil it used in 1974. Imports became a less significant source of oil, accounting for only 57 percent of oil use in 1986. The ratio rose to 63 percent for the remainder of the decade. The Pacific region also trimmed import-dependence prior to 1986 and then started to import a greater share of the oil it used.

While it lasted, the quest for energy self-sufficiency increased conservation efforts, stimulated domestic production, and encouraged diversification. The quest faltered in 1985 and with its demise the environmental imperative assumed preeminence.

THE RISE AND RENEWAL OF THE ENVIRONMENTAL IMPERATIVE

The environmental movement gathered considerable influence before 1973, lost some of its way when nations became preoccupied with energy self-sufficiency, then later regained leverage as the self-sufficiency imperative diminished. Environmental issues surfaced in Washington in the late 1960s. The issues became household concepts on Earth Day 1970, when hundreds of thousands of people around the world demonstrated their concern about environmental degradation. The early phases of the movement spurred the U.S. government to pass the National Environmental Policy Act (NEPA), establish the Environmental Protection Agency, and ratify the 1970 Clean Air Act. International efforts quickly followed American initiatives. The United Nations sponsored the 1972 Stockholm Conference to focus international attention on problems ranging from soil and water degradation to atmospheric pollution. The oil crises then stifled the movement. Immediate economic exigencies took priority over apparently less-pressing environmental issues—until two big events in the mid-1980s reignited the environmental imperatives: the oil-price collapse marked the apparent end of energy insecurity and the explosion at Chernobyl reminded the world that it needed to tend to the hazards it had created. Environmentalism had returned.

Debates over Alaska's oil reserves vividly symbolize the rise, pause, and renewal of the environmental effort. American geologists discovered Prudhoe Bay's monstrous oil fields in 1968 and expected to deliver the oil to markets in the lower states within three years. Great plans were undertaken but abruptly thwarted when, in the wake of the catastrophic Santa Barbara oil spill of 1969, environmentalists won a court injunction to halt development. The injunction held until the 1973 oil crisis prompted an emergency go-ahead on the plan. It then took only four years to develop the infrastructure that could transport the oil from Alaska's North Slope to American markets. Proponents of Alaskan oil development, hoping that energy-security concerns would once again override environmental concerns, vigorously advocated development of the Alaskan National Wildlife Reserve (ANWR) oil resources. The estimated 6 billion bbl of recoverable oil could lift reserves in the United States by 20 percent and extend the life expectancy of oil production from 10 to 12 years. The environmental/energy-security debate raged until October 1992, when the U.S. Senate moved to prohibit ANWR drilling. Environmentalists had regained the leverage they lost in 1973. The post-1985 sense of energy security, combined with a number of monumental environmental catastrophes—such as the *Exxon Valdez* oil spill and the Chernobyl calamity—lend great support to this second phase of the environmental movement.

Two salient aspects of the new environmentalism—its concern with global warming and its concentration in the industrialized world—will shape the environmental imperative's impact on energy markets. Concerns about global warming will draw greater attention to the ways in which energy consumption threatens to damage the earth's atmosphere. Global burning of fossil fuels currently spews more than 5 billion tons of carbon into the air each year. These carbon emissions, the most significant contributor to global warming, amount to more than a ton for every person on the planet. Oil use accounts for about 45 percent of the energy-based carbon emissions, coal for about 38 percent, and natural gas for 17 percent. Efforts to control global warming will favor less carbon-abundant fuels and restrict the use of great carbon producers. Measured in terms of pounds of carbon per million Btus, direct combustion of fossil fuels produces a wide range of carbon emissions: natural gas, 118; gasoline, 190; coal, 210. A car that averages 20 mpg produces one pound of carbon for every mile driven. Electricity production is a remarkably carbon-intensive enterprise. In using coal to generate 1 million Btus of electricity, utilities produce nearly 700 pounds of carbon. The second characteristic, the environmental movement's concentration in the industrialized world, will limit its impact on hazardous energy use in the developing nations—which consume only 25 percent of the world's energy but 40 percent of its coal. The Rio 1992 (environment) Summit proved that these nations cannot afford to comply with many of the proposed improvements. Directly or indirectly, the new environmentalism will impact each fuel market.

OIL AND THE ENVIRONMENTAL IMPERATIVE

The new environmental imperative will impact oil exploration and production (E&P), transportation, refining, and consumption. It will likely increase petroleum product prices and petroleum import-dependence throughout the OECD. The outcome of the ANWR debate suggests that the environmental imperative will restrict E&P activities throughout the OECD. Less E&P activity translates, over the long run, into greater import-dependence. Public reaction to the *Exxon Valdez* and to the January 1993 Scottish oil spill indicate widespread support of legislation that will require greater use of double-hulled tankers and other spill-slowing technologies. Use of these technologies will also raise product prices. Environmental concerns are increasing product specifications and refining costs, especially in the United States and Europe. European refiners alone will have to spend close to $15 billion during the 1990s in order to comply with the mandated reductions in gasoline's lead content, diesel fuel's sulfur content, and the harmful ingredients in most other petroleum products. The environmentally driven financial strains have forced many OECD refiners out of business and increased the probability that OECD nations will ultimately increase their imports of petroleum products. If consumers can find substitutes for the environmentally improved but more expensive products, then refiners will have to bear the improvement cost. Otherwise, as with transport fuels and home heating oil, the consumer will pay more, even if ecology taxes are not imposed.

NATURAL GAS AND THE ENVIRONMENTAL IMPERATIVE

The environmental imperative promises, at least in theory, to boost the demand for natural gas. Natural gas is comparatively clean-burning and its production and transport entail relatively small environmental risk. The U.S. Energy Policy Act of 1992 describes natural gas as an "abundant, environmentally benign and inexpensive substitute for insecure foreign oil" that can "cut auto emissions, reduce acid rain, supply independent power producers and utilities and lower oil imports." The government evidently regards natural gas as a solution to both environmental and security needs. It remains to be seen, however, whether the environmental advantages of gas will translate into greater market share, either in the United States or in other countries. The greatest potential for increased gas demand lies not with the industrial sector, the biggest user of natural gas, but with electric power producers who consistently use about 15 percent of American gas supplies. The 1990 Clean Air Act Amendments require utilities to cut sulfur dioxide emissions from the 1980 level of 17.4 million tons to 8.95 million tons in 2000. This requirement clearly favors gas in new power plant production and encourages the switch to gas in existing plants. Utilities and nonutility generators will also tend toward gas because gas-powered plants involve low construction and operation costs. Russia's political stability will shape the future of Europe's gas use and OECD investment will determine the developing world's gas use. It seems doubtful that gas will replace much oil in the transportation sector.

COAL AND THE ENVIRONMENTAL IMPERATIVE

More than other fuels, coal has the power to acidify lakes, destroy forests, and cause serious respiratory illness. Over the past decade France, the United Kingdom, West Germany, and the former Soviet Union have all cut back on the use of coal: France by switching to nuclear energy, the former Soviet Union by tapping its abundant natural gas reserves. Just recently the governments in the United Kingdom and West Germany caused a furor by attempting to shut down a major portion of their coal-mining capacity as unproductive, unprofitable, and environmentally undesirable.

Coal, nonetheless, possesses distinct advantages, not the least of which are its relative abundance and generous geographical distribution throughout most of the world. Proven coal reserves are some four to five times more abundant than comparable reserves of oil and natural gas. Judging by reserves-to-production ratios at the end of 1991, indicating the number of years remaining reserves would last if production were to continue at present levels, North America has coal enough to last 260 years; Europe, 472 years; Africa, 336 years; Asia and Australia, 196 years. Of all the major regions of the world, only Latin America has negligible endowments, possessing no more than 1.1 percent of the world's coal reserves. Of the major countries, Japan has only 0.1 percent (BP 1992: 26).

Given its relative abundance, coal will undoubtedly continue to play an important role in the energy arena. Proponents of coal use argue that two emerging trends could reduce coal's environmental drawbacks. First, more efficient combustion can reduce the amount of coal needed to produce a given level of heat or electricity. Even before the oil crises forced a reassessment of fuel use, technological improvements had boosted coal-burning efficiency from 5 percent in the early part of the century to nearly 40 percent. A second technological drive—to reduce emissions from every ton of coal that is burned—has also made great strides. Scrubbers typically capture 90 percent of sulfur emissions. Fluidized-bed combustion and coal-gasification also provide ways to use coal's energy without ravaging the atmosphere. All of these advances, which can make coal environmentally more acceptable, increase the cost of coal consumption. Scrubbers, for example, can add as much as 40 percent to power plant construction costs and 35 percent to operational costs. Industrialized nations will be able to fund these adjustments. They will remain heavily coal-dependent, but will use coal in more environmentally tolerable ways. Of the developing nations, China, which has 11 percent of the world's proven coal reserves, is chronically short of hard currency to purchase foreign oil, and currently accounts for 25 percent of global coal use, is unlikely to make these changes. Coal consumption in China will climb, as will the environmental harm.

NUCLEAR POWER AND THE ENVIRONMENTAL IMPERATIVES

Environmentalists have good reason to regard nuclear power as both the best hope for clean power and the worst of all environmental hazards. While nuclear power can produce electricity without exacerbating the greenhouse effect, it poses the constant threat of a reactor malfunction. It could produce another Three Mile Island or another Chernobyl. The process also generates costly, hazardous nuclear waste. Different countries weigh the costs and benefits in different ways. With the exception of Sweden, France has made the most concentrated effort to develop and exploit its nuclear capabilities. From the inception of its program, France has insisted on standardization to reduce construction, operation, servicing, and safety regulation costs. By forgoing constructive innovations that competitive design and bidding might introduce, France has been able to telescope construction schedules from site selection to triggering of the reactor within a narrow time span of six years, less than half the average time for completion of a nuclear facility in the United States. Over the past 20 years France has installed sufficient nuclear power to satisfy 31 percent of its total energy needs and more than 67 percent of its domestic demand for electricity. Sweden derives 45 percent of its total energy from nuclear power; Switzerland, 24 percent (BP 1992: 34).

The United States has encountered severe problems in expanding its civilian nuclear program. Its first generation of nuclear reactors—light-water reactors adapted from nuclear submarines—had little protection against sudden, violent changes in temperature. At Three Mile Island the reactor reached the meltdown stage within two and a half hours of the accident. Technological advances have increased reactors' size but not their inherent safety. Federally regulated safeguards have raised operating costs beyond the most pessimistic predictions. More than 100 nuclear projects planned since 1974 have been canceled. Of the 111 existing nuclear plants, 24 may close by 1999. Without major scientific advances, environmental liabilities will overpower nuclear's assets as a source of energy security in the United States and elsewhere. Sweden, for example, which has the largest proportional domestic nuclear capacity, has moved to ban all nuclear power by 2010. Some people, however, still remain optimistic. With new and better designs they see a safe and productive future for the industry. With rapidly depleting fossil fuel reserves in the OECD countries and growing dependence on foreign suppliers, they argue that nuclear energy is the only viable path toward energy independence. The U.S. government, for its part, remains open. In January 1993 the Department of Energy announced it would provide $150 million to help defray the cost of two studies devoted to new nuclear power plant designs.

CONCLUSIONS

The oil crises of 1973 and 1979–80 ravaged the global economy and cast many countries into heated pursuit of energy self-sufficiency. That drive for energy and economic independence made many nations, but especially the industrialized economies of the OECD, intensify their conservation efforts, escalate their domestic energy production, and increase their attempts to diversify fuel consumption. Each of these efforts made great strides before 1985 but then faltered in the wake of the oil-price collapse. In the interim, the environmental movement gained steam. It had gathered momentum until the early 1970s but was demoted to a secondary concern when the oil crises confronted countries with the threat of economic chaos. At about the same time that the collapse in global oil prices convinced many nations to slow their pursuits of energy self-sufficiency, the Chernobyl explosion reignited worldwide concerns about environmental degradation. A number of other ecological disasters reinforced that concern. Whereas the self-sufficiency imperative favored nuclear power and coal, the environmental imperative opposes them. Oil, the apparent villain of the self-sufficiency drive, gets mixed reviews from the environmental imperative—notwithstanding OPEC's effort to present oil as part of the environmental solution. Natural gas has emerged as the darling of both imperatives, and will gain market share if the needed infrastructure is installed. Both voices will be heard, but the environmental voice, for now, will be heard more clearly.

REFERENCES

The British Petroleum Company (BP). *Statistical Review of World Energy*. London: BP, 1992.
Cambridge Energy Research Associates (CERA). *Electric Power Trends*, Cambridge, MA: CERA, 1992a.
————. *Natural Gas Trends: North America*. Cambridge, MA: CERA, 1992b.
————. *World Oil Trends*. Cambridge, MA: CERA, 1993.
International Energy Agency (IEA). *Energy Balances of OECD Countries*. Paris: IEA, 1991.
United Nations. *Human Development Report*. New York: Oxford University Press, 1992.

Chapter 4

Oil Pricing

J. Cale Case

How much should a barrel of oil cost? This is an often-asked question that has no easy answer. Oil is a strategic and valuable resource. It is frequently associated with supply uncertainty. The question of whether or not we are running out of oil is one of major concern.

Economics has focused on natural resource availability since its inception. Early writings on the possibility of world resource production being unable to keep pace with a growing population led to economics' designation as the "dismal science."[1] However, despite centuries of predictions that we are running out, most natural resources, including oil, are still in plentiful supply. Real prices for extractive natural resources have, almost uniformly, declined with time as improvements in the technology of mining, refining, and utilization have occurred.

This chapter considers how the price of oil is determined—it discusses the relevant economic theory of oil pricing, analyzes the the empirical evidence regarding pricing tendencies, and concludes by speculating on future price trends.

OIL PRICING: THE THEORY

This section begins with a discussion of supply and demand analysis and considers theoretical opportunity cost models that predict increasing resource scarcity. The traditional model is expanded to allow for improving technology, market failures, and uncertainty.

Supply and Demand

Market prices for any commodity represent the product of two forces: supply and demand. Supply is a function that describes how much of a good or service will be provided by producers, given certain conditions. Similarly, demand is a function describing how much of a good or service will be desired by consumers, under specified conditions. In their most simple formulation, both relationships can be expressed as functions of the price of the instant good or service.

The supply function is almost always upward sloping in price-quantity space. It illustrates the fact that firms are willing to supply *more* of a good or service as price increases. Conversely, the demand function is almost always downward sloping when charted in price-quantity space, reflecting consumers' desire to purchase increasing quantities as price falls.

For a hypothetical oil market the intersection of the supply and demand schedules, known as the equilibrium point, is the only price-quantity combination that satisfies both buyers' and sellers' desires and clears the market. If price is higher than the equilibrium price, sellers want to sell more oil than buyers want to buy, and the lack of buyers will cause sellers to lower prices. If price is lower than the equilibrium, buyers want to buy more oil than sellers want to sell and, as a consequence, price is bid upward. Changes in factors such as consumers' incomes and preferences, weather, population, price, and the availability of substitute goods or goods that are used in association with oil can cause the demand curve to shift. The supply curve can also shift due to cost-lowering technological innovations, changes in the prices of inputs, altering of producers' expectations regarding the future, the discovery of additional oil reserves, and other factors.

An important concept is how responsive the quantities demanded and supplied are to changes in market prices. This effect is measured in economics by a term known as "elasticity." If demand is very responsive to changes in the price of the instant good, then it is known as "elastic." Alternatively, if demand does not change very much with a price change, it is known as "inelastic." The process for supply is the same. Elasticity is different for each point along the demand and supply curves. Thus, we can observe little response due to price changes within a particular range, say at the lower end of the price spectrum, and significant response in another range, possibly at the higher end of the price spectrum. Both demand and supply are more elastic in the long term than in the short term, as buyers and sellers are better able to make price-driven adjustments over a longer time period.

If markets are competitive (i.e., composed of many individual buyers and sellers) then each market participant takes the price determined by the market equilibrium as a given. They can do nothing, acting unilaterally, to impact the price. Alternatively, markets with a single buyer, known as a monopsony, or a single seller, known as a monopoly, or both, can impact price unilaterally. A single buyer can refuse to purchase and exercise some control over the market price. Similarly, a monopolist can withhold supplies and drive up the market price.

Thus, the price of oil will be influenced by all the factors that influence either demand or supply and determine equilibrium.

Nonrenewable Resources Extraction Models

Imagine that you are an oil producer and that you have full knowledge of the extent of your reserves. Further, assume that you can access your reserves under constant marginal (additional) production costs and that you sell oil in a competitive market. These assumptions mean that your production costs are independent of the speed at which you remove oil and that you have the option of pumping all of your oil from your reserves in a relatively short time period.

At any point in time you have two options: remove the oil or leave it where it is. Since your goal is to maximize your returns over time, your decision must take into account the possibility of removing and selling all of the oil, investing the proceeds, and earning an annual return of say, r percent.

The opportunity to earn an annual return of r is essential to price determination. In order to decide to leave your oil in reserves, you must be assured that the price to be received in the future will cover your marginal extraction costs, *as well as the forgone interest that you could have earned if you had removed and sold the oil today*. The amount received above your marginal extraction cost is frequently referred to as a royalty.

Note that the above discussion holds for a competitive market. This result will also hold if all reserves are under the control of a single benevolent manager whose objective is to maximize social returns over time. (This case should not be confused with that of a privately motivated monopolist, which will be discussed later in this subsection.) Again, since the total amount of oil is fixed, "mining" and accepting payment for the oil today forgoes an alternative benefit to future members of society. Similarly, to receive a payment for oil in the future, society must forgo the opportunity to provide benefits to members in the present. Thus, in order to maximize societal welfare over time, oil prices will increase by trade-off between present and future members. The trade-off is measured by the social discount rate, s.[2]

While the above analysis produces interesting results regarding how price should increase, a more sophisticated analysis would attempt to better capture extraction cost differentials. One theory is that extraction costs will continue to increase as deposits of increasing difficulty are mined. It is easy to find examples of this in the oil business. When "Colonel" Ed Drake drilled the world's first commercial oil well in 1869 near Titusville, Pennsylvania, the "oil finding" business was relatively simple. Wells were shallow, and in some cases oil even flowed naturally to the surface. Today, discoveries are much more difficult to achieve. Oil wells are deeper and frequently offshore, requiring substantial up-front expenditures, and may take years to bear fruit when new fields are opened up. Since no rational producer will produce oil at a loss, price must always at least equal the marginal cost of the most recently tapped, and therefore the most costly, resource.

Of course, producing oil resources may have considerable lives and thus when marginal (expensive) resources are being utilized, older and cheaper resources will still be producing. Those resources with lower marginal costs than the most expensive resources brought on line will earn an extra "rent" equal to the difference between the marginal cost of their resource and the marginal cost of the most expensive resource being economically utilized.[3]

The above result regarding extraction costs, plus the opportunity cost implications discussed earlier, form the core of the traditional theory of nonrenewable resources, the most complete early exposition of which was developed by Harold Hotelling.[4] The model predicts that prices will continue to increase as long as demand sustains them. If alternative sources of energy exist as a "backstop," price increases will cease once the backstop price is reached. Further, the existence of a backstop resource will alter the oil price path as well as the initial oil royalty.

The biggest drawback of the traditional model is its presumed static technology. Once technology is allowed to improve, the fundamental result of increasing prices can be dampened and even reversed.

A more realistic model would allow oil recovery to become cheaper as technologies progress. Improvements in geology and seismology, and drilling, recovery, refinery, and transportation techniques all work to lower extraction costs, potentially offsetting increases predicted by the Hotelling model.

Market Failures

Market failures also impact the price path of petroleum products. When a market failure occurs, market allocation fails to lead to the most socially desirable outcome. Four cases of market failure impacting petroleum prices are discussed in this section: the problem of common property resources; divergence between private and social rates of discount; market structure deficiencies of monopoly, oligopoly, and cartels; and externalities.

Common Property Resources

One market failure surrounds the fact that oil pools are frequently common property resources. When several producers share rights to the same oil pool, each may have an incentive to pump extra oil to attempt to get the jump on his or her competitors and increase the relative share of pool profits. The result is that the pool is depleted more rapidly than it otherwise would be.[5] The problem is further compounded due to the physics of oil reservoirs, whereby overrapid extraction may reduce the total recoverability of the resource.

Divergence Between Private and Social Discount Rates

Another market failure surrounds differences between the private rate of interest, r, and the social rate of discount, s. Recall that r represents the trade-off between present and future activity for a private firm, and s measures the same trade-off from a social perspective. Most researchers would agree that they are not equal, and that $r > s$.

Two reasons are frequently cited for this divergence: the distorting effects of taxes, and the existence of a private "risk premium." The burden of taxes, such as corporate income taxes, requires firms to earn an extra return above that of the nontaxed "social" investor. Individual firms also face higher levels of risk because they lack the social investor's ability to spread risk across all projects. To compensate firms and encourage them to take this risk, an extra premium is required of the return.

Another school of thought holds that the appropriate social discount rate has little if anything to do with the rate of interest determined in capital markets. These writers argue that any such "private investor-derived" return does not measure concern for future generations.[6]

If the rate of interest determined in private capital markets exceeds the rate appropriate for judging societal trade-offs through time, then the rate of resource extraction conducted by autonomous private firms may be too rapid.

Monopoly, Oligopoly, and Cartels

Market structure issues play a critical role in oil pricing. Recall that the simple model presumes that oil producers cannot affect the price of the resource. Oil markets were assumed to be competitive—that is, composed of many buyers and sellers, each of which cannot unilaterally impact the price of the resource. However, the simple model does not adequately describe a world characterized by huge multinational firms, government monopolies, and cartels.

Monopoly represents a situation in which one producer supplies the market. A monopoly may be a "natural monopoly," whereby decreasing costs can lead to a single firm serving the market at the lowest possible cost, *providing appropriate regulatory actions are taken by government.* This is the so-called good monopoly. Other bad monopolies may exist because of government charter or endorsement, unfair competitive tactics, or alternative sources of market power. Consumers who purchase from a bad monopolist will most likely face higher prices than from competitive suppliers, leading to a reduction in the rate of resource use. However, some researchers have shown that while the monopoly price for an extractive resource is initially above that of the competitive price, it will rise more slowly so that in the long term, the prices are nearly the same.[7]

An oligopoly is a market structure dominated by a small number of relatively large firms. When making price/production decisions, each of the major firms must take into account the reactions that will be generated among competitors. Oligopolies often provide an almost irresistible urge for firms to collude in setting price and production targets.

A cartel is an association of producers that collude to simulate the monopoly outcome by restricting output. Cartels are frequently successful in increasing returns to members. However, cartels also face stability problems. Unless some mechanism exists to verify and enforce each member's quota, significant incentive exists for individual members to cheat by overproducing to take advantage of the higher, cartel-generated, prices. As more and more members cheat, the price-increasing efforts of the organization will cease to work, at least until things are reorganized for another try.

Externalities

The final type of market failure that may impact oil markets involves externalities. Externalities are impacts that accrue to third parties as a consequence of a production or consumption decision. Some types of externalities may be particularly troublesome. For example, a decision to consume petroleum by using gas in one's car may cause damage to other parties due to the associated air pollution. As a consequence, a private decision to consume gasoline, which weighs private costs and benefits, may not coincide with an optimal social decision, which would also consider costs imposed on third parties. The end result is that negative uncompensated externalities cause oil consumption to be greater than it otherwise should be.[8]

Uncertainty

The final extension of the simple model would be to include uncertainty. It is simply not known how much oil is left, how much is recoverable, and how technology will improve the ability to extract it. Such uncertainty regarding the size of the resource stock will tend to increase present prices above what they otherwise would be, and as more oil is discovered, prices will be depressed. Similarly, new discoveries of a substitute resource, such as natural gas for boiler fuel, will also depress prices. Similarly, uncertainty regarding the market application of backstop technology will tend to maintain higher present oil prices.

OIL PRICING: THE EVIDENCE

Despite theoretical support for increasing price paths, the notion of offsetting (indeed swamping) impacts of increased extraction efficiencies seems to be winning handily. The most famous study in this area was conducted by H. J. Barnett and C. Morse, who analyzed the price paths of agricultural, forestry, fishing, and extractive minerals—including petroleum.[9] Their findings strongly indicate that technological innovations and lower costs, rather than increasing Hotelling-style royalties, have driven the price paths of extractive resources, including oil, since at least the middle 1800s.

W. D. Nordhaus confirmed the Barnett and Morse study for the period 1900 to 1970, and found decreasing unit costs for all extractive resources except for copper.[10] Almost all researchers continue to find no evidence of increasing resource scarcity for extractive resources. However, G. M. Brown and B. C. Field found increasing prices for coal, lead, phosphorus, and zinc, but not oil, using an alternative specification that compared resource prices with the returns paid to capital.[11] V. K. Smith found that while extractive resource prices continued to decrease, the *rate* of decrease was declining.[12] Bucking the trend of downward prices for petroleum and other resources, P. W. MacAvoy suggested that the price increases of the 1970s would have happened without OPEC.[13]

Research in this area is proceeding. Evidence throughout the 1980s and 1990s shows that the decline in unit prices for petroleum products is continuing. The most recent extension of the Barnett and Morse work was undertaken by M. A. Adelman, who concluded that oil prices are likely to remain depressed unless OPEC reasserts a major role.[14]

Market Structure and Political Power

A lot of oil companies are very large. Twenty companies have annual revenues in excess of $10 billion (U.S.). Much of the writings on the political economy of oil have focused on the evils of these large multinational firms, often with special emphasis on U.S.-sanctioned wickedness vis-à-vis developing nations.[15] Today, industry concentration is smaller than historical levels, and the biggest oil players are governments, not firms, and with governments may lie many of the problems.

While the world's oil markets are far from being dominated by any one firm or company, within many countries monopoly provision by governmental or quasigovernmental entity is the rule. In these nations, consumers are likely to pay higher prices than in countries with competitive markets. Frequently, higher prices are justified as an attempt to more optimally influence people's behavior and force reduced consumption of petroleum—as well as provide revenue for other government projects. Perhaps just as frequently, higher prices are a product of government inefficiency, bloat, and corruption. Tax policies can play a similar role in generating higher prices and do not require government provision for collecting the subsidy flow. Lately, taxes have been frequently suggested as a mechanism to correct for externalities.

What about the impact of OPEC? Clearly, the OPEC cartel has the potential to enormously impact prices—at least in the short term. Witness the $3 to $32 increase in the price of oil during the eight-year period from 1972 until 1980. However, prices soon renewed their decline, and today stand near pre-1972 levels (in real terms). OPEC has not been able to support substantial increases, and oil markets have become somewhat more shockproof (e.g., the surprisingly small amount of disruption brought about by the recent Gulf War). The OPEC-driven price increases stimulated exploration and brought more oil to world markets, as well as encouraged Germany, Japan, and the United States to establish strategic reserves. OPEC has, except for a brief period following the Gulf War, had to survive with chronic current excess production capacity among the larger members.

One point is clear, however. Restraint, either communal, through OPEC, or through the unilateral actions of the Gulf States nations (especially Saudi Arabia), has had significant impact. Very low-cost, high-quality Saudi supplies could capture almost the entire world market, providing enormous returns to the country. These returns would likely exceed the present value of proceeds from any other price path. However, the simple fact remains that Saudi Arabia and the other nations of the Gulf States do not avail themselves of this opportunity. This action has required a combination of pro rata reductions among larger members and unilateral actions of Saudi Arabia. Thus, the conclusion may be that while OPEC has not had much particular success as of late in increasing prices, it has been very successful at preventing prices from falling as far as they otherwise would have.[16]

In the end, the cartel will likely hold together as each member has too much to lose from its collapse. However, little success will likely occur in raising prices. Volatility among members remains a possibility, albeit perhaps a declining one.

CONCLUSION

It is hoped that this chapter has helped to answer questions regarding how the price of oil is determined. Overwhelmingly, oil prices have declined over time following the Barnett and Morse model of resource scarcity. Our ability to find, transport, and process oil has continued to increase.

We are good at describing the past, but how about predicting the future? Even bigger questions remain: Will oil prices continue their stable to downward trend? Or will the physical limits of world supplies come into play to reverse the trend to date? We cannot escape these nagging questions.

Let's take a closer look at the experience in finding oil in one of the most thoroughly explored places on the globe, the continental United States. Some 90 percent of all the oil wells drilled in the world have been drilled in the lower 48 states. The results, based solely upon U.S. experience, would seem to indicate Hotelling-style increases. We cannot escape some basic indications of scarcity. Average lift prices in the United States are in the range of $15–$20 per barrel, while the same figures in Saudi Arabia are $1 to $4. The average U.S. well produces approximately 14 barrels/day, while the average Saudi well produces nearly 12,000 barrels/day. The United States, once the world's largest producer, has seen its share of the world's proven reserves fall below 4 percent.

Fortunately for the people of this world, the U.S. experience is an exception, and the earth still has a fabulous oil potential. Newly opened areas in the former Soviet Union and Eastern Europe, Latin America, China, and elsewhere all offer a promising future. Of particular significance, Russia has the potential to rival Middle Eastern production, although currently its reserves are more on par with the United States.

It seems obvious that if the U.S. experience was the world's, then we probably would see generalized increasing costs today. This would seem to imply that when the rest of the world becomes as picked over and as utilized as the United States has, costs will go up. As time progresses, demand will increase with a more developed world. We hope our knowledge of finding, producing, and possibly recycling will continue to increase, as well as our skill of using petroleum more efficiently, and will provide similar price paths for the next several decades. Then, perhaps, improved backstop technology may make the price of petroleum irrelevant.

NOTES

1. Thomas Robert Malthus, *An Essay on the Principle of Population as it Affects the Future Improvement of Society, with Remarks on the Speculations of Mr. Godwin, M. Condorcet, and other Writers*, published anonymously in 1798.

2. Implicit in this discussion are several heroic assumptions about the ability of our resource manager to determine the social welfare function. Fundamentally, we have assumed that returns from resource utilization (or nonutilization) have the same benefit regardless to whom the benefits occur. For more on this subject the reader is referred to J. de V. Graaff, *Theoretical Welfare Economics* (Cambridge: Cambridge University Press, 1957, reprinted 1979).

3. The notion of increasing marginal cost of utilization and economic rents was formulated by D. Ricardo, *Principles of Political Economy and Taxation* (London: Everyman, 1926: originally published in 1817).

4. H. Hotelling, "The Economics of Exhaustible Resources," *Journal of Political Economy* 39 (1931): 137–175.

5. The problem of so-called common property resources has been treated in economics for a considerable period. See, for example, H. S. Gordon, "The Economic Theory of a Common Property Resource: The Fishery," *Journal of Political Economy* 62 (April 1954).

6. See, for example, S. A. Marglin, "The Social Rate of Discount and the Optimal Rate of Investment," *Quarterly Journal of Economics* 77 (1963): 95–112.

7. See Partha Das Gupta and Geoffrey M. Heal, *Economic Theory of Exhaustible Resources* (Cambridge: Cambridge University Press, 1979), Chapter 6.

8. The key here is "uncompensated." External impacts of oil consumption may be partially or fully compensated by the existence of population control laws that embody society's preferences for a clean environment.

9. H. J. Barnett and C. Morse, *Scarcity and Growth: The Economics of Natural Resource Scarcity* (Baltimore: Johns Hopkins University Press, 1963).

10. See W. D. Nordhaus, "Resources as Constraint on Growth," *American Economic Review* 64 (1974): 22–26.

11. G. M. Brown and B. C. Field, "Implication of Alternative Measures of Natural Resource Scarcity," *Journal of Political Economy* 86 (1978): 229–243.

12. V. K. Smith, "Natural Resource Scarcity: A Statistical Analysis," *Review of Economics and Statistics* 61 (1979): 423–427.

13. Paul W. MacAvoy, *Crude Oil Prices as Determined by OPEC and Market Fundamentals* (Cambridge, MA: Ballinger, 1982).

14. M. A. Adelman, "Mineral Depletion, with Special Reference to Petroleum," *Re-

view of Economics and Statistics 72 (1990): 1–10; and "Modelling World Oil Supply," *Energy Journal* 14(1) (1988): 1–32.

15. See, for example, Robert Engler, *The Politics of Oil: Private Power and Democratic Directions* (Chicago: University of Chicago Press, 1961); and Michael Tanzer, *The Political Economy of International Oil and the Underdeveloped Countries* (Boston: Beacon Press, 1969).

16. See Adelman (1988) for more on this point.

Chapter 5

Spot, Options, and Futures Oil Markets

Robert A. Biolsi

Trading in the world's oil markets in the past 15 years has changed dramatically with the advent of derivative securities for oil and other petroleum products. Prior to the 1979 Iranian revolution, much of the oil market was dominated by long-term contracts with oil companies. Efforts, particularly those by OPEC, to control the supply of oil during the 1970s led, however, to the transition from long-term deals to spot market trading. With the trend toward short-term spot trading, risk and uncertainty regarding where equilibrium prices for petroleum would go became a prominent feature of the petroleum markets. It was with the development of spot trading, along with the surrounding uncertainty in the petroleum markets during this time, that in turn led to the successful development of derivatives on petroleum products.

These derivatives include oil futures contracts that currently trade on the New York Mercantile Exchange (NYMEX), the International Petroleum Exchange in London, and the Singapore International Monetary Exchange. Each of these exchanges trades options on oil as well. In recent years, over-the-counter markets have grown dramatically in terms of Swap agreements, as well as various types of exotic options. Since their introduction in the late 1970s and early 1980s, petroleum-related commodities have become the most actively traded commodity derivatives in the world.

Paradoxically, derivative contracts on petroleum became an integral part of the oil market on the heels of an attempt to fix prices by major producing countries. As will be discussed, futures and other types of derivative products are generally designed to offset the risk of fluctuating prices. In 1979 in the aftermath of the Iranian revolution, OPEC agreed to lift oil prices to $32 per barrel. Having such a target price would typically reduce the desirability of trading futures and options, since there would seem to be little profit incentive for traders to take positions on which direction the market was heading. However, attempting to establish a price floor at an unsustainably high level set off such huge turmoil and price volatility in the oil markets, that the value of futures, options, and relative derivative contracts became important for the oil industry.

DERIVATIVE MARKET OVERVIEW

Derivative securities come in various classifications. Forward agreements, as well as futures contracts, represent agreements to buy or sell a particular commodity or asset at a predetermined price on a specified future date. While alike in their basic terms, they differ in some important aspects. Futures contracts are standardized, while forward contracts are not necessarily so. For example, the crude oil futures contract traded on NYMEX calls for the purchase or sale of 1,000 barrels of light ''sweet'' crude oil for delivery in Cushing, Oklahoma. Forward contracts can vary with the grade of oil being delivered, the future date at which it is to be delivered, as well as the quantity that is to be delivered.

In addition, while forward contracts involve a single cash transaction at the expiration of the contract, futures contracts are ''marked-to-market.'' The exchange, through its clearinghouse mechanism, takes the opposite side of each transaction. The clearinghouse is simply the association of the exchange's collective clearing members. Clearing members are firms that take responsibility for honoring contract performance for each trader. For each party agreeing to buy (''go long'') oil, the clearinghouse agrees to sell. For each trader agreeing to sell (''go short''), the clearinghouse agrees to buy. By doing so, the exchange can virtually guarantee performance on its contracts by using the entire association of its clearing members to guarantee performance on each trade. This guarantee process is further enhanced with the concept of margins. These performance bonds require both sides to deposit certain sums of money into their respective accounts to insure that they both be in a position to meet their losses. Their accounts are then marked-to-market, a process whereby gains and losses are credited to their accounts on a daily basis. Consequently, futures contracts generally carry a AAA credit rating.

In contrast, forward contracts carry a credit that is only as good as the individual parties. Such markets are typical of trading in Brent crude oil in the North Sea. In the event of a large change in prices, there is a single large cash flow that can magnify the credit risk that is involved. In early 1986 a major default occurred as prices fell from about $30 to about $10 per barrel.[1]

Futures contracts also contain other characteristics and protections that are not typical of forward contracts. Among these are price and position limits. For example, NYMEX limits the allowable price fluctuation on certain of its contracts to $15/barrel/day.[2] By doing so, the market is thought to gain additional time to adjust to fundamental changes in prices. In addition, the exchanges limit the total amount of positions any single trader can hold in order to limit the possibility of traders manipulating the market.

ECONOMIC ROLE OF FUTURES MARKETS

Futures contracts got off to a rather hesitant start in the oil market. Several attempts by the Cotton Exchange (1971) and the Chicago Board of Trade (1975) were unsuccessful. This was probably due to the underlying nature of the cash market, where the norm of long-term deals limited the uncertainty of price behavior for the industry. The first successful petroleum-based contract was on #2 heating oil on NYMEX in 1978. This contract called for delivery of 42,000 gallons of #2 heating oil in New York harbor. While it was not greatly utilized at first, the industry gradually became accustomed to trading futures. By the early 1980s, it became one of the most actively traded commodity futures contracts in the world. This was followed by crude oil futures in 1983 and unleaded gasoline futures in 1984, also on NYMEX. Today these contracts represent the most actively traded contracts in the world, averaging more than 200,000 contracts traded per day in 1992.

For the oil markets, the futures markets play three critical economic functions in providing a price hedging mechanism, a price discovery function, and market liquidity. The success of energy futures in the last ten years is one measure of how valuable these contracts are in today's energy industry.

Hedging

In particular, futures contracts play an important role in providing a hedging mechanism for the oil industry. As mentioned previously, the oil industry underwent a transition from a long-term deal market to a day-to-day spot market in the 1980s. No longer could producers rely on long-term price agreements to help remove the uncertainty involved in drilling and exploration. Independent refiners faced increasing uncertainty over their costs for crude oil. In a market faced by abrupt supply shocks and sharp swings in demand, an enormous increase in risk faced participants in the oil markets. Prices fell from $40/barrel in the early 1980s to less than $10/barrel in 1986 for crude oil. Heating oil would experience a drop from $1.15/gallon in December 1979 to less than $.30 in 1986. During the Gulf crisis, crude oil would swing from $40/barrel in October 1990 to $19/barrel in April 1991 on NYMEX.

By hedging, producers and consumers of oil could help shield themselves from the volatile nature of oil prices through much of the period after 1979. Take, for example, the position of a producer who is ''long'' the cash commodity. Suppose the producer anticipates selling 1,000 barrels of crude oil a day at $20/barrel. Assuming the futures price can be locked in also at $20/barrel, a short hedge entails selling futures contracts to provide the producer with price insurance. If prices fall to $19/barrel, the producer stands to lose $1/barrel on his production output, but will gain $1/barrel on the futures position.

Of course, rising prices will entail losses on the futures position, which would then be offset by gains to the cash position. The essential point in this analysis is that the short hedge for the producer locks in the selling price for the production stream. In return for this downside price protection, however, any potential upside for rising prices is foregone.

For consumers of crude oil, such as gasoline or heating oil refiners, a long hedge can be utilized to provide price insurance. Such oil consumers tend to be "short" oil; that is, they need to buy it for refining purposes. For example, a refiner could be anticipating buying 1,000 barrels/day to refine into gasoline at $20/barrel. To offset the risk of rising prices, the producer can go long the futures contracts. In this way if prices should rise to $21/barrel, and the refiner has difficulty passing along the cost increase to the consumer, the profit margin of the refiner will not be adversely impacted. The addition $1/barrel that will be paid by the refiner for the crude oil will be offset by the $1/barrel that the refiner will make on the associated futures contract.

The above examples assume that the cash price of oil and the futures price move perfectly in tandem with one another. In setting the standardized terms and conditions for their contracts, futures exchanges take great care to insure "convergence" between the spot and futures markets. That is, they establish arbitrage mechanisms to help insure that the futures price at the expiration of the contract converges to the underlying cash market.

Specifically, they could call for the physical delivery of the underlying commodity. The most actively traded crude oil futures contract traded on NYMEX calls for the physical delivery of light sweet crude oil in Cushing, Oklahoma. This site was chosen because it is the nexus of several major crude oil pipelines, allowing for relatively easy delivery. If the futures price were to diverge too far from the underlying cash price, traders would be in a position to "arbitrage" the two markets, forcing them back in line. For example, suppose that just prior to expiration, the spot market price was greater than the futures price. Traders would be in a position to sell their crude oil inventories at the "expensive" price, and replace them at the "cheap" futures price by buying the futures contract. In sufficient volumes, this arbitrage would force the futures price higher and the cash price lower. Conversely, if the spot market price was less than the futures price, all traders could sell oil for delivery at the high futures price and transact to buy spot supplies to deliver against the contract. Again, prices would be forced to converge as futures prices would come under selling pressure and spot prices would firm.

However, hedgers must be aware of the fact that the correlation need not be perfect because of basis risks (which refers to the lack of correlation between futures and cash prices). This basis risk is most often attributed to the fact that there is a quality differential between the commodity traded in the cash or spot market and that which underlies the futures contract. For example, the most widely traded crude oil futures contract is traded on NYMEX. Six different grades of light sweet crude oil are deliverable under the contract, but the futures are generally priced as West Texas intermediate crude. However, if hedgers are looking for price protection for "sour" (high sulfur content) crude oil, they may find that the price movement in the futures contract is not exactly offset by the cash commodity. For example, the correlation between Alaskan North Slope crude and NYMEX futures is only about 0.8.

To minimize this basis risk, exchanges have sought to introduce futures contracts for different grades of crude oil. The Singapore International Money Exchange and NYMEX have introduced futures contracts based upon crude oil with high levels of sulfur (sour). However, these contracts have generated very little interest, for reasons to be explained.

Price Discovery

Prior to the introduction of actively traded futures contracts, the real price of oil was shrouded in secrecy. Cash transactions were subject to negotiation. Physical traders would have to make multiple calls to get a sense of where the price of crude oil was at a given moment in time. Today, only a quick look at a wire service screen gives the market's determination of where a price is at a given time. The reason is that virtually the entire oil industry participates in the futures markets. Between NYMEX and the International Petroleum Exchange more than 100 million notational barrels of oil futures traded per day in 1992, about four times the total output of OPEC!

It was often thought that futures prices were derived from the underlying cash prices. Today in a very real sense the opposite is the case. Cash market traders look to the futures markets to determine where their physical trades should be valued. Even for those grades of crude oil where there is no matching liquid futures market, such as for sour grades of oil, the futures market plays a major role in pricing. Many spot transactions are now executed at a differential below the futures price. This is perhaps one reason why contracts based on a sour crude delivery have not met with that much success. The sweet crude hedge based on the futures contracts satisfies most of the industry's hedging needs.

Price discovery takes place in the futures market because of the transparency that results through the mechanism of ''open outcry.'' With open outcry, traders on the floor of the exchanges shout out the prices they are willing to buy and sell at for the entire floor community to hear. Transaction prices are then quickly disseminated over wire services to virtually the entire petroleum industry. As noted, the spot market tends to be much more secretive.

Liquidity

Futures contracts also allow oil company traders to avoid entering into long-term agreements. Prior to the introduction of futures contracts, most oil deals were long-term (five to ten years) in nature. However, as OPEC countries gained control over worldwide oil supplies, short-term transactions became the rule. With supply inelastic, while demand was becoming progressively more elastic with the rise in prices, market prices became increasingly more volatile.

Futures contracts give oil companies the facility to enter into long-term cash market contracts but keep liquid by offsetting them with futures contracts. For example, an oil company may agree to buy 100,000 barrels/day of oil for five years in the cash market at $20/barrel. If its circumstances change in the future whereby it no longer needs or desires to continue purchasing the oil, a very convenient means to back out of the contract is simply to sell futures contracts against it. While the futures contracts may not guarantee they will be able to sell the oil for $20/barrel, it would effectively unwind the physical delivery properties of the cash deal.

In fact more than 95 percent of all petroleum futures contracts do not involve the actual delivery of the petroleum product. On the International Petroleum Exchange, all contracts are cash settled. On NYMEX most contracts actually are offset before expiration. Physical delivery of the product represents only a very small percentage of all contracts traded. However, the fact that physical delivery is possible plays an important role in insuring that futures prices converge to actual cash prices.

OPTION MARKETS

Options on petroleum futures are often perceived to be substantially different from that of futures. However, in reality, they are closely related instruments.[3] Technically, the buyer of a call (put) option has the right, not the obligation, to buy (sell) the petroleum futures contract at a prespecified price within a certain time period. This designated price is known as the strike or exercise price.

Options can be viewed as complementary to futures contracts for hedging and speculative purposes. Futures have symmetric risk/reward profiles, while options are asymmetric. The futures contract risk/reward profile is symmetric about the price at which a futures contract is entered. For a long crude oil futures position, for example, profits result from rising prices (a one-dollar rise in price translates into a one-dollar rise in the value of the position, and vice versa). The risk/reward profile for options is asymmetric. A long crude oil call option increases in value as the futures price increases (albeit generally not on a one-for-one basis). However, losses, or decreases in value, are limited to the premium paid, regardless of how low prices fall.

The asymmetric risk/reward profiles of options and combined futures/options strategies allow commercial oil company hedgers to fine-tune their exposures to a much greater degree than futures alone would allow. This asymmetry of risk and reward also is attractive to speculators, who, by providing risk capital, will contribute substantially to the liquidity of the petroleum options market.

For example, a call option may specify the right to go long a futures contract at $20/barrel. If the futures price is at $21 on expiration day, the holder of the option would have the incentive to exercise the option for a $1/barrel profit. Mathematically, the holder of the call option has the right to go long the futures at $20/barrel and could then turn around and sell the futures at $21/barrel. The higher the price of the futures at expiration, the proportionately greater the value of the call option. If the futures are trading at less than $20 on expiration day, the call option holder has an incentive to let the option expire worthless.

Conversely, since the buyer of the put option has the right to sell the underlying futures contract at the exercise price, he or she stands to profit as the futures price falls. For example, the holder of a put option with a $20 exercise price has the right to sell the underlying futures contract at $20. If by expiration the price of the underlying futures should fall to $19/barrel, the put option will be valued at $1/barrel as the holder can buy the futures at $19 and then sell them for $20. The lower the price of the futures at expiration, the proportionately greater the value of the put option. If the futures are trading at more than $20 on expiration day, the put option holder has an incentive to let the option expire worthless.

So in the above examples, whenever the option buyers exercised their options, it came at the expense of the seller. If the option should expire worthless, the seller simply keeps the option premium. However, unlike the buyer, who can simply let the option expire worthless, for sellers, in return for the income from the sale of the initial premium, the losses can be virtually unlimited.

Unlike futures contracts, options can be viewed similarly to that of an insurance policy, hence the use of the term "premium" instead of "price" for the option. The strike price can be viewed as being very similar to an insurance deductible. For call options, the higher the strike price, the lower the premium of the option. This follows since the higher strike price implies a higher insurance "deductible." For example, the crude oil call option with a strike price of $25 will always be less in value than the corresponding $20 call option. This flexibility in choosing strike prices allows the trader to tailor the option to meet the cost concerns and hedging needs of his or her firm.

While the pricing of options is beyond the scope of this chapter, one of the characteristics of price plays a major role in the economic role in options on futures contracts. Specifically, in option pricing theory, the option price embeds an implied forecast of volatility for the underlying futures contract. In fact, academic studies have concluded that this is in fact the best forecast of the magnitude of future fluctuations in the petroleum markets. This can be extremely useful information for industry participants.

For example, on the eve of the Gulf War in January 1991, with crude oil trading at about $30, the March $30 crude oil options on NYMEX implied a forecast of about 57 percent volatility. With options, volatility is almost always quoted as an annualized percent of contract value. Therefore since this option had only 23 days to expire, the implied volatility would be prorated to the time left to expiration. Assuming that the percent return on crude oil is normally distributed, the implied forecast of a 99 percent confidence interval for crude oil over a one-day time interval would have been plus or minus $8.92/barrel[4] for any given day over the interval. When trading began in the immediate aftermath of the initiation of hostilities on January 17, 1991, March crude oil prices fell $9.66/barrel. The option-implied volatility seemed to give a good estimate of the market's future volatility, which in turn gives the industry a quantitative measure for its hedging needs.

Recent trends in the oil over-the-counter markets have seen the development of more exotic types of options. Average price, or Asian options, have payoffs that depend on the average price over a period of time, typically over the course of a month, and the strike price. With these options, it not only depends upon where the futures settle at expiration, but also what pattern of futures prices transpired over the averaging period.

"Crack Spread" options have also become popular over-the-counter instruments. The name is derived from the refining process where crude oil is "cracked" into heating oil and gasoline components. These options derive their value from the differential between refined products and crude oil. This option has the desirable characteristic that it provides a hedge for an integrated oil company's profit margin rather than the level of prices. For example, if crude oil and gasoline prices both fall in tandem with one another, a vertically integrated oil company will not suffer any loss in terms of its profit margin. However, if crude oil increases faster than the price of gasoline (i.e., the spread narrows), the oil company can suffer losses even though prices are rising. It is just such a scenario that has made these "Crack Spread" options popular with the petroleum industry.

There are many other types of exotic options that are beyond the scope of this section, including "Lookback," "Knockout," and "Down and Out" options. All of these options have unique characteristics that provide hedges for given unique scenarios. The industry appears to be continuously searching for instruments by which it can tailor hedges to its own unique circumstances. The use of options in the petroleum industry seems to be evolving in order to meet this need.

SWAP MARKETS

Following on the heels of the tremendous success enjoyed by Swap agreements in the interest rate and currency markets, Swap agreements have become a popular hedging vehicle in the petroleum markets in recent years. Essentially, a Swap agreement calls for the exchange of cash flows between two parties based on the relative move of an index price relative to a fixed reference price. Typically, the index price will be a widely disseminated price such as an oil cash price from a trade publication or even a futures price from one of the exchanges, such as NYMEX.

As an example, suppose a producer expects to sell 1,000 barrels of light sweet crude oil per month for the next three years. Suppose further that the current price is $20/barrel, and that the producer would like to lock this price in. A Swap agreement offers the one way of doing this. As the price, based on an index, falls below $20, the counter party will be obligated to pay the producer the difference between the index price and the reference price of $20. For example, if the index falls to $19, the counter party would be obligated to pay the difference, $1 ($20 − $19) times 1,000 barrels. As index prices rise above $20 the producer becomes obligated to pay the counter party the difference in prices. For example, if the index price rises to $21, the producer is required to pay the counter party $1,000.

The counter party could be a Swap dealer, such as a bank, or another industry participant who has the opposite petroleum price risk of the producer. For example, an independent refiner may have concerns about crude oil rising in price, since it would squeeze the profit margins for refining gasoline. In this case, the refiner through the Swap could effectively lock in the $20/barrel price over the three-year period.

Note that the Swap cash flows involve only the difference in prices, not the entire amount of the notational value of the Swap. Also, the resettlement dates are customized according to the needs of the participants. For example, they could be monthly, quarterly, or semiannually. The fixed reference price is often an average of a "strip" of futures prices going out a similar length of time.

Swaps offer an advantage over futures hedges in that they don't entail the possible daily cash flow exchanges of marking-to-market. Also, industry participants may have bumped into the position limit ceilings imposed by the exchanges, and no longer have the exchange available to them. However, they are disadvantageous in the credit risk that is involved. The credit quality of the Swap is only as good as the credit quality of the two parties involved. Moreover, Swaps are not as liquid as futures contracts. While it is not impossible to get out of the Swap agreement prior to its maturity, it would likely entail some penalty to do so.

NOTES

1. See Weiner (1991) for an excellent analysis of the difference in default risk between forward and futures contracts.

2. At the time of writing (early 1994), the two closest to expiration contracts have the $15/barrel daily limit. Other expiration months have a $1.50/barrel daily limit.

3. A long futures contract can actually be replicated by buying a call option at a given exercise price and expiration date and selling the put option with the same exercise price and expiration date. Conversely, a short futures contract can be replicated by selling a call option at a given exercise price and expiration date and buying the put option with the same exercise price and expiration date, plus the exercise price.

4. Since crude oil was trading at about $30.29, and the option had 23 days to expiration, a 99 percent confidence interval could be created by multiplying the futures price times 2.58 times the one-day prorated volatility of the square root of 1/250, where 250 is the number of trading days in a year.

REFERENCES

Razavi, Hossein. "The New Era of Petroleum Trading: Spot Oil, Spot-Related Contracts, and Futures Markets," World Bank Technical Paper No. 96, 1989.

Treat, John Elting, Simon Cowie, Frederick Davidson, Margaret Duffie, Steven Errera, Philip Gotthelf, Joel Miller, Timothy Murphy, Guy Rouquette, and Phillip Verleger Jr. *Energy Futures: Trading Opportunities for the 1980s*. Tulsa: PennWell Books, 1984.

Weiner, Robert. "Default Risk and the Difference Between Forward and Futures Markets: An Empirical Case-Study." Working Paper No. 212, Columbia Center for the Study of Futures Markets, 1991.

Chapter 6

Marketing of Oil in the United States

Carolyn E. Predmore

This chapter looks at the marketing of oil from the wellhead to the consumer and beyond. Oil companies are not just interested in promoting their oil products, they are also interested in enhancing the image of the company. Oil companies as well as other branded companies try to build brand equity for their products. They want the customer to have a clear picture of what the company products are, how well they work, and what the company stands for. Marketing helps the oil companies achieve a differential advantage within the public's mind.

Using information garnered from the marketing department, the oil company can control the product, its price, its promotion, and its distribution. There are, however, uncontrollable factors including society, technology, government, customers, competition, the economy, and politics. The marketing department in a company may not be called upon to react to all of these influences in order to build brand equity, but certainly it has dealt with all of these issues at different times.

The effects of decisions concerning product, price, promotion, and distribution at each stage in the movement of oil will be examined in this chapter. However, the marketing of oil does not stop there. Oil companies are very aware that public opinion can sway governmental regulations either for or against the industry. The oil companies not only market their products, they market themselves to the local community, the country, and the world. This chapter will also look at some of the extensive programs oil companies have to enhance their corporate image in the United States and worldwide.

THE OIL WELL—THE BEGINNING

It is easiest to understand the marketing of oil if the movement of a barrel of oil is followed from the wellhead to the consumer. Oil is found by drilling installations of either established oil companies with entire refining and selling operations or smaller companies with only drilling capabilities, or wildcat firms (Channing L. Bete Co. 1979). A small company will sell the barrel of oil on the market because it will not have the facilities to process it further.

A large oil company may keep the oil it finds on land owned or leased by the company to complete the refining process at another company installation for further processing. However, a large company may also sell the barrel of oil in the marketplace if there is more profit to be earned that way. At Exxon, each division acts as a profit center, responsible for the costs of its raw materials and the revenues of its processed materials. The decisions on any given day depend on the market rate for the product they produce in order to provide the highest profit (Patterson, 1993).

TRANSPORTATION

From the oil well, the barrel of oil is transported by tanker, barge, rail tankcar, truck, or pipeline to the refinery, where the decision is made concerning what products to make. There were 115 companies operating 224 refineries in the United States in 1987 (Temple, Barker and Sloane 1988). Pipelines have come to be a major mode of transportation for oil and oil products since World War II. There are more than 227,000 miles of pipeline in the United States. Shipping oil through a pipeline is quiet, efficient, and cheap. It cost approximately one cent to move a gallon of oil from Texas to New York in 1984. Pipeline construction, on the other hand, is costly. The pipeline that moves oil from Texas to New York so cheaply cost over $370 million to build in 1964.

Pipelines can vary in size from a 56-inch-diameter main trunk line to a 2-inch gathering line. Gathering lines bring the oil from the oil field to the storage supply areas. The crude oil trunk pipelines carry the oil from the supply storage to the refinery and the product trunk pipelines transport the refined oil and gas from the refinery to distribution centers. Pipelines are generally routed underground to reduce chances of the pipeline being injured and to remove the pipe from view. However, in Alaska the pipeline was placed above ground to protect the permafrost and the pipeline from damage and was the most expensive pipeline built to date (American Petroleum Institute 1984).

Tankers can be oceangoing vessels of up to 1,300 feet in length or small barges designed to work in local harbors where the draft may be less than six feet at low water (American Petroleum Institute 1984). These local barges help to transport supplies to local distributors.

Rail tank cars vary in size from 4,000 to 33,000 gallons in volume and help transport oil and other petroleum products long distances. Tank cars may be insulated to prevent temperature variation within the product, which helps maintain the integrity of the products and helps in the removal of the products at destination (American Petroleum Institute 1984). Trucks carry oil and oil products nearly everywhere. The largest trucks can carry 8,000 to 10,000 gallons per truckload, allowing trucks to provide service to distributors and retail outlets anywhere where barges, rail cars, and pipelines do not go. Often the final journey to a retail outlet or to a consumer is by truck.

At any point in time the transportation system of one refinery will be carrying approximately 50 million gallons from the refinery processing points to the final consumer. There are over 3,000 different products that can be distilled out of a barrel of crude petroleum (*The Downstream* 1986). These products also form the raw materials for other products such as records, plastics, synthetic fabrics, and so on. The variety covers gasoline, home heating oil, asphalt, aviation fuel, as well as rubbing alcohol and others. The refinery decides what products to produce depending on the needs of the company and the expected usage levels of the population that the refinery and its customers serve. Additionally, not all refineries produce all types of products. ARCO does not refine the heavier products like aviation fuel and asphalt (ARCO 1990).

It would be impossible to cover all of the 3,000 products resulting from the refining of oil to the final consumer, so two consumer products most heavily used in the United States will be covered here: home heating oil and gasoline.

HOME HEATING OIL

Home heating oil is distilled from crude oil and then sold to consumers through two different distribution channels. Refineries may have direct sales to industrial customers, such as schools, hospitals, and other institutions, which use entire truckloads of oil, are located near the refinery, and will have contracts with the refinery for continuous oil delivery. The refinery is interested in loading up its own trucks and unloading the oil very quickly and then turning around and repeating the process. Refineries are not interested in transporting heating oil any distance, as they do not have the transportation system set up to efficiently serve the public and gain a profit.

There have been exceptions to this rule in the past. Exxon had a home heating oil delivery division around Perth Amboy, New Jersey, until about 1980. The customers were those people who had homes near the Exxon refinery in Perth Amboy. Exxon realized that it did not want to expand that aspect of the business, so discontinued it (Patterson 1993). It was not cost effective. The local oil companies were able to deliver oil to individual home customers more efficiently.

The more traditional route for home heating oil is for local heating oil distributors to buy the oil from the refinery. It is then transported to the local distributors' holding tanks until it is loaded into a truck for a regular delivery route. Many of these home heating oil companies have grown with the home heating industry, which began with the whale oil industry in the early years of this country. Local peddlers set up regular customer routes to sell whale oil. In 1860 kerosene was the choice for home lighting (*The Downstream* 1986).

Once the customers' needs changed from lighting to heating, the same businesses that had begun with whale oil sold the new home heating oil. They had the delivery systems in place, they had the transportation system working, and they had the customer base. Refineries do not want to assume additional risk by expanding into large-volume direct customer sales in competition with established local businesses (Patterson 1993).

The price of home heating oil varies according to the amount of reserve that the refineries have. If the winter turns out to be fairly mild, the refineries will have an excess of home heating oil. The price of the oil will drop so that the refineries will be able to sell the oil to make room for increased production of gasoline for the summer months.

There are many ways that the price of heating oil can be pushed higher due to demand, weather conditions, transportation problems, political events, and so on. The job of the oil companies is to try to forecast events so that inventories can be maintained as close to the demand level as possible. Companies try to get customers to sign contracts of a year or more to buy heating oil from one firm. Customers are set up on a regular delivery system so that they should never run out of heating oil, especially during the winter heating season. Customers may have some loyalty to local oil companies, but any company that tries to push and maintain higher prices alone will find that customers will gravitate to the lower priced competitors or the company with better service (Patterson 1993).

There are a variety of promotional tactics that oil companies will use in order to persuade customers to contract with them. Many customers are influenced by a free service contract, furnace cleaning, or coupons that the oil company can provide. Many customers dread the possibility of a cold winter morning dawning where the inside of the house is as cold as the outside. The better an oil company can assuage that fear, the more likely the customer will buy oil from that company on a continual basis.

Oil companies also compete with other heating fuels for customers. There is a continual battle for people to change from oil heat to gas or electric central systems. In addition, since the oil crises in the 1970s and 1980s, there has been a return to wood-fired stoves and more interest in coal-fired stoves and furnaces. Home heating oil companies do not operate in a vacuum and must work to continually please their customers in order to retain their business.

GASOLINE

Gasoline is distilled from the barrel of crude oil at the refinery. If the company can make more profit by keeping the gasoline and selling it through its branded stations, then the barrel of gasoline is sold to a branded dealer at dealer tank-wagon prices (by the truckful or DTW; Temple et al. 1988). Branded dealers can be salary stations that the company owns and operates with salaried personnel. Branded dealers may also be franchisees who pay fees to the company for the use of the brand name, buy all of their gasoline from the company, and benefit from the national advertising that the company produces (Temple et al. 1988).

Refineries may also sell gasoline to another company for sale to the public, depending on the daily prices of the gasoline market (Patterson 1993). Those stations will not bear the branded name of the gasoline, but will have the same-quality gasoline. The company obviously has much less control over these outlets than those previously discussed. Distributors may be "unbranded" and selling either unbranded gasoline or a private brand of gasoline to private branded stations or unbranded stations. Distributors may also be branded under the name of one or more refineries or they may be both unbranded and branded (Temple et al. 1988). Approximately 82 percent of the gasoline stations in the United States are run by either franchise owners or are independent stations. Chain marketers buy gasoline in bulk and sell through their chain of salary-operated stations (Temple et al. 1988).

From the time the barrel of oil has been pumped from the ground at the wellhead until the customer has the gasoline put into the car, almost three weeks have passed. In that time, the open market for the product has been examined and reexamined to see where the best price can be obtained.

Service Stations

Companies have been examining the service structure of the gasoline station for several years and have developed several types of stations and levels of service in order to remain competitive. Within the gasoline market there are 10,000 independent distributors and over 160,000 retail outlets (Temple et al. 1988). Oil companies have found that using branded stations for distribution of gasoline has helped them better estimate demand and plan for the future. By giving the public some way to differentiate between stations, through either the quality of the gasoline or customer service, some brand loyalty is established.

Salary-Operated and Lessee Stations

Gasoline stations have three basic formats, salary-operated, lessee dealerships, and open dealer stations. Salary-operated stations are usually owned by the company, which pays a salary to all of the station personnel. The company is then responsible for the facility and equipment, retail prices, hours of operation, and all operating policies. These stations represented about 4.5 percent of the stations in 1986 (Temple et al. 1988). Having salary-run stations allows the oil company to experiment with a variety of marketing strategies and plans. It affords the company a direct line of communication with the customer and a chance to learn about potential problems before they escalate.

With a lessee dealer, the land, buildings, and major equipment are owned or leased by a refiner or a distributor, which then leases the setup to the dealer. These lessee dealers are independent business owners who are responsible for the other equipment, inventories, and personnel. The relationship between distributor and lessee dealer is usually defined by a contract that is renewed periodically (Temple et al. 1988).

Open Dealers

Open dealers are independent businesspeople who either own the station or rent it from an entity other than an oil company. These dealers contract with refiners or distributors for their inventories of gasoline and other supplies. The use of dealers allows the oil companies to reduce the number of personnel on salary and to share some of the risk involved in the retailing of gasoline (Temple et al. 1988).

The original gas station in the United States sold gasoline, tires, batteries, and accessories. The stations had service bays and mechanics on hand who could service your car. As of 1984, 29 percent of the gasoline stations were still full-service stations (American Petroleum Institute 1984). Since the oil embargoes of the 1970s, the industry has seen a leveling of oil consumption in industrialized countries. The oil companies have had to work harder to remain profitable. Older refineries have either been reconditioned or shut down. As of 1986, 175 refineries have been decommissioned (*The Downstream* 1986). The number of gasoline stations has also declined precipitously from 226,500 in 1972 to the 117,000 that receive a majority of the station income from gasoline and services (Temple et al. 1988).

Over the past 20 years, the major oil companies have been experimenting with gasoline stations without service areas. That space has often been taken up by a convenience outlet store selling staples (milk, bread, etc.) as well as fast foods and impulse items. Recently, some stations have received more than 50 percent of their revenues from the convenience store products (Temple et al. 1988).

Self-Service

Another type of station that has been increasing in popularity has been the self-service station where customers pump their own gasoline. Some states still prohibit their existence (i.e., New Jersey) as well as individual towns within more liberal states (i.e., Huntington, New York). About 78 percent of the gasoline sold in the United States is sold from self-service stations or from the self-service lane at more traditional gas stations (Temple et al. 1988). Many motorists view self-service as a means to save time by not waiting for an attendant to respond. Usually gasoline is priced lower for the self-service lane or station and the hours of operation may be extended to 24 hours, giving customers flexibility as well as savings.

This effort to streamline the gasoline station has enabled the personnel to work more efficiently and keep a cleaner appearance surrounding the station.

Customers seem to have found specialty service businesses to take care of the work previously done by service stations, such as brake repair, transmission repair, oil changes, and lubrication. Gasoline stations do not need to be complete service centers in all locations. In fact, "the service and parts market share of gasoline service stations has declined from 16.8 percent in 1970 to 7.8 percent in 1985" and motor oil sales at service stations have declined to only 16 percent of the market (Temple et al. 1988). Many gasoline stations only sell gas. They do it quickly and in great quantities.

COMPETITION

There is tremendous competition between the branded gasoline stations for customers. Gasoline companies realize that many customers do not perceive any difference between brands of gasoline and will go to the station that is least expensive, in the best location, or is the cleanest (Patterson 1993). Therefore, the public is shown print and broadcast advertising touting the cleanliness of the stations, the helpfulness of the personnel, and the ease of buying gasoline with the companies' credit cards.

Speed and Ease of Use

Some oil companies have eliminated customer credit. ARCO decided in the 1980s to concentrate on high-volume cash operations with self-service. With this strategy, ARCO has been able to maintain lower prices to the public. Those lower prices have offset the lack of amenities such as oil checks or windshield cleaning (ARCO 1990). As repair services were eliminated from the gasoline stations, ARCO opened automotive service centers that provide engine tune-ups and brake and air-conditioning repairs. A new focus for the 100 service specialty shops are smog inspections and emission-control repairs. This new focus is reflected in the renaming of the shops to "Smog Pros" (ARCO 1990).

Cash Purchases

As banks have incorporated the automatic teller machine, some gasoline stations are encouraging their customers to purchase gasoline with the debt card. The gasoline is bought at the cash price and customers do not have to carry cash with them (American Petroleum Institute 1984). Other gasoline stations have joined with major banking networks in the area and have installed automatic teller machines in the station to facilitate cash transactions. Some gas stations have reverted to running sales promotions, such as a free glass with every fill-up of gasoline. Each station is trying to encourage station loyalty, if not brand loyalty.

New gasolines are formulated as the demand for better performance increases. Oil companies have to be able to enhance the octane ratings of their gasoline without resorting to leaded additives in order to comply with national statutes (*The Downstream* 1986). In the winter months, gasoline must be oxygenated to reduce airborne pollutants. Gasoline formulations also differ depending on the region of the country in which they will be sold. The altitude of the area must also be taken into consideration in the refining process (American Petroleum Institute 1984).

Brand Equity

The companies want to demonstrate their differential advantages so that they build a value into each brand—brand equity. The level of service, price, quality of the products, and availability as well as company reputation as a caring member of the community all combine to define the differential advantage. There are several methods the companies can use to display their community spirit. One of these is to enhance communication between employees throughout the company.

Oil companies not only market to the final consumer, but to all the people involved with the company in order to enhance the company image and reputation. Informational publications for employees that cover a myriad of topics ranging from strategic planning for the coming year for the company to light-calorie, low-fat cooking recipes to promote better health have been provided. Honors for worker excellence are noted, employee profiles are given, notices of new operations are given, as well as information about new innovations. Employees can write to the editor about their concerns and get written responses.

Promotional Campaigns

Another method used to illustrate community leadership is involvement in support of educational and special programs. For example, Exxon launched three new promotional campaigns in order to raise money for college scholarships and the U.S. Special Olympics.

Texaco helps to underwrite the costs of the Teacher Training Institute in partnership with WNET, the public television station in New York City. This program instructs teachers how to use video information effectively in the classroom, particularly science, technology, and environmentally based videos. Also in New York, the company helps sponsor the Reading Recovery Pilot Program. The program identifies children with reading problems early in their educational careers and then effects early intervention of three to four months. This project is examining the benefits of early intervention versus waiting until remedial reading courses must be used. Monetary awards for scholarships for high school students have been granted.

By helping to provide good entertainment, companies may enjoy enhanced reputations. Entertainment can range the gamut from amusement parks to the performing arts. Exxon has teamed with Disney to be partners at Euro Disney.

Esso France is one of 12 corporate sponsors at Euro Disney and is the official supplier of oil products to Euro Disney. The exhibits provide a glimpse of life in 1910 with a car dealership of the era while also maintaining the only gasoline station on the property selling both gasoline and diesel fuel. The station office sells Esso memorabilia as well as food and drink. Esso has enhanced its reputation as a company selling a quality product at a good price with good service through this close association with Euro Disney. Esso enjoys this advantage and is seeking to use this consumer perception to become number one in the European gasoline market (Dedera 1992).

Exxon has been energetically building stations in the former East Germany. At the end of 1992, there were 47 stations built. These are high-volume stations with convenience stores and car washes to satisfy the public. The company is looking for opportunities to expand into Poland and Hungary in the near future (Exxon 1992).

Involvement in the performing arts has become another way to show community support by major organizations. The weekly Saturday radio broadcasts of the Metropolitan Opera over the past 50 years have been sponsored by Texaco. The company has also helped sponsor the telecasts of the Metropolitan Opera and began to cosponsor the ''Great Performances'' broadcasts on public television.

Although the Olympics may not be classified as a performing art, they elicit many positive emotions and beliefs about competitors, the countries, and the world. Support for the Olympics can be used by corporations as indicators of pride in citizenship and achievement. Sponsoring individual team sports of the U.S. Olympics teams helps to form and maintain close relationships between the company and the athletes. Many of a company's slogans (in this case, Texaco) remind their customers of the commitment made to the Olympic games. It is another way to stand apart from the other branded gasoline companies.

Additionally, oil companies sponsor many health-care programs to be good community neighbors and enhance their image.

It is especially important for oil companies to display their awareness of environmental issues and to demonstrate programs that reduce hazards. Additionally, they try to promote the emergence of a healthier environment in order to counteract the negative publicity of oil spills and other accidents. The general public needs to be convinced that the oil companies are good neighbors. After the oil spill of the *Exxon Valdez* in Alaska's Prince William Sound, oil companies have been trying to increase their involvement with environmental research. Exxon has started cosponsoring an Alaskan environmental study on the moose population. It is being accomplished with the work of the U.S. Forest Service (Matthews 1992). Research is delving into all aspects of moose life— foraging, birth, death, wintering-over habits, effects of snow conditions on moose activity, climate records—and trying to determine optimal moose living conditions in the Alaskan ecosystem.

Texaco also has been involved in promoting tree-planting all over the United

States since 1991 for a cost of $1 million a year in conjunction with the American Forestry Association.

CONCLUSION

In summary, the oil companies try to meet the needs of their customers of gasoline, home heating oil, and other products by producing enough for their needs, in the right quantities, and distributed to the desired places at the right time. The competition within the oil industry ranges from major oil companies to small niche companies for every aspect of marketing from the wellhead to the final consumer. Promotional campaigns stress the products for sale as well as community services provided in order to create brand equity. The companies try to successfully create a perception of differential advantages either through customer service, community service, superior products, or a combination of factors in order to gain brand loyalty. It is the successful catering to the customers' needs and wants through marketing, blended with the needs of the company, that promotes longevity of the brand.

REFERENCES

American Petroleum Institute. "Facts About Oil." Washington, DC: API, 1984.
ARCO Products: The Energy of People, 1990.
Channing L. Bete Co. *The ABC's of Oil*. Greenfield, Mass.: Channing L. Bete Co., Inc., 1979.
Corporon, Bill. "Plan Tells Where We're Going and How to Get There, Says Longwell," *Exxon Today* 1(18) (December 14, 1992).
Davis, Bob. "Marketing Kicks Off Fall with Three Promotions." *Exxon Today* 1(14) (September 28, 1992).
Dedera, Don. "The Magic Begins: Esso at Euro Disney." *The Lamp* 74(4) (1992).
The Downstream. Exxon Corporation, April 1986.
Exxon Annual Report, 1992.
Matthews, Downs. "Moose and Man at Portage Flats." *The Lamp* 74(4) (1992).
Patterson, Larry. Marketing Advisor, Exxon Company International, January 26, 1993.
Temple, Barker and Sloane, Inc. "Gasoline Marketing in the 1980's: Structure, Practices, and Public Pricing." May 1988.
Texaco Annual Report. "The Energy to Go Farther," 1991.

Chapter 7

Refined Product Prices

John T. Boepple

Although OPEC production policies, security of supply concerns, and other geopolitical factors often take precedence over market forces as determinants of international crude oil prices, refined product prices are invariably established by a matrix of supply/demand pressure for refined products, the cost structure of refined processes, and the level of crude oil prices.

Refined product prices vary throughout the world as a result of regional differences in market structure, product quality specifications, environmental legislation, proximity to major markets, and supply/demand requirements. However, these differences are ultimately constrained by freight costs to move products from one region to another, because in today's global and increasingly transparent market, whenever price differentials exceed freight costs, traders and others will take advantage of the opportunities to arbitrage the discrepancies.

While freight economics strongly influence interregional price relationships, within each major refining center, all major product prices are heavily dependent on the characteristics of the region's refineries and are linked through the technical characteristics and variable margin of the area's incremental producer. The price differentials between major refined products also reflect the underlying economics of key refining technologies as well as supply/demand pressures. This chapter will highlight the linkages between refined product prices and refining processes in more detail and cite recent product pricing trends in several of the world's major refining centers that illustrate these linkages.

A region's refined product prices are primarily influenced by the cost structure and yield pattern for the refinery configuration most representative of the region's incremental producer of refined products. When a region's refining capacity is not fully utilized, it is hypothesized that prices for each major product are formed so that the incremental producer's variable margin is slightly positive, providing an incentive to process the additional crude oil needed to satisfy the last increment of the region's product supply requirements. For example, if the price of heavy fuel oil declines, the prices of light refined products (i.e., gasoline and diesel) typically rise, so that a positive variable margin for the incremental crude oil processor is maintained.

When a region's refining capacity is fully utilized and incremental crude oil processing is not an option, a different mechanism governs product prices. In this case prices reflect the additional cost of importing the product from another region.

The price differential between light and heavy refined products is a key refining economics parameter that strongly influences refined product prices. Key factors impacting this price differential in international markets are:

• world's capacity to produce crude oil relative to consumption
• product demand mix
• mix of crude oils available to refiners
• availability of fuel oil conversion capacity in refineries

The underlying economics of the refinery processes for resid conversion heavily influence the maximum and minimum diesel/fuel oil price differentials in major refining centers. In the long term, reinvestment economics for catalytic cracking and coking provide a ceiling for this differential while in the shorter term, incremental processing economics for these processes provide a floor for the differential.

Developments in global markets over the past 20 years have demonstrated the impact of each of these factors on the diesel/fuel oil price differential, a proxy for the price differential between light and heavy refined products. Most recently, events during the 1990 Persian Gulf crisis caused the diesel/fuel oil differential to sharply increase for about a year. During that period, the sudden loss of Kuwaiti and Iraqi crude oil production reduced the world's capacity to produce crude oil. The gap between supply and demand was filled largely by increased production of heavier crude oils from Venezuela and Saudi Arabia, resulting in a heavier mix of crude oils for refiners. Heightened demand for light products and the destruction of Kuwait's complex refineries also contributed to the differential's sharp escalation.

Another price differential, between premium and regular gasoline prices at the refinery gate, is an important indicator of gasoline production economics. This differential is closely linked to the economics of the catalytic reforming process and historically has reflected the availability of catalytic reforming capacity in a refining region. For example, the differential in the U.S. Gulf Coast rose sharply during the second half of the 1980s when the complete removal of lead from gasoline and higher gasoline demand strained the region's available catalytic reforming capacity to its limits.

The technical and market factors that influence the diesel/fuel oil and premium/regular gasoline price differentials illustrate the linkages between refined product price differentials and major refinery processes. Price differentials between other major refined products similarly are influenced by other refinery processes. This dependence of product price differentials on refinery processes, together with the postulated role of the incremental producer's yield structure on price formation, clearly demonstrates the linkages between refined product prices and refining.

REFINERY CONFIGURATIONS

The operating costs and product yields of an oil refinery are both dependent on its process unit configuration and the type of crude oil processed. The following refinery configurations, listed in order of increasing processing capability, span the range of refineries operating throughout the world.

- "Topping" refineries refer to plants that include only atmospheric distillation units to separate crude oil into streams that meet the product specifications for major refined products. Gasoline is not usually produced in a topping refinery, except in some developing countries where lower octane specifications apply and tetra ethyl lead addition is still permitted.
- "Hydroskimming" refineries consist of crude oil atmospheric distillation, naphtha catalytic reforming and often middle distillate hydrotreating units.
- "Cracking" refineries include vacuum, as well as atmospheric, distillation and use a catalytic conversion process, either fluidized catalytic cracking or hydrocracking, to upgrade the vacuum distillates.
- "Deep Conversion" refineries include units such as delayed coking or resid hydrocracking to process the residue from vacuum distillation. Deep conversion refineries have the ability to maximize light product yields and eliminate residual fuel oil production or reduce it to low levels.

REFINERY MARGINS

Types of Refinery Margins

Refinery margins can be calculated on several different bases, all of which are used within the industry for different purposes:

- variable margins (cost base reflects only variable operating costs)
- cash cost margins (includes fixed operating costs)
- full cost margins (includes depreciation)

The variable margin indicates whether additional crude oil processing is profitable for an incremental yield structure. That is, crude and incremental utility costs are taken into consideration, but manpower and other fixed costs are not because they should not change with incremental crude processing.

The cash cost margin, based on revenues for the refinery's entire production, provides an indication of a refinery's overall economics and profitability. All cash operating costs, such as those for manpower and maintenance, are taken into account, but depreciation and other noncash items are excluded from the calculation.

The full-cost margin indicates profitability in accounting terms and more closely mirrors the profitability reported by refining companies in their financial statements. The prevailing practice in the industry is to calculate refining margins using spot crude and product prices. This is because the spot market represents the most widely reported value of crude oils and refinery output. This does not, however, reflect the full margin achieved by some refineries that purchase crude and/or sell product on contract bases.

Technical Factors

When a region's refining capacity is not fully utilized, its refined product prices are primarily influenced by the yield pattern for the refinery configuration most representative of the region's incremental producer of refined products, obtained from the region's swing source of crude oil supply.

If a region's refining capacity is fully utilized, its product prices reflect the additional cost of importing product from another region. In this case the higher products will result in wider margins for the region's refiners.

The refinery configuration used to produce a region's last increment of product supplies often does not reflect a specific refinery, but usually represents the available configuration and yields obtained for the last 5 percent of refinery throughput. Over a 12-month period, the variable margin of the incremental refinery configuration will usually be slightly positive (25 to 50 cents per barrel) in order to provide the necessary incentive to process the additional crude oil needed to satisfy the last increment of the region's product supply requirements.

Over a shorter time horizon (daily or monthly), the variable margin of the incremental producer is more volatile, due to product inventory factors, seasonal changes in product demand, and abrupt changes in crude oil prices due to political factors. At times, the variable margin of a region's "typical" incremental producer will turn negative. Reductions in the industry's utilization rate usually occur when a negative variable margin persists for more than a week.

Analyzing historical variable margins for a refining center provides an excellent indication of the type of configuration that is influencing its refined product prices. For the U.S. Gulf Coast area, the yields and variable costs of a hydroskimming configuration including vacuum distillation have recently established prices for major refined products. Although there are no longer any larger hydroskimming refineries operating on the U.S. Gulf Coast, cracking and coking refineries typically fully utilize their conversion capacity, but have some primary distillation and catalytic reforming capacity available for use on a discretionary basis, provided it generates a positive variable margin.

The situation in Europe, where crude distillation capacity is available but most reforming capacity recently has been fully utilized, is somewhat different. The yields and variable costs of a topping configuration have recently been the key technical factors influencing European prices for refined products.

Asian markets have recently been the strongest for refined products as the region's higher economic growth rates and relatively low levels of per capita oil consumption have resulted in steady increases in oil demand. As a result, the region's refinery capacity has been fully utilized and there has been an ongoing need to import all major products into the region. Thus, the region's incremental producer has recently been an exporter to Asia, located outside the region (in Europe or the United States).

Under these circumstances, the variable topping margin in Singapore has been higher than it would have been if crude oil processing capacity had been available in the region. The premium reflects the higher costs associated with refined product shipping, relative to crude oil shipping.

Historical Market Developments

Table 7.1 presents variable margins since 1985 for crude oil processing in the world's three key refining centers. For each refining center, the variable margin shown applies to the same refinery configuration throughout the period. For the U.S. Gulf Coast area, margins for a hydroskimming configuration including vacuum distillation processing a light sweet crude oil are presented. Margins for a topping configuration processing a sour Mideast crude oil are shown for Rotterdam and Singapore.

The variable margin trend is most consistent for the U.S. Gulf Coast (USGC) region, averaging 45 cents/barrel during the period. This pattern indicates that the hydroskimming configuration including vacuum distillation has been a reasonable representation of the incremental producer's operations throughout the period. The largest deviations from the average occurred in 1986, 1987, and 1990—periods of especially volatile crude oil prices.

Although the variable margins for all three centers were negative in 1987, the historical margin patterns for Rotterdam and Singapore are different from the U.S. Gulf Coast pattern. In both Rotterdam and Singapore, a topping configuration was clearly uneconomic in 1985, suggesting that the incremental producers in both regions at the time were utilizing a more complex process configuration yielding a higher value product mix.

Variable margins for a topping configuration remained negative in Rotterdam through 1988 and it was only in 1989 that a topping configuration began to mirror the operations of the incremental producer. By that time, capacity reductions and demand growth had combined to tighten the European supply/demand

Table 7.1
Crude Oil Variable Margins, 1985–93 ($/barrel crude)

Refining Center:	USGC	ROTTERDAM	SINGAPORE
Refining Configuration:	Hydroskimming [1]	Topping	Topping
1985	0.51	(0.60)	(0.97)
1986	1.01	0.85	0.43
1987	(0.49)	(0.30)	(0.10)
1988	0.69	(0.35)	0.51
1989	0.46	0.68	1.45
1990	1.03	0.34	1.34
1991	0.17	1.23	2.52
1992	0.24	0.49	0.75
1st nine mos. 1993	0.47	(0.31)	1.48

[1] Hydroskimming including vacuum distillation

balance. Since 1989 the variable topping margin has averaged 50 cents per barrel, in line with expectations for the incremental producer.

The average of the U.S. Gulf Coast variable margins shown for a hydroskimmer with vacuum distillation producing heavy vacuum gasoil for sale was about 20 cents/barrel greater than the average Rotterdam variable margin for a topping configuration during the 1985–93 period. However, it should be recognized that if the Rotterdam yield structure for a topping configuration had been assumed for the U.S. Gulf Coast, the resultant USGC variable margin would have been negative throughout the period, by an average of more than $1/barrel. Its average for the period would have been about $1.25/barrel less than the average Rotterdam variable margin.

The variable topping margin in Singapore since 1989 has averaged about $1.50/barrel. This pattern is consistent with the observed full utilization of refining capacity in the region and highlights that the region's incremental producer recently has not been a refiner in the region. During the period, the Asian region's incremental product needs have generally been supplied by European refiners, with Asian prices reflecting European product prices plus the cost of freight to India. India is the western edge of the normal supply zone for Singapore refiners.

REFINED PRODUCT PRICE DIFFERENTIALS

Product price differentials in absolute terms are important refining economics parameters that also strongly influence refined product prices. In the world's major refining centers, these price differentials are established by regional supply and demand pressures, but ultimately they are transmitted to other regions through changes in the international trade of crude oils and refined products. As a result, developments in one region are soon reflected in similar price differential trends around the world.

Price differentials have floors and ceilings that are directly related to the economics of key refining processes. For example, the minimum diesel/fuel oil price differential typically reflects variable cost economics for a fuel oil upgrading process, such as coking, while the differential's maximum long-term trend reflects reinvestment economics for the process.

Product price differentials between diesel and fuel oil, jet fuel and diesel, diesel and gasoline, naphtha and gasoline, low-sulfur and high-sulfur fuel oil, and premium gasoline and regular gasoline are all important product price differentials. This chapter will focus on only two of these: the diesel/fuel oil price differential and the premium/regular gasoline price differential.

The diesel/fuel oil price differential, especially when viewed as a proxy for the price differential between all light and heavy refined products, is a key refining parameter. In addition to reflecting the price gap between light and heavy products, it also governs the profitability of the industry's major capital investments in fuel oil upgrading facilities.

The premium/regular gasoline price differential reflects gasoline production economics and provides an indication of a region's supply/demand balance for gasoline.

Diesel/Fuel Oil Price Differential

Technical Factors

The key factors influencing the diesel/fuel oil price differentials in international markets are:

- *Capacity to Produce Crude Oil Relative to Consumption.* When the world's capacity to produce crude oil approaches consumption, the price of diesel, which has few substitutes, rises relative to the price of fuel oil, which has readily available substitutes such as coal and natural gas. However, when the world's capacity to produce crude oil exceeds consumption, the differential is lower because of the availability of excess refining capacity and the tendency of producing countries to produce more light crude to make up for their revenue losses.

- *Product Demand Mix.* The relative demand of gasoline, middle distillate, and fuel oil in the world market affects the diesel/fuel oil price differential. The product mix is influenced by short-term factors, such as a war or major coal strike, and long-term factors, which determine the relative demand growth rates for the major products. The key long-term factor affecting transportation fuels (gasoline and diesel) demand is economic growth. In addition to economic growth, fuel oil demand is affected by the price and availability of substitute fuels.

- *Available Crude Mix.* The mix of light and heavy crude oils made available to the world market by producers affects the diesel/fuel oil price differential. For example, the increase in the production of lighter, high-diesel-yield non-OPEC crudes, such as those from the North Sea during the early 1980s and the decrease in the production of heavier Mideast crudes, tended to reduce the diesel/fuel oil price differential.

- *Resid Conversion Capacity Available in Refineries.* Capital-intensive, long-lead-time investments in additional resid conversion capacity (cat crackers, visbreakers, hydrocrackers, and cokers) can be made to offset changes in the product mix or crude mix. Additions to the world's resid conversion capacity tend to reduce the diesel/fuel oil price differential.

The underlying economics of the refinery processes for resid conversion mentioned above heavily influence the maximum and minimum diesel/fuel oil price differentials in major refining centers. In the long term, reinvestment economics for catalytic cracking and coking provide a ceiling for this differential, while in the shorter term incremental processing economics for these processes provide a floor for the differential.

Historical Market Developments

Major variations in the diesel/fuel oil price differential can be attributed to developments causing major changes in one or more of the above factors that affect the differential. The differentials between diesel (also referred to as gasoil) and high-sulfur fuel oil prices in Rotterdam have historically reflected changes in the international refined products markets. Some of the key developments affecting the differential in Rotterdam during the past 20 years include:

- The period of tight crude oil supply during the Arab oil embargo in 1973 and 1974 caused the differential to increase from $7/barrel up to a peak of $29/barrel.

- In the 1978/79 period, tight crude supplies during the Iranian crisis caused the differential to rise from $8/barrel up to a peak of $35/barrel.

- Between 1982 and 1985 the differential declined due to increases in high-diesel-yield North Sea crude oil production and the start-up of major resid conversion capacity in the United States, Western Europe, and Mideast.

- Late in 1984 the differential declined to a low of $3/barrel due to the British coal miners' strike, which increased fuel oil demand by 0.5 million barrels/day.

- The differential shot up to $14/barrel late in 1985 when cold weather and low heating oil inventories resulted in an unusually high seasonal demand for diesel.

- When oil prices plummeted in 1986, stimulating demand for fuel oil through substitution, the differential dropped to $4/barrel.

- During the 1988–89 period, the differential rose from $5 to $9/barrel as fuel oil prices remained weak due to pressures from competing fuels such as natural gas and coal. However, strong economic growth increased the demand for lighter products when little new refining capacity was being commissioned.

- Iraq's invasion of Kuwait in August 1990 had a profound effect on the differential, causing it to shoot up from $9/barrel to $17/barrel in early 1991. As discussed below, the invasion impacted all the key factors affecting the differential.

  —The shutdown of Kuwait's crude oil production and the UN-sanctioned embargo of Iraqi production reduced the world's short-term capacity to produce crude oil below its level of consumption.

  —The product mix also shifted abruptly toward lighter products as jet fuel and other middle distillates were stockpiled in the Persian Gulf to supply the military's requirements, while higher fuel oil prices eroded its competitive position in many markets.

  —The crude mix available to refiners also got heavier as the production of heavier crudes in Saudi Arabia and Venezuela filled most of the shortfall in the world's crude oil needs following the loss of Iraqi and Kuwaiti production.

  —The shutdown and destruction of Kuwait's refineries with their extensive fuel oil upgrading capabilities resulted in an overnight reduction in the world's resid conversion capacity of about 7 percent.

- During 1992 and 1993, the diesel/fuel oil differential dropped from $14/barrel at the end of 1991 to $12/barrel in mid-1993 as many of the 1990–91 developments have been reversed, as described below.

  —Additional non-OPEC crude oil production capacity in the North Sea and other areas increased the world's capacity to produce crude oil. This occurred when recessions in Europe and Japan tempered the demand for oil.

  —The demand mix of oil products was little changed, although fuel oil demand in the United States appears to have bottomed out as higher natural gas prices improved the competitiveness of fuel oil for consumers with dual fuel capabilities.

  —The available crude mix has gotten lighter as Saudi Arabia and Venezuela preferentially reduced their lower-revenue, heavy crude oil production when their OPEC production quotas were reduced. In addition, increased North Sea and Nigerian crude oil and condensate production has increased the availability of lighter crude oils.

  —The recommissioning of Kuwait's resid conversion facilities and the start-up of new or expanded catalytic crackers, hydrocrackers, and cokers has increased the availability of resid conversion capacity.

Premium/Regular Gasoline Price Differential

Technical Factors

The price differential between premium and regular gasoline in a major refining center reflects the market value of octane in the region. For example, in the United States the difference in octane between the most commonly traded unleaded premium and unleaded regular grades is about five octane numbers. Thus a 5 cent/gallon differential between their prices implies an octane value of 1 cent/gallon/octane number.

The premium/regular gasoline price differential in the market is closely linked to the economics of the catalytic reforming process, which is the key process that most refiners use to adjust the octane number of their gasoline pool. The octane of reformate, the major product from a catalytic reforming unit, can be increased by raising the unit's reaction temperature. However, the reformate's higher value is offset by reduced yield, increased plant energy consumption, higher catalyst deactivation rate, and usually a reduction in the unit's throughput capacity. These additional processing costs can be used to calculate the costs of incremental octane production.

Historical Market Developments

The premium/regular gasoline price differentials in the U.S. Gulf Coast steadily increased during the second half of the 1980s from 4.0 cents/gallon in 1985 to 7.3 cents/gallon in 1988. The increasing differential reflected a tightening of the octane balance and increased utilization of catalytic reforming units as lead was completely removed from gasoline. During this period the demand for gasoline also rose 643,000 barrels per day, or 90 percent, and unleaded premium gasoline's share of sales also rose.

The value of octane in U.S. markets during the late 1980s usually exceeded the variable cost of octane production via catalytic reforming, reflecting high utilization rates for these units. The premium over variable costs was about 0.5 cents/gallon/octane number in 1986, 1987, and 1989, and shot up to 1 cent/gallon/octane number in 1988. In addition, the strong price differentials attracted increased trans-Atlantic imports from Western Europe, a price-sensitive supply source. Gasoline imports from Western Europe rose from 45,000 barrels/day in 1984 to 142,000 barrels/day in 1988.

During the second half of 1990, the fly-up in crude oil and gasoline prices and the economic recession negatively impacted total U.S. gasoline sales and also led to some consumer resistance to premium grades. As a result, total gasoline sales dropped 2 percent and unleaded premium's share of gasoline sales fell to 18.5 percent in 1991 from a peak of 23.5 percent in 1989—an overall drop in unleaded premium gasoline sales of 18 percent.

Reflecting the weaker demand for unleaded premium gasoline, the price differential between premium and regular grades dropped to 3.7 cents/gallon in 1991, compared to 5.6 cents/gallon in 1990. This lower differential persisted in 1992 and 1993, even though U.S. gasoline demand increased about 4 percent. The addition of significant volumes of high-octane oxygenates, mandated under the 1990 amendments to the Clean Air Act for about 30 percent of U.S. gasoline sold during the winter, has increased the gasoline production capability of U.S. refineries. In response to the lower value of octane in the United States, gasoline imports from Europe dropped by nearly 50 percent between 1988 and 1992, to 84,000 barrels/day in 1992.

CONCLUSION

This chapter has presented the technical and market factors that influence two key product price differentials. This discussion has described the linkages between these two differentials and major refinery processes, further demonstrating the linkages between refined product prices and refining. Price differentials between other major refined products are similarly influenced by refinery processes.

PART II

THE POLITICAL ECONOMY OF
GLOBAL OIL MARKETS

Chapter 8

OPEC: Past, Present, and Future

Massood V. Samii

It is difficult to find an international organization, particularly one from the developing countries, that has received as much attention in the economic literature and international press as the Organization of Petroleum Exporting Countries. Having control of more than 77 percent of the world's oil reserves and over 50 percent of the world's oil export[1] has provided it with a unique role as the driving force behind the international oil market.

OPEC was initially established in September 1960 in Baghdad in response to a unilateral decision of oil companies to reduce posted prices of oil. The founding members—Iran, Iraq, Kuwait, Saudi Arabia, and Venezuela—stated a number of objectives for the organization, among which were for OPEC to achieve a fair rate of return on its oil export, oil price stabilization, and regulation of oil output. Based on the declaration, the organization's policies would take into account the interest of both producing and consuming countries.

That members shall study and formulate a system to ensure the stabilization of prices by, among other things, the regulation of production, with due regard to the interests of the producing and consuming nations, and to the necessity of securing a steady income to the producing countries, an efficient, economic and regular supply of this source of energy to consuming nations, and a fair return on their capital to those investing in the petroleum industry.[2]

OPEC's success in preventing oil companies from reducing posted prices throughout the 1960s was overshadowed by sharp increases in crude oil prices in the 1970s and early 1980s. Measuring OPEC's success in terms of dollar income would lead to the conclusion that the organization was highly successful in those periods. Yet some OPEC officials and oil market analysts recognize that, in the long run, sharp price increases would become a destabilizing force for the international oil market and oil price.

The 1980s witnessed a shift in the oil market balance and in OPEC's power. Excess oil supplies and sharp price fluctuations, along with political factors, including inter-OPEC conflicts and war, and a shift in the strategic objectives of individual member countries, raised questions regarding OPEC's influence on the global oil market and, more importantly, the future of the organization.

This chapter, after reviewing a number of models of OPEC behavior, focuses on the changing strategy of OPEC as a consequence of structural changes in the international oil market. It also reflects on the future of OPEC.

OPEC AND THE OIL MARKET

While OPEC has been at the center of discussion and debate relating to the oil market and oil prices, there are different theories regarding its actual role in influencing international oil prices and, more generally, the structure of the international oil market.

There are models that attribute the evolution of oil prices to factors other than OPEC decisions. They argue that the role of OPEC has not been crucial in shaping the course of international oil prices. In the *Property Right Theory*, Ali Johany (1979) explained the oil price adjustment of 1973–74 in light of the shift of ownership of oil reserves from international oil companies with short planning horizons to OPEC member countries with longer planning horizons. Such differences in planning horizons and its consequence on the social discount rate resulted in a slower rate of oil exploitation by oil producing countries leading to higher oil prices.

In the *Globalization Theory*, Cyrus Bina (1985) argued that internationalization of the oil market resulted in the equalization of crude oil prices internationally at the highest international price level. This represents the marginal social cost of oil production of the highest cost producing countries.[3] The Globalization Theory eliminates price differential on the basis of variance in the average production cost of different regions.

The *Political Theory* of crude oil prices evolution argues that international oil prices and international political developments, particularly in the Middle East, are closely related. It maintains that it is the latter that has been the main factor in setting the course of crude oil prices. Regional political considerations such as the Arab-Israeli War or the Iran-Iraq War and internal upheavals and revolutions have impacted the supply of oil and consequently crude oil prices.

Finally, there is the *theory that attributes changes* in crude oil prices to supply and demand factors, rather than OPEC action. Imbalances between demand and supply of oil are, in turn, the result of excess changes in crude oil prices (MacAvoy 1982; Mead 1980). Demand for oil between 1970 and 1973 increased by about 10 mbd, while non-OPEC production only increased by 3 mbd (more than 2 mbd from centrally planned economies). This resulted in an additional 7 mbd demand for OPEC oil in three years. The demand for OPEC oil had reached the organization's maximum sustainable capacity. Therefore, any further increase in demand would have led to a shortage of oil and an increase in crude oil prices. The crisis may have been expedited by the 1972 Arab-Israeli War and Arab oil embargo.

A number of empirical studies have attempted to test the relation between OPEC's price decision and spot crude prices or product prices. These studies— Verleger (1982), Fitzgerald and Pollio (1984), Lowinger and Ram (1984), and Loderer (1985)—have attempted to show empirically that there is a causality between official OPEC oil prices and the market price of oil. They have attempted to show that the causality runs from market prices to official prices. However, Samii, Weiner, and Wirl (1989), have shown that while there is causality between OPEC's official prices and market prices, the causality is not unidirectional. The logical conclusion, therefore, is that while OPEC decisions have been important in shaping the course of the oil market and prices, there were other factors that were as instrumental in effecting the oil market in the last two decades.

OPEC DECISION MAKING

OPEC's decision making is commonly described in the context of a revenue-maximizing cartel with individual members following the price leader, namely Saudi Arabia. Such a simplistic model fails to take into account the complexity of the economic, financial, and political interests of individual member countries resulting in varied strategies from individual countries within OPEC. To understand OPEC's conduct in the process of decision making, it is essential to focus on each member country's decision parameters rather than the assumption of a collective approach of a cartel.

Each member country of OPEC attempts to identify crude oil prices and supply levels that maximize its social benefit prior to each OPEC conference. An OPEC conference provides a forum to argue and attempt to convince others within the organization to accept its position. Since OPEC agreement must be unanimous and the objectives of individual member countries are different, the probability of the failure of OPEC conferences far outweighs its possible success.

The social benefit that each individual member country attempts to maximize would not necessarily coincide with the traditional neoclassical revenue maximization of the Hotelling type, nor would it necessarily coincide with the maximization of the social welfare of OPEC as a group. Individual countries' social welfare is determined by economic and financial conditions, oil-related factors, as well as political factors.

Hossein Razavi (1984) has attempted to explain OPEC's behavior with the use of the *Coalition Theory*. The Coalition Theory argues that individual players each attempt to optimize their position independently. They then form a coalition, within which they negotiate to reach their individual objectives. As long as a collective approach moves individuals toward their defined position, the coalition is successful and individual members gain from participation in it. OPEC member countries are highly heterogenous in terms of population, financial needs, oil reserve, oil production capacity, financial requirements, and per capita income. They also have diversified political and cultural structures and internal political ties. The overall objective of the coalition emerges from the collective agreement of the individual members. If members of the coalition are highly heterogenous, then they may never reach an agreement.

Despite their differences, OPEC member countries have historically clustered around two extreme groups and an in-between group. The first group, led by Saudi Arabia and including Kuwait, the United Arab Emirates, and Qatar, has been arguing for an increase in supplies and moderate pricing. The second group, led by Iran and including Libya and Algeria insists on the organization restraining its output in favor of higher prices. The remaining members shift positions and ally themselves with each of the two groups, depending on circumstances.

Factors that have shaped the policy of the group led by Saudi Arabia included relatively high production reserve ratio and high per capita production capacity, implying that both private cost and social cost of oil production are relatively low. Moreover, they have high per capita income, low absorptive capacity, and a strong financial situation indicating low short-term need for oil revenue. The high degree of integration of these countries with the Western industrial economies indicates that there is great concern in preventing a negative impact of higher oil prices on those economies.

Politically, members of this group are closely aligned with the Western countries and therefore the political and economic stability of these countries is at the top of this group's objectives. They also have very little parliamentary accountability. The absence of an elected parliament removes any debate on the government's public policy. These economic, financial, and political factors point to the strategy of high output and moderate prices.

The second group is somewhat more diverse. For example, while Algeria has limited oil reserves, Iran's oil reserves are quite high. However, Iran's production capacity was limited in the 1980s because of the war with Iraq and the neglect of its oil reservoir. Iran and Algeria both have high absorptive capacity and Iran and Libya have limited integration to global economies. All three countries have high financial requirements, either because of their foreign debt or their limited foreign exchange reserves. For them, there is a benefit from increases in oil revenue in the near term. Therefore, they take a short-term view in formulating their oil policy.

Politically, the three countries have had limited ties to the West, with Iran (after the fall of the shah in 1978) and Libya having considerable anti-West sentiment. While Iranian support for the Islamic Fundamentalist Movement in

Algeria has created a faction between Iran and Algeria, this has not affected their oil policies. These countries are interested in having higher current oil revenues at the expense of future income.

The members of third group—Venezuela, Ecuador,[4] Gabon, Nigeria, and Indonesia—while in terms of financial and economic conditions are close to the second group, quite often align themselves with the first group, mainly because of political considerations. This group, however, at crucial times has shifted its position.

The economic debate within OPEC has been formulated in the context of price sensitivity of demand (price elasticity of demand). The group that argues for higher oil prices focuses on the short-run elasticity of demand. It maintains that since demand is price inelastic in the short run, an increase in price (even if it is accompanied with the needed cut in output) will result in an increase in revenue. However, the other group takes a long-term view, arguing that the long-run price elasticity of demand is higher than one, therefore any short-run gain in revenue, as a result of higher prices, will lead to substantial loss in the long run.[5]

One must also consider the position of Iraq. During its first few days of the war with Iran, Iraq lost most of its export capacity, as did Iran. While it has a substantial reserve and production capacity, because of limited export possibilities it was unable to play a leading role in OPEC. Upon the conclusion of the war with Iran and the building of its export capacity, it began to emerge as a leading force in the organization. However, its invasion of Kuwait in 1990 and subsequent developments resulted in the isolation of that country within OPEC and, once again, substantial loss of its production and export capacities. While Iraq has a large oil reserve and export capacity, it can become a major player in the oil market only if it solves its international and domestic political problems.

Finally, the analysis would be incomplete without mentioning the relationship between Iran and Saudi Arabia, the two most important oil producers within OPEC. In the aftermath of the fall of the shah, the center of the Islamic Republic of Iran's foreign policy was the export of its revolution to the neighboring countries. In retaliation, Arab countries in the Persian Gulf organized the Gulf Cooperation Council (GCC). This organization was viewed by the Islamic government of Iran as highly pro-West and anti-Islam. The support of the GCC for Iraq during the war further reinforced their suspicions of the organization and particularly its leading member, Saudi Arabia. The result was a great deal of hostility between the two countries during the 1980s. This hostility was also reflected in the negotiations at OPEC conferences. However, the Islamic Republic of Iran's foreign policy after the war and, more generally, with the emergence of seemingly political pragmatism has resulted, to some extent, in reducing the conflict with its southern neighbors.

INSTITUTIONAL STRUCTURE OF OPEC DECISION MAKING

The highest decision-making body in OPEC is the OPEC Conference, which consists of oil ministers from individual member countries (occasionally, a cabinet minister other than the oil minister represents his country). In the Conference, each minister has one vote and all votes are treated equally. All decisions that require a resolution, such as those relating to prices and production, require unanimous approval. Therefore, each member country can effectively veto a Conference decision. Ordinarily, the OPEC ministerial Conference meets twice a year; once in late spring and then again in late November or early December. However, if it is deemed necessary, Extraordinary Conferences can be called in order to address a specific issue, such as overproduction by member countries or a major decline in oil prices. Extraordinary Conferences can also pass resolutions. Finally, ministers can meet in a Consultative Conference to discuss issues and exchange views. A consultative meeting of ministers cannot issue resolutions unless the status of the meeting is changed to an Extraordinary Conference.

The OPEC Conference receives analytical reports and official recommendations from a number of different sources, including ministerial committees, the Economic Commission Board of OPEC, and the expert meeting set up to deal with specific issues. Ministerial committees are set up by the Conference to address specific concerns and recommend courses of action. For example: OPEC's Long-Term Strategy Committee was set up in the 1970s and 1980s to develop an overall strategy for OPEC, not only for OPEC pricing and production but also regarding relations with other developing countries and industrial countries.

The Economic Commission Board of OPEC (ECB) consists of energy and economic experts who represent each individual member country. They meet twice a year, prior to each Ordinary Conference, to review the global energy and economic situation as well as the oil market conditions. The analyses and recommendations of the ECB become the basis for ministerial discussion and debate on various policy measures and their implications. The ECB discussion and position of each country's representative could be viewed as an early indication of that individual country's posture in the Conference. Besides the ECB, there have been committees that address specific subjects, such as crude oil price differential, product pricing, and price indexation. Their reports are used either by the ECB or by specific ministerial meetings.

Finally, there is the OPEC Secretariat, which is responsible for research and studies that become the foundation of each committee's analysis and report. The Secretariat's research staff consists of a number of energy and economic experts who are engaged in the modeling of international energy and oil markets, oil market analysis, and surveying the results of research from other institutions. The Secretariat's research division consists of three departments: the Economic and Finance Department, responsible for energy and economic analysis; the Energy Department, responsible for energy and oil market studies and modeling; and the Data Services Department, responsible for data collection and processing.

OPEC STRATEGY AND CHANGING STRUCTURE OF THE INTERNATIONAL OIL MARKET

Structural changes in the international oil market after the 1973–74 oil price adjustment resulted in an internal debate regarding the role of the organization in the international oil market (or, more generally, in the global economy) and its future strategy. Two major debates, in the late 1970s and in the mid-1980s, resulted in shifts in the strategy of the organization.

The initial objective of the organization, as it was noted earlier, was to develop a negotiating force vis-à-vis multinational oil companies and prevent further deterioration in the "posted price" of oil. While it succeeded in doing so in the 1960s, it failed to prevent the decline in the purchasing power of oil caused by international inflation. The breakdown of the Bretton Woods system and the subsequent fall of parity of the U.S. dollar against major currencies further reduced the purchasing power of oil.

The oil price adjustment of 1973–74 not only restored the purchasing power of crude oil, but resulted in the improvement of its real prices. Debate shifted in 1976 to the future strategy of OPEC. The internal debate centered on whether the organization should continue to strive for higher prices or attempt to find a formula for crude oil price stability. The OPEC long-term strategy addressed this issue and proposed a formula for price indexation. While the formula for price indexation was discussed within the ministerial Conferences, the organization failed to reach any agreement on this issue. In fact, because of a shortfall in crude oil supplies caused by the Iranian revolution and by the Iran-Iraq War, oil prices increased sharply. This made the issue of price indexation moot.

A number of major developments in the early 1980s resulted in a further shift in OPEC strategy. The sharp fall in demand for OPEC oil between 1979 and 1985, the increase in the role of spot crude oil prices in international oil trading, the emergence of the oil future and forward market, and the net black crude oil pricing by OPEC member countries all indicated that there is a need for another shift in OPEC's strategy from fixing crude oil prices to that of regulating oil prices.

Realizing that its official prices at $28 were way out of line from market, prices were floated in March 1985. The floating of prices happened de facto when the organization failed to reach an agreement in its Geneva conference in March 1985. After a year of floating crude oil prices (during which time spot crude prices fell to as low as $8/barrel), OPEC managed to reach an agreement in November 1986. The new agreement was a milestone for the organization, since it shifted overall strategy from controlling crude oil prices to that of managing prices through supply control.[6] However, a target price of $18.00 was set and subsequently raised.

Overnight, the Iraq-Kuwait War removed the oil supply of both countries from the market, resulting in crude oil prices once again moving into the $30.00 range, despite the official OPEC target price of $21.00 and efforts of other member countries to increase output to maximum sustainable capacity to support the target price. Although crude oil prices eventually receded to their prewar levels, the events illustrated how fragile the balance between supply and demand is in that market.

In the 1990s, a number of political and economic changes have taken place in the Persian Gulf region that will directly impact OPEC's decision making. The two most important factors are the seemingly increasing political moderation of the Islamic Republic of Iran and the increase of the financial and foreign exchange needs of Kuwait and Saudi Arabia.

The Persian Gulf War had two important consequences: it removed substantial amounts of supplies from the market, and it had a negative impact on the financial and economic situations of Kuwait and Saudi Arabia. The Persian Gulf War resulted in Iraq, Kuwait, and Saudi Arabia becoming in dire need of oil revenues for their economic development. Kuwait, one of the richest countries in the world, exhausted its "fund for future generations." Iraq's financial and economic situation is even worse, and Saudi Arabia is currently running a huge account deficit. This leads to the conclusion that once these countries develop production and export capacity, they will attempt to fully utilize it.

FUTURE OF OPEC

OPEC's role has changed over time from setting crude oil prices to regulating the international oil market through production programming and management. Structural changes in the international oil market have created a situation that makes it impossible for OPEC to return to fixed crude oil pricing. OPEC, at best, could only attempt to regulate the oil market through supply policy.

Even the organization's ability to regulate the market depends upon demand for OPEC oil in relation to its production capacity and the financial needs of its individual member countries. If the demand for OPEC oil reaches OPEC production capacity, oil prices will increase, irrespective of OPEC policy. When demand for OPEC oil falls far below its production capacity, it also becomes difficult for the organization to regulate the market, since financial requirements of individual member countries would entice them to exceed their allocated quotas, hence weakening crude oil price and the price structure.[7] An analysis of the relation between the demand for OPEC oil and OPEC production capacity indicates that sharp price fluctuations have occurred when the demand for OPEC oil has reached either of the two limits.

While there is debate on the future supply and demand for crude oil, a number of analysts project a tightening of supply and demand for oil by the end of the

1990s. Increase in demand for oil, partly because of an increase in economic activity and partly in response to lower oil prices in real terms, along with stagnation of non-OPEC oil supplies, would indicate that there would be a call on OPEC to raise its output to balance the market.

Moreover, most OPEC member countries are producing closer to their production capacity. Only a few members are in a position to increase their output, all of whom are in the Persian Gulf. Since crude oil production of non-OPEC oil producers are at maximum production, any further increase in global oil supplies must come from only a few countries.

These countries are already major players in the international oil market in terms of their oil reserves and production. Between them, the Persian oil producers have nearly 64 percent of the world's oil reserves, 24 percent of the world's oil production, and 32 percent of global export.[8] In essence, the strong position of the Persian Gulf oil producers in the international oil market will become even more important in the future. Therefore, the future of OPEC would be highly associated with that of the Persian Gulf oil producers and their ability to increase output in the face of increases in demand. Historically, Saudi Arabia had played the role of "swing producer." It had increased its output in the case of shortage and reduced output in production for declining demand. In 1985 it refused to continue such a role when it was forced to cut output to below 2 mbd to maintain balance in the market. Saudi Arabia's role of swing producer inevitably will be shared by other Persian Gulf oil producers.

CONCLUSION

This chapter argues that while OPEC has been influential in affecting crude oil prices, it has not behaved according to the traditional model of a profit-maximizing cartel. This is attributed to the differences of view among its member countries regarding optimum price quantity relations for themselves and for the organization. Each member's view is defined independently by its internal social cost and benefit functions. These functions include a complex set of variables such as oil reserve, oil production capacity, absorptive capacity of the economy, financial situation of the country, internal political structure, and international political tendencies.

Since these factors have been quite diverse among individual member countries, their views of optimal price and supply have been quite different. Differences have been so great that the organization at times has moved to the brink of demise. To determine the future of OPEC, it is essential to see the consequences of recent events on the policy of individual member countries.

By focusing on the two leading groups within OPEC, it appears that their political, economic, and financial views are directionally converging as a result of recent political development in the Middle East. This does not imply that there are no differences within the organization. Rather, it suggests that there has been a shift in inter-OPEC relations. Improved relations and less divergent economies of leading OPEC countries may lead to a more cohesive organization.

However, given the structural changes in the oil market, OPEC no longer will be able or willing to fix crude oil prices. What the organization can strive to achieve is more stable crude oil prices over the long run.

In the long run, OPEC's ability to stabilize the oil market by adjusting its output to satisfy demand for its oil will depend on the collective production capacity of the organization. To increase production capacity, massive investment in exploration and development must take place. With the current financial condition of individual member countries, the possibility of such investment to enhance production and export capacity seems to be low.

The most appropriate candidates to increase production and export capacity are the Persian Gulf oil producers with their substantial oil reserves. If demand for oil continues to grow at the rate of the late 1980s and early 1990s, OPEC will be hard-pressed to maintain a balance in the international oil market, even with increases in output from Persian Gulf oil producing countries. In such a situation, prices will increase not because of OPEC, but despite it. Such price increases should not be viewed as oligopolistic prices or as the success or failure of OPEC, but rather a reflection of the dynamic adjustment of the oil market.

NOTES

1. OPEC Annual Statistics Review (1991).

2. Seymour *OPEC Instrument of Change* (1980), p. 37.

3. Lorensten, Roland, and Anahiem (1985) have estimated the cost of crude oil production, including capital cost, for North Sea oil fields. For some fields, such as Heather and Tarten, they have estimated about $24 per barrel.

4. Ecuador left OPEC in 1992 in protest over its oil quota.

5. The debate of the OPEC Long-Term Strategy Committee focused on this issue. See *Petroleum Intelligence Weekly*, "The Recommendation of OPEC Weighed at Taif," May 12, 1980.

6. For the discussion of this agreement and the shift in OPEC strategy, see Samii (1987).

7. For discussion of relation between OPEC capacity and organization's ability to stabilize the oil market, see Samii and Clemenz (1988).

8. Data refer to 1990, before Iraq's invasion of Kuwait.

REFERENCES

Adelman, Morris. "OPEC as a Cartel." In James Griffin and David Teece (eds.), *OPEC: Behavior and World Oil Prices*. Winchester, MA: Allen Unwin, 1982, 55–75.

Bina, Cyrus. "Limits of OPEC Pricing: OPEC Profits and the Nature of Global Oil Accumulation." *OPEC Review*, Spring 1990.

————. *The Economy of the Oil Crisis*. New York: St. Martin's Press, 1985.

Fitzgerald, Desmond and Gerald Pollio. "The Relation Between Spot and Official Crude Oil Prices." *OPEC Review* 8 (1984): 341–349.

Gately, Dermot. "A Ten-Year Retrospective: OPEC and the World Oil Market." *Journal of Economic Literature* 22(3) 1984: 1100–1114.

Hotelling, Harold. "The Economics of Exhaustible Resources." *Journal of Political Economy* 39 (1931): 137–175.

Johany, Ali. "OPEC and Price of Oil: Cartelization or Alternation of Property Rights." *Journal of Energy and Development*, Autumn 1979: 72–80.

Loderer, Claudi. "A Test of OPEC Cartel Hypothesis: 1974–1983." *Journal of Finance* 40 (1985): 991–1008.

Loretsen, Lorents, Kgell Roland, and Asbjorn Aaheim. "Cost Structure and Profitability of North Sea Oil and Gas Fields." In Olav Bgerkholl and Eric Offerdal (eds.), *Macroeconomic Prospects of a Small Oil Exporting Country.* Dordrecht: Marhius Nijhoff, 1985.

Lowinger, Thomas and Ram Rati. "Product Values as Determinant of OPEC's Official Crude Oil Prices: Additional Results." *Review of Economics and Statistics* 66 (1984): 691–695.

MacAvoy, Paul. *Crude Oil Prices as Determined by OPEC and Market Fundamentals.* Cambridge, MA: Ballinger, 1982.

Mead, Walter G. "The OPEC Cartel Thesis Reexamined: Price Constraints from Oil Substitutes." *Journal of Energy and Development*, Spring 1986: 213–242.

OPEC Annual Statistical Review. Vienna: OPEC Secretariat, 1991.

Pindyck, Robert S. "Gains to Producers from Cartelization of Exhaustible Resources." *Review of Economics and Statistics* (1978): 238–251.

Razavi, Hossein. "An Economic Model of OPEC Coalition." *Southern Economic Journal*, October 1984: 419–428.

Razavi, Hossein and Massood Samii. "Speculative Demand for Oil." *OPEC Review* 7 (1983): 86–101.

Samii, Massood. "OPEC's Return to Fixed Oil Pricing." *Energy Policy*, October 1987: 421–432.

———. "The Organization of Petroleum Exporting Countries and the Oil Market: Different Views." *Journal of Energy and Development*, Fall 1985: 159–173.

Samii, Massood and Claude Clemenz. "Exchange Rate Fluctuations and Stability in the Oil Market." *Energy Policy*, August 1988: 415–423.

Samii, Massood, Robert Weiner, and Franz Wirl. "Determinants of Crude Oil Prices: OPEC Versus Speculators." Energy Environment Policy Center, Harvard University Discussion Paper E—89–05, 1989.

Seymour, Ian. *OPEC Instruments of Change.* London, Macmillan, 1980.

Verleger, Philip Jr. "The Determinant of Official OPEC Crude Prices." *Review of Economics and Statistics*, 64 (1982): 177–183.

Chapter 9

The International Energy Agency

Siamack Shojai

On November 15, 1974, in response to the Organization of Arab Petroleum Exporting Countries' (OAPEC) oil embargo against the United States and the Netherlands, the Council of the Organization for Economic Cooperation and Development decided to establish the International Energy Agency (IEA) under the auspices of OECD. In Chapter 10, Lowell S. Feld provides a thorough discussion of the oil crisis of 1973. Here, it suffices to say that the Arab oil embargo was in response to the U.S. support of Israel in the Arab-Israeli War of October 1973. Initially, the embargo did not cause a major increase in the price of oil. In addition, the embargo was not applied uniformly to all the European Community (EC) countries. For example, France and the United Kingdom were exempt but West Germany, Italy, and others were subject to a gradual oil shipment reduction. Thus, the response and attitude of the OECD countries was in disarray and there seemed to be no consensus as how to deal with the embargo (Smith 1988). However, in December 1973 oil prices jumped over $12/barrel and it became obvious that the OECD countries had to come to a consensus if they wished a successful response to the crisis.

The European Community had already taken oil stockpiling measures since the late 1960s. In 1972, pursuant to creating a Community Energy Policy, directives had been issued to raise the emergency oil stocks from an average of 65 days to 90 days of consumption. At this time, the energy policy of the EC consisted of securing oil supplies at economically acceptable prices. The response of the EC members to the Arab-Israeli War was to distance themselves from the conflict. The NATO members refused to cooperate with the United States in adopting a common NATO policy toward the crisis. Meanwhile, France, Italy, and West Germany were engaged in unilateral negotiations with the oil producing countries in an attempt to secure their own oil supplies. To the dismay of the United States, in early 1974 the European Council had already accepted the Arab League's proposal to establish a Euro-Arab Dialogue in search of a cooperative solution to the oil crisis. In contrast, the United States had proposed the creation of an Energy Action Group to establish a common and coordinated response to the crisis. France was adamantly opposed to such a proposal (Van Der Linde and Lefeber 1988).

In February 1974 the U.S. government invited the EC members to Washington for an energy conference. The American proposal to create a United Energy Consuming group was rejected and instead the IEA was established. France did not join the IEA; but the other 12 participating countries agreed on establishing an International Energy Program.

THE IEA'S GOALS AND STRUCTURE

From its inception the IEA adopted the following four major goals:

1. To establish an emergency oil supply sharing program during major oil supply disruptions.
2. To reduce dependency on imported oil by encouraging conservation, research, and development of alternative sources of energy.
3. To promote cooperation between oil producing and oil consuming countries in an effort to establish a stable international oil market.
4. To gather and disseminate information on the international oil market.

To achieve these goals, the IEA has been engaged in several activities such as establishing an information-sharing system among the members as well as many international and domestic oil companies, encouraging long-term energy policies in the member countries, and establishing an emergency oil sharing program (Badger 1988). Major information-gathering and data-collection activities have resulted in several significant periodical publications by the IEA. Also, the dissemination of information gathered on total oil supplies and distribution by international oil companies contributes to reduction of undue pressure on prices, due to competing and multiple bids for the available stock of oil in the spot market during an emergency situation.

The organization chart of the IEA shows the four major entities that carry out its mandates. These include a Governing Board, a Management Committee, many Standing Groups, and the Secretariat. R. T. Smith (1988) provides an excellent discussion of the tasks and membership of various Standing Groups within the IEA. He describes the IEA's decision-making process and explains the voting system utilized at the ministerial level. The voting power of the members is determined based on an oil consumption formula that takes into consideration the relative oil consumption of the members. A larger oil consuming member receives more votes than a smaller member. In addition, each member has three general votes. The IEA's decisions are adopted based on a majority rule. The IEA has relations with many intergovernmental organizations, such as the Latin American Energy Organization. It also maintains relations with nongovernmental organizations, such as the Association of the Coal Producers of the European Community.

OIL SHARING PROGRAM

The IEA has formal and informal arrangements to deal with oil supply disruptions. Informal actions include stockdraws and demand restraint. These measures are needed in the early stages of a significant supply disruption of any size. However, a loss of at least 7 percent of supply constitutes a major disruption that brings the formal measures into play. In 1979, after the fall of the shah of Iran, the oil market lost 5 percent of its supply. This did not trigger adoption of formal measures; nevertheless, oil prices rose by about 160 percent and remained at that level for almost two and a half years. This led to an agreement at the July 11, 1984, meeting of the IEA to devise a mechanism to deal with smaller disruptions (Toner 1987). G. Toner provides an excellent account of the events that led to this agreement.

D. B. Badger (1988) argues that the 1984 agreement reflected a shift in the philosophy of the IEA from a "last resort" to a "first use" attitude. According to the last resort philosophy, stockdraws should be used as a last measure after demand restraints have been put in place. This measure can be more effective at times of production capacity constraints. Proponents of early use of stockdraws argue that when the potential capacity to produce is substantial and a permanent excess production capacity exists, early use of stockdraws prevents the occurrence of a panic situation similar to the one experienced in the 1979 market. A major portion of the emergency oil stocks are owned by and under the direct control of the member governments. Private oil companies are also required to carry emergency stockpiles.

The formal emergency sharing plan comes into play in the face of a loss of at least 7 percent of supply. In accordance to the formal plan, governments and oil companies share the necessary information about oil supplies and stockpiles. A sharing formula is utilized, which allocates the total supply available to the members based on their share of total oil consumption in a base year. The international oil companies will redirect their imported oil from countries with a surplus to countries with a deficit. A deficit or a surplus is the difference between a member's actual supply (domestic output plus imported oil) and its share of the total available supply. The sharing takes place at the going market price. This program is intended to cope with temporary short-term market disruptions, and dealing with long-term structural movements is left to market competition. The program prevents IEA members from bidding up the spot prices by competing with each other. Nonmember competition can still bid up the prices in a major disruption, particularly when a substantial uncertainty about future supply leads to severe buyer competition in the spot market. For example, France, among many other countries, attempted to purchase oil for its state-owned refineries in the 1979 episode (Toner 1987).

EFFECTIVENESS OF THE INTERNATIONAL ENERGY PROGRAM

Many authors have studied the effectiveness and desirability of the International Energy Program (IEP) (Okogu 1992; Toner 1987; Horwich and Weimer 1988a, 1988b). A major oil supply disruption can boost prices and this in turn can cause a deterioration of the terms of trade for oil importing countries and a real transfer of resources to oil exporters. The impact and long-term macroeconomic effects of oil shocks are well known. However, any attempt by governments to manage the oil market during a crisis and avoid price hikes can cause inefficiencies in consumption and production, and a misallocation of resources. The opponents of the IEP argue that the program was not effective in dealing with the crises of 1979, 1981, and 1991. Those in favor of the IEA argue that a loose coalition of oil importers is better than no action when the importers are faced with a loose association of oil exporters such as OPEC.

In the face of an oil supply shock, oil importers have two options. First, they can let market discipline correct the situation and allocate existing oil supplies. The economic, social, and political hardships that follow because of higher oil prices pressure the governments of oil importing countries to take action and deal with the situation as a matter of public policy. Second, government policy can take the form of coordinated supply-sharing with other affected countries as well as measures to restrain demand. Oil import quotas, oil import fees (taxes), targeted oil imports, and a mixed response are among possible actions available to policymakers. In a recent study of the IEA (Horwich and Weimer 1988a), Horwich and others concluded that the price should be allowed to clear the markets except when the terms of trade loss outweigh efficiency gains.

On May 11, 1987, U.S. Secretary of Energy John S. Herrington addressed the Miministerial Meeting of the IEA and stated:

We have found that continued reliance on the market to set prices and allocate energy supplies and investments is the best long-term strategy for sustaining a strong national oil industry, assuring our economic prosperity, and bolstering our energy security. We also found that the economic costs of an oil import fee far outweigh any security benefits, and therefore, an oil import fee has been rejected (Department of State Bulletin 1987: 47).

Later in 1993 the Clinton administration rejected the imposition of an oil import fee, even in the face of huge budget deficits. Oil import quotas are also considered inferior to other demand restraint measures. Bohi and Toman (1988), like many others, favor stock draws during an emergency. However, in Chapter

19 of this book they argue that in the long term energy security can be achieved through renewed efforts in research and development, and the development of alternative sources of energy.

Smith (1988) argues that the IEA has done more harm than good to the stability of the oil market. He presents an elaborate analysis of the IEP and concludes that it has not been effective in dealing with oil crises in the past. However, the events during the Persian Gulf crisis of 1990 shed additional light in appraising the IEA's performance. The Iraqi invasion of Kuwait resulted in a sharp decline in the world's oil supply. The IEA was reluctant to activate the emergency sharing program until the outbreak of Desert Storm. Even then, it was only the United States that allowed draws on its strategic reserves of up to 2 million bpd. The IEA has been sharply criticized for its slow response and lack of action in the early stages of the crisis (Morse, 1990; Verleger 1990).

CONCLUSION

This chapter has provided a brief discussion of the IEA, its origin, objectives, and structure. It has also presented a survey of recent literature on policy actions available to oil importing countries and the emergency response of the IEA to major oil supply disruptions.

It is concluded that the general feeling of various analysts is that the existence of the IEA is preferable to its abolishment. The agency has been instrumental in devising better responses to short-term oil crises as well as to long-term energy security needs through advocating energy efficiency, conservation, research and development, and environmental imperatives.

REFERENCES

Badger, D. B., Jr. "International Cooperation During Oil Supply Disruptions: The Role of the International Energy Agency." In Horwich and Weimer 1988a.

Bohi, D. R. and M. A. Toman. "Restructuring the IEA Crisis Management Program to Serve Members' Interests Better." In Horwich and Weimer 1988a.

Department of State Bulletin, July 1987.

Horwich, G. and D. L. Weimer. *Responding to the International Oil Crisis.* Washington, DC: American Enterprise Institute, 1988a.

———. "The Economics of International Oil Sharing." *Energy Journal* 9(4) (1988b).

Morse, E. N. "The Coming Oil Revolution." *Foreign Affairs*, Winter 1990.

Okogu, B. E. "What Use the IEA Emergency Stockpiles? A Price-based Model of Oil Management." *Energy Journal* 13(1), (1992).

Smith, R. "International Energy Cooperation: The Mismatch Between IEA Policy Actions and Policy Goals." In Horwich and Weimer 1988a.

Toner, G. "The International Energy Agency and the Development of the Stocks Decision." *Energy Policy*, February 1987, pp. 40–58.

Van Der Linde, J. G. and R. Lefeber. "International Energy Agency Captures the Development of European Community Energy Law.'' *Journal of World Trade* 22(5), (October 1988): 5–25.

Verleger, P. K. Jr. "The Theory of Price Shortage." *American Economic Review* 29 (1990): pp. 1254–1262.

Chapter 10

Oil Markets in Crisis: Major Oil Supply Disruptions Since 1973

Lowell S. Feld

It has now been more than 20 years since the world was shaken by the first in a series of "oil shocks." Before 1973, oil had been one of the most stable commodities, in terms of both price and reliability of supply. In fact, oil had for decades been so cheap, so plentiful, and so easily transportable that it had become the most desirable energy source for powering modern civilization. To fill Western societies' seemingly insatiable demand for oil, a great international network of large oil companies had evolved over the years. These corporations effectively controlled exploration, production, and marketing of oil, while also enjoying most of the profits associated with these activities. Meanwhile, the countries in which oil happened to be located were becoming increasingly disenchanted with this arrangement. For the most part, however, oil producing countries could do little about this situation until 1973. In that year, the countries seized an opportunity to change the situation, and world oil markets have not been the same since.

HISTORICAL BACKGROUND

Over the past 40 years, there have been 13 significant disruptions of oil supplies from the Middle East (see Table 10.1). Chronologically, by far the largest number of Middle East oil supply disruptions occurred in the 1970s (7), with 2 each taking place in the 1950s and 1960s, and 1 each in the 1980s and 1990s. These disruptions have varied in terms of cause, ranging from damage to oil facilities to war or other forms of civil unrest. They have also varied widely in terms of severity, although the vast majority have been relatively small (i.e., the 300,000 bpd oil supply loss in the case of the 1976 Lebanese civil war) and/or short-lived (i.e., the 1-month, 700,000 bpd disruption to a Saudi oilfield in May

Table 10.1
Middle East Oil Supply Disruptions Since 1951

Dates of Net Oil Supply Disruption	Duration (Months of Net Supply Disruption)	Average Gross Supply Shortfall (Million B/D)	Reason for Oil Supply Disruption
3/51-10/54	44	0.7	Iranian oilfields nationalized May 1, following months of unrest and strikes in Abadan area.
11/56-3/57	4	2	Suez War
12/66-3/67	3	0.7	Syrian Transit Fee Dispute
6/67-8/67	2	2	Six Day War
5/70-1/71	9	1.3	Libyan price controversy; damage to Tapline
4/71-8/71	5	0.6	Algerian-French nationalization struggle
3/73-5/73	2	0.5	Unrest in Lebanon; damage to transit facilities
10/73-3/74	6	2.6	October Arab-Israeli War;
4/76	2	0.3	Civil war in Lebanon;
5/77	1	0.7	Damage to Saudi oil field
11/78	6	3.5	Iranian revolution
10/80	3	3.3	Outbreak of Iran-Iraq War
8/90	3	4.6	Iraqi invasion of Kuwait

Sources for this table include: U.S. Department of Energy, *Strategic Petroleum Reserve: Analysis of Size Options* (DOE/IE-0016, 2/90); U.S. Energy Information Administration, *Energy Situation Analysis Report* (8/14/90, 8/16/90, 8/20/90, 10/29/90); Lowell S. Feld and John H. Herbert, "Oil Stocks and Crises," in *Geopolitics of Energy* 12 (December 1990).
Average gross oil supply shortfalls are calculated using a baseline of average oil production during a three-month period preceding the disruption.

1977). In general, the crises of the 1950s and 1960s resulted in little significant change in world oil prices. Even the relatively large 2 mbd gross[1] oil supply disruptions caused by the 1956 and 1967 Arab-Israeli Wars had almost no price impact. The small impact of these early crises was due primarily to surplus oil production capacity in the United States and flexible oil distribution networks maintained by the major oil companies.[2]

This situation began to change significantly in the early 1970s, however, as world oil consumption grew rapidly while oil production capacity (particularly in the United States) failed to keep pace. In addition, fundamental changes were taking place in the world oil market, as control of oil resources shifted steadily away from the major oil companies and toward the producing countries.[3] By

1973 the push for greater "participation" by producing nations had coincided with a progressively tighter oil market (as oil demand outstripped supply) and an increasingly tense situation on the Arab-Israeli front to create a "worst case scenario" for a major disruption in world oil supplies.[4] In October 1973 the "worst" occurred—namely, the first of four major oil supply disruptions over the next two decades.[5]

MAJOR OIL CRISIS NO. 1: THE 1973 ARAB OIL EMBARGO

On October 6, 1973, Egyptian forces crossed the Suez Canal into the Israeli-occupied Sinai Peninsula, marking the start of the fourth Arab-Israeli War, as well as the end of the relatively stable world oil market of the post-World War II era. Ten days later, on October 16, the "Gulf Six" Arab oil producing countries (Iraq, Kuwait, Qatar, Saudi Arabia, the United Arab Emirates, and Bahrain) met in Kuwait, where they agreed both to cut oil production by 5 percent immediately (with more cuts threatened) and unilaterally to raise the posted price of Saudi Light marker crude by 70 percent, from $3.01 to $5.12 per barrel.[6] This initial decision to unleash the "oil weapon" in response to the U.S. emergency airlift of military equipment to Israel (which began on October 13) was followed a few days later by a ban on oil exports from Arab OPEC members to the United States and the Netherlands (subsequently extended to include South Africa, Rhodesia, and Portugal).

On November 5, despite the existence of a stable cease-fire, the oil embargo was further reinforced by an announced 25 percent cut in Arab OPEC production.[7] As a result, Arab members of OPEC produced only 15.5 mbd in November, compared to around 20 mbd in September. Meanwhile, as a result of the war, oil production had also been disrupted in Syria, Egypt, and the Israeli-occupied Sinai Peninsula (Abu Rudeis fields). On the eve of the outbreak of hostilities, Egypt had been producing 225,000 bpd, Israel 105,000 bpd, and Syria 126,000 bpd. By November Egypt's production had declined by nearly 90 percent, to only 29,000 bpd, with Israel producing only 48,000 bpd, and Syria just 53,000 bpd.

At its peak in November and December 1973, these oil supply reductions taken as a whole resulted in a gross supply disruption in "market economies' " (i.e., the entire world minus the Communist countries) oil production of more than 4 mbd compared to average levels for the three months (July–September) preceding the crisis.[8] Even taking into account limited amounts of increased production from various non-Arab countries (mainly Iran and Nigeria), market economies' oil production was effectively reduced in November and December by around 3.7 mbd from July–September average production.

This oil supply disruption, although large, at first resulted in only small oil price increases. Oil prices began to rise more rapidly beginning in December, however, partly in response to a decision that month by the Gulf Six to increase the posted price of marker crude by 128 percent (from $5.12 to $11.65/barrel) effective January 1, 1974. Also during December, Arab OPEC oil production remained almost constant from November, at about 15.8 mbd. The effect of this continuing supply disruption was being reflected to an increasing degree in world oil prices. The average price of imported oil (at that time known as the "refinery gate price") in the United States, for instance, reached $7.84/barrel in December (from $4.78 in September and $5.84 in November), increasing to over $12 (using a slightly different measure, called the "imported refiner acquisition cost," or IRAC) in February 1974. In March oil prices began to level off as the Arab-Israeli crisis eased, partly as a result of U.S. Secretary of State Henry Kissinger's continuing "shuttle diplomacy" efforts. Finally, on March 17, Arab oil exporters decided to terminate their oil embargo of the United States. This move marked the formal end of the worst oil crisis ever to that point, but did not result in a decrease in oil prices. In fact, by the end of 1975 the IRAC had *increased* by another $2, to nearly $15/barrel. More than anything, this was a definitive sign that OPEC had effectively seized control of world oil markets and, with them, the price of oil.

MAJOR OIL CRISIS NO. 2: THE IRANIAN REVOLUTION OF 1978/79

Over the next three years, though, OPEC did not attempt to push oil prices any higher, apparently satisfied with the increases to date. In late 1978, however, this stability was shattered by the second major oil crisis of the decade—the Iranian revolution. On September 8, 1978, following months of increasing turmoil, martial law was declared in Iran. By October, strikes in the oil sector had succeeded in effectively shutting down the Iranian economy. In November, Iranian crude oil production fell to only 3.5 mbd, around 40 percent below its preceding three-month average production level of about 5.8 mbd. By the end of December, with the Iranian revolution in full swing, Iranian oil production plummeted even further, to around 500,000 bpd. On December 30, the shah effectively ceded power by appointing Shahpour Bakhtiar to head a new constitutional government, and by agreeing to leave Iran "temporarily," which he did on January 16, 1979. Finally, on February 1, 1980, Ayatollah Khomeini returned to Iran, where he and his supporters soon succeeded in seizing power from forces loyal to Premier Bakhtiar.

The full impact on oil prices of the oil supply disruption caused by the Iranian revolution was not felt immediately. In fact, for the six-month period from November 1978 to April 1979 (Crisis No. 2), during which the average gross supply shortfall was around 3.5 mbd (peaking at 5.1 mbd in January and February 1979), the IRAC increased by only 20 percent, from $14.63 in October 1978 to $17.58 per barrel in April 1979. In comparison, during the 1973 Arab oil embargo (Crisis No. 1), which had involved a smaller average gross supply shortfall of about 2.6 mbd over six months, prices increased by over 160 percent, from $4.78 to $12.73/barrel.

How does one explain this much smaller price increase resulting from the Iranian revolution (Crisis 2) compared to the Arab Oil Embargo (Crisis 2), even though Crisis 2 represented a larger gross supply shortfall than Crisis 1? One possibility is to look at differences in Saudi behavior during Crises 1 and 2. First, although the Saudis were an integral part of the decision to impose and implement an oil embargo on countries considered pro-Israel in Crisis 1, in Crisis 2 the Saudis neither caused nor aided the Iranian revolution and its consequent supply disruption. On the contrary, during the initial months of Crisis 2, the Saudis actively worked to maximize their own production, thereby partially offsetting the loss of Iranian production and moderating the consequent price hike. Thus, the Saudis steadily increased their production from 7.1 mbd in August to 10.4 mbd in December, before reducing to 9.8 mbd in the first quarter of 1979. Other OPEC countries also stepped in to help make up the shortfall, particularly Iraq (3.3. mbd in February vs. 2.9 mbd in October), Kuwait (2.6 mbd vs. 2.1 mbd) and Nigeria (2.4 mbd vs. 2.1 mbd). The net result of these supply increases by February was to offset over 2.5 mbd of the Iranian supply loss.

By March 1979 the worst of the crisis appeared to be over. Iranian production had recovered to 2.54 mbd (from 700,000 bpd in January and February), the remaining net supply shortfall had fallen below 300,000 bpd (less than 1 percent of world oil production), and oil prices appeared to have stabilized (with IRAC around $16 per barrel). By April, in fact, with Iranian production up to 4.2 mbd, market economies' oil production had more than recovered its precrisis level. It was just at this point of apparent calm, however, that oil prices exploded, reaching $23 per barrel by July.

Once again, Saudi behavior has been cited as critical by many analysts.[9] In this case, Saudi Arabia's decision of April 1979 not to extend its first-quarter production ceiling into the second quarter, effectively resulting in a 1 mbd production cut (to 8.8 mbd), is seen by some analysts as exacerbating, if not actually causing, the subsequent price increases.[10] This is not completely supported by the facts. For one thing, despite the Saudi production cut, overall market economies' production in April increased by over 1 mbd from March. Market economies' production continued to increase through July, when the Saudis finally restored production to first-quarter levels. By this point, oil prices had increased by 31 percent from April levels (from $17.58 to $23.09/barrel). Following the July resumption of Saudi production at 9.8 mbd, prices did not fall (as would be expected if Saudi behavior was assumed to be critical), but in fact continued to rise rapidly, reaching nearly $29/barrel by year's end. Thus, the evidence tends to refute the conclusion that Saudi production restraints were responsible for the oil price increases that occurred in this stage of the crisis.

A better explanation for the rapid escalation of oil prices throughout the spring and summer of 1979 can be found by looking not at the supply side but at the demand side of the equation, particularly oil stockbuilding behavior by major oil importing countries. The outbreak of the Iranian revolution in the fourth quarter of 1978 occurred at a time in which OECD oil stocks were at 3.1 billion barrels, or about 73 days of consumption.[11] By the first quarter of 1979, however, these stocks had been drawn down significantly to 2.8 billion barrels, the equivalent of only 61 days of consumption—the lowest level in at least five years. Given strong world demand for oil, the unstable international supply situation, past price increases, and fear of even worse to come, this low level of stocks caused a massive wave of crude oil stockbuilding.

Beginning in the spring of 1979, and continuing through the summer, consumers frantically built stocks at the rate of nearly 1 mbd. By the third quarter, this rapid stockbuilding behavior had succeeded in not only rebuilding OECD stocks to normal levels, but also in boosting them to record high levels (3.3 billion barrels, or 85 days' worth of OECD consumption). This stockbuilding resulted in a classic vicious cycle situation. In this case, an initial, real oil supply disruption caused apprehension among oil traders regarding future supply difficulties. This then prompted buyers to attempt to hedge by building stocks. As a result, buyers bid against one another for available oil supplies on the increasingly important spot market, causing demand to increase and further aggravating the upward price spiral begun by the actual supply disruption. Lack of coordination among consuming nations further exacerbated matters, while many oil producers were more than happy to take advantage of this situation by pushing up prices even further.

As a result of this situation, the IRAC increased another $7.47 (to over $25/ barrel) between April, when the oil supply disruption caused by the Iranian revolution had essentially ended, and October, following the summer of stockbuilding. At this point, oil prices were given a further upward push by the seizure of U.S. embassy personnel as hostages by Iranian militants on November 4, 1979. In response, President Carter on November 12 ordered an embargo on Iranian oil imports into the United States, and three days later Iran responded by canceling all contracts with U.S. oil companies. Three other events that potentially threatened even further disruption to Persian Gulf oil supplies took place soon afterward: (1) in late November, Islamic fundamentalists seized the Great Mosque in Mecca, and were dislodged only with great difficulty and loss of life; (2) in December, protests broke out in Saudi Arabia's main oil producing region—the eastern al-Hasa province—by the Shi'a Muslim minority; and (3) in late December, Soviet troops invaded Afghanistan. These actions, combined with continued stockbuilding, fueled anxiety levels that helped push the IRAC over $33 by March 1980—a 24 percent increase in less than five months. By the summer of 1980, oil prices finally began to level off, with OECD stocks having reached around 103 days of consumption (nearly 20 days more than in the comparable period the previous year). A period of price stability now seemed possible, barring any new crisis. Just such a crisis, however, soon erupted.

MAJOR OIL CRISIS NO. 3: OUTBREAK OF THE IRAN-IRAQ WAR AND 1980s OIL GLUT

On September 23, 1980, Iraq invaded Iran, threatening the world's third major oil shock in seven years. Through damage to the two countries' oil transportation and production facilities, the outbreak of the Iran-Iraq War caused an initial gross oil supply loss of 3.9 mbd. Due to production increases from Saudi Arabia, Nigeria, and others, however, the *net* world oil supply shortfall reached only 3.3 mbd in October. Still, this was a major oil supply disruption, comparable in magnitude to levels reached during Crisis No. 2. Unlike Crisis 2, however, Crisis 3 did not result in a major increase in world oil prices. Why not?

First and foremost, OECD oil stocks at the outbreak of Crisis 3 remained at record high levels (about 100 days' of OECD consumption). This provided a significant amount of breathing room, both in physical and psychological terms, which was not present at the outset of Crisis 2. This breathing room, combined with better coordination among consuming countries, helped prevent the kind of panic buying witnessed in Crisis 2. Second, a high level of spare world oil production capacity was present at the outbreak of Crisis 3, in contrast to the situation at the start of Crisis 2. This was largely due to a significant decrease in world oil demand caused by the massive price increases of the previous two years. As a result of a near doubling in prices caused by Crisis 2, world crude oil demand had fallen nearly 7 mbd, from 63 mbd in October 1978 to only 56 mbd in October 1980.

Brought on line, the spare oil production capacity available at the outset of Crisis 3 had by November 1980 reduced the world oil production shortfall to only 2.4 mbd below its July–September average level, despite the fact that Iraqi production was down by more than 90 percent (or 2.8 mbd) and Iranian production by nearly 50 percent (or 680,000 bpd). In fact, by December, only two months after Crisis 3 had begun, market economies' oil production had recovered to less than 1 mbd below July–September average levels. This was primarily due to the ability and willingness of countries with spare production capacity (particularly Saudi Arabia, Kuwait, Nigeria, and the United Kingdom) to make up production lost from Iran and Iraq. As a result, the physical and psychological effects of the initial oil supply disruption were minimized, thus helping to reduce the price impact of Crisis 3. In fact, at year's end, the IRAC price had increased only 3 percent from September, and U.S. gasoline prices had actually remained flat. In sum, Crisis 3, although sizable in terms of its level of disruption, did not result in any major increases in oil prices.

The oil price increases resulting from the oil crises of the 1970s resulted in major shifts in world energy markets during the 1980s. Among others, these included a significant decrease in energy intensity[12] (i.e., the amount of energy consumed per unit of output) and a major decrease in world crude oil demand (from more than 62 mbd in 1979 to under 53 mbd in 1983).[13] At the same time, the high oil prices of the 1970s prompted increased exploration and production among non-OPEC countries (particularly Mexico, the United Kingdom, and Norway[14]). The net result of these changes was a sharp decrease in OPEC production (from 31 mbd in 1979 to less than 17 mbd in 1985) and market share (from a high of 68 percent in 1974 to only 38 percent in 1985). During the same period, the decline in OPEC production caused a huge increase in OPEC excess oil production capacity.

By the mid-1980s the result of these trends was a large glut of oil on world markets, and a resultant deterioration in real oil prices. The IRAC price, for instance, fell slowly but steadily from its high in 1980 of $51.96/barrel (in constant 1990 dollars), to only $31.98/barrel in 1985. By 1985 Saudi Arabia had seen its share of the shrinking OPEC production total decline from over 40 percent in 1981 to little more than 20 percent in 1985. As a result of its efforts at playing swing producer and attempting to prop up oil prices, Saudi Arabia had seen its oil production fall to barely over 2 mbd (from over 10 mbd in 1981), and its oil export revenues collapse from $100 billion (in constant 1980 dollars) in 1981 to only $27 billion in 1985. Finally, in late 1985, Saudi Arabia decided that it had had enough. As a result of the Saudi decision to abandon its role as swing producer within OPEC and instead to increase its own production, Saudi oil output rebounded by early 1986 to over 4.5 mbd. Not surprisingly, this only worsened the prevailing world oil glut, triggering a price collapse. The market now demonstrated that price shocks did not always have to be in the upward direction, with the IRAC falling during 1986 to less than $17 a barrel (in constant 1990 dollars), less than one-third its 1980 level.

The oil price collapse of the mid-1980s contributed to a less-than-surprising trend: a reversal of the favorable oil consumption, production, and energy intensity developments that followed the price spikes of the 1970s. Thus, by 1989, OECD oil consumption had rebounded nearly 4 mbd from its 1983 low of just under 34 mbd. Non-OPEC crude oil production, which had increased from 31.5 mbd in 1979 to 37.7 mbd in 1988, began to level off. As a result, demand for OPEC oil began to increase. Consequently, OPEC countries began to utilize their oil production capacities at higher rates.[15] By 1989, in fact, OPEC capacity utilization had rebounded to 80 percent, from a low of 62 percent in 1985. At the same time, U.S. net oil imports, which had bottomed out at 4.3 mbd in 1982, surpassed 7 mbd in 1989, and neared 8 mbd in 1990. And finally, some of the reductions in energy intensity that had taken place since the 1970s began to reverse; as an example, new car fuel efficiency in the United States actually declined from 1987 to 1988, as lower oil prices prompted many people to purchase larger cars once again. As the decade of the 1990s began, therefore, the power balance in world oil markets between producers and consumers appeared (on the surface at least) to be shifting back toward the producers once again (following the producers' ascendancy in the 1970s and relative decline in the 1980s).

Beneath the surface, however, world oil markets at the start of the 1990s had changed greatly over the preceding 20 years. On the oil consumption side, significant changes had taken place in the way oil was bought and sold, largely through the development of oil spot and futures markets. The opening of the New York Mercantile Exchange to oil trading (on March 30, 1983) represented in many ways as dramatic a shift in world oil markets as the decline of the Seven Sisters or the rise of OPEC. The price of oil would now be set as much by the open market as by oil producers or companies. At the same time, major consuming countries were moving to insulate themselves against any future oil supply disruptions by the stockpiling of strategic oil reserves. The United States, for instance, began pumping oil into Louisiana salt domes as part of its effort aimed at creating a Strategic Petroleum Reserve (SPR). Finally, fundamental changes were also taking place in oil producing countries. Among the most important of these changes was an increasing level of dependence on the huge oil export revenues that had resulted from the price spikes of the 1970s. During the 1980s, oil producers came to rely on these revenues as a means of achieving national economic growth, political and social stability, and military strength. The 1985/86 oil price collapse was therefore traumatic for many oil producing countries. In most cases, these countries attempted to adjust to the resulting new reality of greatly diminished oil revenues. In some cases, however, reality was hard to take.

PRELUDE TO MAJOR OIL CRISIS NO. 4: THE CASE OF IRAQ

Even more so than monarchies or sheikhdoms like Saudi Arabia and Kuwait, Ba'athist Iraq had grown dependent on oil revenues. To finance an ambitious economic and social agenda, combined with its dreams of regional military ascendancy, Iraq's ruling Ba'ath party regime (headed by President Saddam Hussein) had need of huge sums of money. This need became even more apparent as a result of Iraq's devastating ten-year war with Iran. In the aftermath of this terrible war, Iraq was faced with a foreign debt of over $80 billion (including $50 billion to Gulf Arab countries that supported Iraq against Iran), soaring inflation, huge reconstruction costs, and the return of nearly 1 million soldiers, many looking for jobs. Under these circumstances, low oil revenues were, not surprisingly, unwelcome by an Iraqi leadership that had staked a good part of its political legitimacy on the promise of economic development and material prosperity for its rapidly growing population.

Given the high degree of importance attached to oil revenues by Iraq's Ba'athist regime, any threat to these revenues was not likely to be accepted willingly. In retrospect, then, it should not have been surprising during the spring and summer of 1990 that a perceived threat to this interest would have been taken by Iraq as a serious provocation. Due primarily to a precipitous decline in oil prices from the beginning of 1990 (IRAC falling from $20.50 in January to $15.15 in June), Iraq's estimated oil revenue had declined from $1.7 billion in January to less than $1 billion in June—a reduction of around 40 percent in only six months.

That such a decline would not be readily accepted by Iraq was soon made apparent in an escalating series of bellicose statements aimed primarily at Kuwait, Saudi Arabia, and the United Arab Emirates, which Iraq identified as the three major OPEC overproducers. Iraqi hostility was aimed particularly at Kuwait, not coincidentally the state nearest to Iraq and least capable of defending itself. On August 2, 1990, this hostility boiled over as Iraq invaded Kuwait.

MAJOR OIL CRISIS NO. 4: THE IRAQI INVASION OF KUWAIT

What was the world oil market situation at the outset of Crisis No. 4? First, petroleum stocks in OECD countries were high in absolute terms, although relative to consumption they had fallen slightly in recent years. Significantly, OECD strategic oil reserves had grown rapidly in the 1980s, to around 850 million barrels, primarily located in the U.S. Strategic Petroleum Reserve (582 million barrels), and in Japan (208 million barrels). Overall, OECD countries were better prepared on August 2, 1990, in terms of stock availability than at the outbreak of Crises 1 and 2, but slightly less so compared to Crisis 3.

Second, market economies' oil production over the first six months of 1990 was the highest in over ten years. Nearly half of this 52 mbd, however, was produced by OPEC members, with almost one-third produced by Persian Gulf countries alone. This continued a trend since 1985 toward steadily increasing OPEC oil production. At the same time, oil consumption in the OECD countries was increasing rapidly. U.S. oil consumption, for instance, was running about 1.5 mbd above its 1985 level of 15.7 mbd. Meanwhile, U.S. production had fallen by around 1.5 mbd between 1985 and 1990. The net result of this decrease in U.S. oil production and increase in U.S. oil consumption over the period was a seemingly inexorable rise in U.S. net oil imports, from only 4.3 mbd in 1985 to nearly 8 mbd in early 1990. As a consequence, U.S. import dependence shot up from only 27 percent in 1985 to over 45 percent in the first half of 1990.

Despite this increase in oil demand since 1985, however, oil prices through July 1990 had remained low. The reasons for this were complex, and were partly due to the existence of significant excess world oil production capacity (of around 5 mbd). From the Iraqi perspective, however, the situation was much simpler to explain. As Saddam Hussein put it in a speech only two weeks before the invasion, low oil prices were the result of a conspiracy between the United States and "some Arab rulers."[16] To further emphasize the point, on July 18 Iraqi Foreign Minister Tariq Aziz presented a memorandum to the Arab League accusing Kuwait of, among other things, a "planned operation to flood the oil market . . . (leading) to the collapse" of prices, and categorized these acts as "tantamount to military aggression."[17]

The Iraqi invasion of Kuwait on August 2, 1990, and UN Security Council Resolution 660 imposing an embargo on exports from Iraq and occupied Kuwait, resulted in a gross disruption to oil world supplies of 4.6 mbd (2.7 mbd from

Iraq and 1.9 mbd from Kuwait). This was prior to offsetting surge production from countries with excess capacity. As in past crises, Saudi Arabia once again was the critical actor in this regard, as the one country possessing considerable surge production ability. In the event, Saudi Arabia moved quickly and aggressively to make up for lost Iraqi and Kuwait oil. As a result of these efforts, Saudi Arabia by November managed to increase its crude oil production by 2.9 mbd over July levels of about 5.4 mbd. This increased Saudi production, combined with increased production from other countries (including the United Arab Emirates, Venezuela, the United States, and the North Sea), by November had essentially eliminated any net oil supply disruption caused by Iraq's invasion of Kuwait. A major gross disruption continued, however, along with a significant increase in oil prices.

In sum, although the *net* oil supply disruption resulting from Iraq's invasion of Kuwait lasted barely three months (August–October), it resulted in a major oil price spike, largely based on fears regarding critical Saudi oil supplies. The price spike peaked in early October (with IRAC over $30/barrel, compared to $16/barrel in July) and then receded, as the influx of Allied troops (Operation Desert Shield) minimized any threat to Saudi Arabia. By January 17, 1991, the day after the onset of the coalition bombing campaign (Operation Desert Storm), the price spike had essentially ended,[18] although the liberation of Kuwait was not completed until February 28. The end of the ground campaign did not, however, immediately remove the 4.6 mbd *gross* oil supply disruption. For one thing, Kuwaiti oil production, processing, and export facilities had been severely sabotaged by Iraqi troops. As a result, Kuwaiti production did not resume until June 1991, and did not achieve prewar levels until February 1993. Second, the UN oil embargo on Iraq was set to continue until Iraq complied with all cease-fire terms and relevant UN resolutions. As of late 1993, Iraq still had not been allowed to export any oil. In one sense, therefore, Crisis 4 did not end with the Allied military victory, but continues to this day.

Despite the absence of Iraq from world oil markets since 1991, however, world oil prices have remained well below OPEC's official goal, largely due to weak demand caused by anemic economic growth in major oil consuming countries. At the same time, revenue-strapped OPEC countries have been reluctant to cut production. As a result, even with Iraq still excluded from exporting oil, OPEC meetings since 1991 have mainly struggled with the challenge of reining in *overproduction*. Ironically, therefore, OPEC's greatest challenge today lies not in coping with any new oil supply disruption, but with the final resolution of the last one (Crisis 4). Some have speculated, in fact, that OPEC's failure to deal effectively with Iraq's return to world oil markets could cause another collapse in oil prices, and even lead to the disintegration of OPEC. Already, one country (Ecuador) has officially left OPEC, while others (Kuwait, Iraq, Venezuela) have threatened to do so. Thus, 20 years after the first oil shock helped OPEC grab control of world oil markets, the organization now faces a potential threat to its very existence.

CONCLUSIONS

What conclusions can be drawn from this examination of the major oil crises of the past 20 years? First, petroleum stocks, both in terms of behavior and levels, played an important role in the development of all four crises. In particular, stockbuilding behavior helped aggravate the severity of Crisis 2, while high stock levels helped prevent Crisis 3 (and possibly Crisis 4) from escalating. Second, the amount of available excess oil production capacity (and the will to use it) has proven critical in all crises. Third, the behavior of Saudi Arabia (as the country possessing much of this excess capacity) has been important, whether in leading the oil embargo in Crisis 1, in possibly exacerbating Crisis 2, or in helping to lessen the severity of Crises 3 and 4. Finally, market psychology has been an important factor in all crises, with significant (although unpredictable and difficult-to-quantify) impacts on the price response to any given physical oil supply disruption.

NOTES

1. A *gross* oil supply disruption is defined as the absolute amount of oil lost to world oil markets (compared to the previous three-month average production level) prior to offsetting increases in production by undisrupted countries. A *net* oil supply disruption takes into account such offsetting oil supply increases.

2. The "major" oil companies included first and foremost the so-called Seven Sisters, as identified by Anthony Sampson in his book, *The Seven Sisters: The Great Oil Companies and the World They Shaped* (New York: Bantam Books, Inc., 1975). Five of these companies were American (Exxon, Standard Oil of California/Socal, Mobil, Gulf, and Texaco); one was British (British Petroleum); and the other Anglo/Dutch (Royal Dutch/Shell).

3. Two events were particularly significant in this regard. In September 1970 Occidental Petroleum Company was pressured by Libya into accepting price and tax increases on Libyan crude. This was followed a few months later by the Teheran agreement (signed on February 14, 1971), in which the major oil companies were forced to accept a 55 percent minimum tax rate, along with an increase in posted prices. These two events were followed by a series of nationalizations of oil interests, in Algeria (February 24, 1971), Iraq (June 1, 1972), Iran (March 16, 1973), and Libya (August/September 1973).

4. For excellent discussions of the struggle for control of world oil resources, see Sampson, *The Seven Sisters*, and Daniel Yergin, *The Prize: The Epic Quest for Oil, Money, and Power* (New York: Simon and Schuster, 1991).

5. A major oil supply disruption is defined as significant in terms of both "gross" and "net" disruption sizes, as well as causing at least some upward impact on prices.

6. Throughout this chapter, oil prices are expressed in nominal dollars per barrel unless otherwise noted.

7. Since oil is a "fungible" commodity (i.e., one that can be easily and inexpensively moved around, is widely distributed, and can be readily refined into a variety of products), an embargo on only certain countries does not ensure that those countries will lose access to oil supplies from the embargoers. The combination, therefore, of both an outright ban

on oil exports to certain countries, along with an overall reduction in oil supplies, can have more impact than either measure carried out independently.

8. Comparison of oil production levels to a three-month average (as opposed to one month) preceding the outbreak of a crisis is considered more meaningful, particularly given monthly fluctuations in production figures.

9. See, for instance, William B. Quandt, *Saudi Arabia in the 1980s: Foreign Policy, Security, and Oil* (Washington, DC: The Brookings Institution, 1981). See also Theodore Moran, ''Modeling OPEC Behavior: Economic and Political Alternatives,'' in James Griffin and David Teece, *OPEC Behavior and World Oil Prices* (London: George Allen & Unwin, 1982).

10. See especially David B. Golub, *When Oil and Politics Mix: Saudi Oil Policy, 1973–1985*, Harvard Middle East Papers No. 4, 1985.

11. Sources of data for this section and elsewhere in the chapter are U.S. Energy Information Administration, *Historical Monthly Energy Review: 1973–1988* (DOE/EIA–0035 [73–88]); *International Energy Annual, 1991* (DOE/EIA–0219 [91]); and internal estimates.

12. The two terms, ''energy efficiency'' and ''energy intensity,'' are often used interchangeably, but they are actually different (although related) concepts. ''Energy efficiency'' is primarily a technical concept, referring to the amount of energy used by equipment or processes under uniform operating conditions. ''Energy intensity,'' on the other hand, describes energy use per unit of output at an aggregate level.

13. As with any other input, economic theory would predict that an increase in energy prices should result in substitution into other factors of production (i.e., labor and/or capital). In general, the law of demand states that the most efficient way to use resources is to use more of them when they are relatively cheap (and less of them when they are relatively expensive).

14. Although oil and gas exploration in British and Norweigian areas of the North Sea had actually begun before 1973, significant production from the region did not begin until the mid 1970s.

15. OPEC oil production capacity is defined as OPEC's maximum sustainable oil production capability over several months. OPEC capacity utilization (output as a share of capacity) is considered an important variable in forecasting oil prices, since prices historically have tended to rise when OPEC capacity utilization was high, and have tended to fall when OPEC capacity utilization was low. For a fuller discussion of this subject, see Dermot Gately, ''A Ten-Year Retrospective: OPEC and the World Oil Market'' in *Journal of Economic Literature* 22 (September 1984).

16. Energy Economics Research Ltd., *Oil & Energy Trends* 15(8) (August 17, 1990).

17. Ibid.

18. In addition to launching the Allied bombing campaign, the January 16 decision by President Bush to draw down the U.S. Strategic Petroleum Reserve is frequently cited as playing an important role in calming market fears and helping to lower oil prices. Following the president's authorization, Secretary of Energy James Watkins immediately ordered the Department of Energy to implement a drawdown of 33.75 million barrels. A ''notice of sale'' for this oil was issued on January 17, 1991, only hours after the initial Allied attack on Iraq. Over the next 45 days, 17.3 million barrels of oil were eventually sold, an average of around 350,000 barrels per day.

Chapter 11

Energy Use and Efficiency in the G-7 Countries

Dominick Salvatore

The energy market in general and the petroleum market in particular have been remarkably unstable during the past two decades, with reduced supply and high prices in the 1970s followed by ample supplies and low prices in the 1980s and early 1990s. While petroleum remains the most important energy source, accounting for some 40 percent of the world energy consumption, there have also been major shifts in the relative importance of the various energy sources during past decades.

There is, in addition, a great deal of disagreement among experts in interpreting the events with regard to the operation of the petroleum market in the 1970s and 1980s. The most widely accepted view concludes that the sharp increase in petroleum prices during the 1973–74 and 1979–80 periods was the classic result of the cartelization of the world oil market by OPEC. A significant number of economists, however, believe instead that the sharp increases in petroleum prices were the result of competitive forces that saw petroleum consumption get close to production capacity, thereby leading to large price increases. These price increases were very large, they argue, because of very low price elasticities. The collapse of oil prices since the early 1980s is given as evidence and vindication that market forces reign supreme and that OPEC is basically irrelevant in influencing petroleum prices.

Considerable uncertainty also exists about future petroleum prices. Past projections have been so far off the mark and have been revised so frequently and drastically that great prudence and meekness is required in any attempt to forecast petroleum prices in the future. For example, the consensus of oil price forecasts compiled by the International Energy Workshop in 1981 predicted real oil prices would be $60/.barrel in 1990. This figure was revised in 1983 to $40/barrel, and again in 1983 to $30/barrel. In June 1990 the actual nominal price of oil was bout $18/barrel and the real price was $16/barrel, proving that such predictions are often incorrect and unreliable.

PETROLEUM PRICES AND CONSUMPTION IN THE G-7 COUNTRIES FROM 1960 TO 1990

The price of petroleum in dollars per barrel at 1985 prices was $5.45 in 1960; it gradually declined to $3.00 in 1970. After 1970, the price of petroleum started to increase but stood at $6.54 in 1973, just before the first petroleum shock. The real price of petroleum shot up to $21.34/barrel in 1974. It then remained more or less constant until 1978. From 1979 to 1981, as a result of the second price shock, the real price of petroleum again increased sharply, reaching the all-time high of $38.46 in 1981. From 1982 to 1986 the price of petroleum collapsed, falling to $12.84 in 1986. The following year it rose to $16.03 and again to $16.85 at the time of Iraq's invasion of Kuwait in 1990. The real price of petroleum subsequently declined again to a price of $12.31/barrel in May 1993.

Petroleum consumption increased sharply in all G-7 countries from 1960 to 1973 as a result of declining petroleum prices, but primarily because of rapid economic growth. Consumption declined somewhat in all G-7 countries[1] from 1973 to 1975 as a result of the first petroleum shock, but resumed its rise from 1976 until the second shock of 1979–81. The second shock was followed by a much larger reduction in petroleum consumption from 1979 to 1984, after which consumption gradually started to rise again.

What were the reasons for the behavior of petroleum consumption during the past two decades? Two factors in particular contributed to the 1973–75 decline in consumption that resulted from the first petroleum shock. Effects of this shock were felt in all G-7 countries with the exception of Canada, which, as a net exporter of petroleum during the 1970s, did not experience a significant reduction in consumption. One such factor is that the price elasticity of petroleum is notoriously low, especially in the short run. The other is that it was widely believed at the time that the sharp increase in petroleum prices could not be sustained. After all, microeconomic theory clearly predicted that cartels are inherently unstable and are inexorably doomed to collapse.

The much sharper reduction in petroleum consumption in all G-7 countries (including Canada) from 1979 to 1983 that resulted from the second petroleum shock was also due to two reasons. The first is that industrial countries, after experiencing the first petroleum shock, had now come to believe that the increase in petroleum prices was indeed sustainable. The second factor is that some of the conservation measures that were introduced after it became clear that the 1973–74 increase in petroleum prices would persist started to bear fruit.

With petroleum prices resuming their decline in 1982, petroleum consumption again started to increase in 1983, especially in the United States and Japan. Lower prices and the end of the improvement in fuel efficiency, or a great slowdown in the improvement, as well as rapid growth were responsible for the fairly rapid increase in petroleum consumption in the G-7 countries during the second half of the 1980s and the early 1990s.

ENERGY SUPPLY BY FUEL TYPE

To examine the change in energy efficiency in each nation over time and relative to one another, it is essential to examine all energy supplies by fuel type. The energy categories that warrant consideration are oil, coal, natural gas, nuclear, hydroelectric, and others. The "others" category includes geothermal, solar, and wind power.

Overall G-7 Countries

In 1960 oil had a 41 percent share of total energy used in the G-7 countries. It rose to 53 percent in 1973 and then gradually declined, falling to about 43 percent in 1991. The share of total energy use provided by coal was 37 percent for the G-7 countries as a group in 1960. It fell to a low of 21 percent in 1974 before gradually increasing to 24 percent in 1991. The share of natural gas was 19 percent in 1960. It rose to 22 percent in 1974 and to 20 percent in 1991. Nuclear power, which was practically nonexistent in 1960, steadily increased to supply about 10 percent of total energy used by the G-7 countries in 1991. The increase in the use of nuclear power, however, seems to have come to a halt since 1986, no doubt as a result of the decline in petroleum prices and from increased consumer opposition in most countries, especially after the Three Mile Island meltdown in the United States and the Chernobyl disaster in the former Soviet Union. Hydroelectric power has remained practically constant over the past three decades, supplying about 2 percent of the total energy use in the G-7 countries as a group. The share of other energy sources has grown since 1960 but accounted for only about 0.5 percent of the total energy use in the G-7 countries as a group in 1991.

United States

In both 1960 and 1974, the share of oil in total U.S. energy use was 46 percent, but had declined to 41 percent by 1991. The share of total energy used provided by coal was 26 percent in the United States in 1960, fell to a low of 21 percent in 1974, and gradually increased to 27 percent by 1991. The share of natural gas was 28 percent in 1960, rose to 30 percent in 1974, but had declined to 23 percent by 1991. Nuclear power, nonexistent in 1960, steadily increased to supply nearly 8 percent of total energy used by 1991. The increase in the use of nuclear power, however, seems to have come to a halt since 1986, because of the decline in petroleum prices and as a result of increased consumer opposition to nuclear power in many countries. The share of hydroelectric power increased from 1.3 percent in 1960 to 1.6 percent in 1974 before declining to 1.2 percent of total energy use in 1991.

Thus, the changes in the relative share of the various energy sources were almost diametrically opposed in the United States as compared with the G-7 countries as a group. Since the United States is as large economically as the other six of the G-7 countries combined, the difference in tendencies in the relative share of energy used in the United States and the other six countries is even greater than those indicated above. This difference is important in explaining why the United States had a slower increase in energy efficiency than the other G-7 countries between 1974 and 1991.

Japan

Compared to the changes in the use of various energy sources in the United States during the past three decades, Japanese changes were dramatic. The share of oil in Japanese energy use rose from 35 percent in 1960 to 75 percent in 1974 before falling to 58 percent in 1991. The share of total energy provided by coal declined from 58 percent in 1960 to 19 percent in 1974 and to 18 percent in 1991. The share of natural gas, which was 1 percent in 1960, increased to 2 percent in 1974 and leaped to 10 percent in 1991. Nuclear power, nonexistent in 1960, supplied nearly 2 percent of Japan's energy needs in 1974 and jumped to 12 percent in 1991. The increase in the use of nuclear power, however, seems to have come to a halt since 1986 in Japan for the same reasons as in the United States and the other G-7 countries. The share of hydroelectric power declined from 6 percent in 1960 to 2 percent in 1974 and stayed at that level until 1991. It should be noted that this is a relative, not an absolute, decline in the use of hydroelectric energy due to the very limited possibilities of expanding this form of energy in view of Japan's small geographical area. The share of other energy sources has grown since 1960 but accounted for less than 0.5 percent of the total energy use in 1991.

Germany

Changes in reliance on various energy uses in Germany during the past three decades were also large, although not quite as great as those that occurred in Japan. The share of oil in German energy use rose from 22 percent in 1960 to 52 percent in 1974 and fell to 40 percent in 1991. The share of total energy provided by coal declined from 77 percent in 1960 to 34 percent in 1974 to 28 percent in 1991. The share of natural gas, which was less than 1 percent in 1960, jumped to 12 percent in 1974 and to 17 percent in 1991. Nuclear power, with a share of less than 0.5 percent in 1960, supplied nearly 1.5 percent of German energy needs in 1974 and jumped to more than 14 percent in 1991. As opposed to the United States and Japan, the share of nuclear power in Germany seems to have continued to expand through 1991, even though its rate of expansion slowed down significantly after 1986. The share of hydroelectric power remained at less than 1 percent over the entire period and other energy sources were nil.

France

France is another country where sharp changes in the share of energy supplied by various sources have occurred since 1960. The changes, however, were dominated by the sharp decline in the share of coal and the dramatic increase in the share of nuclear power. Specifically, the share of oil in French energy use rose from 36 percent in 1960 to 68 percent in 1974 and declined to 41 percent in 1991. The share of total energy provided by coal declined from 56 percent in 1960 to 18 percent in 1974 and to only 11 percent in 1991. The share of natural gas went from 3 percent in 1960 to 8 percent in 1974 and to 11 percent in 1991. The share of nuclear power, which was practically nonexistent in 1960, supplied 2 percent of French energy needs in 1974 and jumped to an incredible 35 percent in 1991. French reliance on nuclear power is nearly 5 times that of the United States and more than 2.5 times that of Germany. While the expansion in the share of nuclear power has come to a halt since 1986, French reliance on nuclear power is far greater than any other country in the world. The share of hydroelectric power in France declined from 4 percent in 1960 to 3 percent in 1974 to less than 2 percent in 1991. The share of other energy sources was practically nil over the entire period.

Italy

Changes in reliance on various energy sources in Italy during the past three decades were large as well as different, both quantitatively and qualitatively, from the changes that occurred in the other G-7 countries. The share of oil in Italian energy use rose from 49 percent in 1960 to 75 percent in 1974 and slipped to 61 percent in 1991. The share of total energy provided by coal declined from 26 percent in 1960 to 8 percent in 1974 before rising slightly to 9 percent in 1991. The share of natural gas was 12 percent of the total energy use in both 1960 and 1974, and doubled to 24 percent by 1991. Nuclear power, practically nonexistent in 1960, provided 1 percent of Italian energy sources in 1974 but was phased out by 1991, the Italian electorate having voted to ban it. The share of hydroelectric power declined from 9 percent in 1960 to 3 percent in 1974 to 2 percent in 1991. Once again, it must be pointed out that this is a relative, not an absolute, decline. By 1960 Italy had practically fully exploited all possibilities for hydroelectric power and, even though the absolute amount of energy supplied by hydroelectric power did not decline, this became less and less important relative to the nation's rapidly rising needs for energy. Other energy sources supplied 4 percent of the national needs in 1960, 2 percent in 1974, and almost 4 percent in 1991.

The United Kingdom

Changes in reliance on various energy sources in the United Kingdom were dominated by the change of the United Kingdom from a petroleum importing country to a petroleum exporting country in the early 1970s. The share of oil in the U.K.'s energy use rose from 28 percent in 1960 to 50 percent in 1974 before falling to 39 percent in 1991. The share of total energy provided by coal declined from 71 percent in 1960 to 32 percent in 1974 to 22 percent in 1991. The share of natural gas, which was less than 1 percent in 1960, jumped to 14 percent in 1974 and to 22 percent in 1991. Nuclear power, with a share of less than 0.4 percent in 1960, supplied about 4 percent of British energy needs in 1974 and jumped to more than 9 percent in 1991 (but, as in other G-7 countries, except Germany, the increase of nuclear power had come to an end by 1986). The share of hydroelectric and other energy sources remained practically nil in the United Kingdom over the entire period.

Canada

Changes in reliance on various energy sources in Canada were more gradual than in most other G-7 countries, similar to those that occurred in the United States during the past three decades. Of course, Canada was also the only country among the G-7 that exported petroleum over the entire period. The share of oil in Canada's energy use declined from 59 percent in 1960 to 53 percent in 1974 to 37 percent in 1991. The share of total energy provided by coal declined from 17 percent in 1960 to 10 percent in 1974 before rising to 17 percent in 1991. The share of natural gas jumped from 12 percent of total energy use in 1960 to 24 percent in 1974 to 26 percent in 1991. Nuclear power, which was practically nonexistent in 1960, supplied about 2 percent of Canadian energy needs in 1974 and jumped to 9 percent in 1991 (but declined slightly since 1986). The share of hydroelectric power remained practically constant at 12 percent over the entire period. Other energy sources were practically nil in Canada over the entire period.

Overall Conclusion

In all G-7 countries, except the United States and Canada, there was an increase in share of petroleum as a source of energy and a reduction in the share of coal during the past three decades. There was a sharp increase in the share of natural gas, except in the United States, where the share of natural gas declined. There was also a sharp increase in nuclear energy in all countries, except in Italy where it was banned. The expansion of atomic energy seems to have come to a halt since 1986, no doubt because of the low price of petroleum and the increased sensitivity to the dangers of atomic energy. The importance of atomic energy in France was spectacular. France may have overestimated the safety of atomic energy and the price of petroleum. It is also interesting that France located most of its atomic reactors near the border with Spain and Italy, so that it benefits from a reduced dependence on imported oil while sharing the potential dangers with its two neighbors. Hydroelectric power supplied less than 2 percent of total energy in all G-7 countries in 1991, except for Canada, where it supplied nearly 12 percent. Finally, for all the talk of alternative energy sources, ''other'' energy sources supplied less than 0.5 percent in all G-7 countries in 1991, except for Italy where it supplied almost 4 percent of total energy uses.

ENERGY EFFICIENCY

In this section we examine the absolute and relative change in energy efficiency in the production of gross domestic product (GDP) in each of the G-7 countries from 1974 to the present. Energy efficiency is defined as the Total Primary Energy Supply (TPES) per unit of dollar GDP. TPES is made up of energy-indigenous production, plus energy imports, minus energy exports, plus international marine bunkers, plus/minus energy stock changes. The unit of measure is one million tons of oil equivalent (mtoe), which is defined as 10^7 kilocalories and is approximately equal to one metric ton of crude oil.

In general, energy efficiency worsened from 1960 to 1974 in all G-7 countries, especially in Italy and Japan (with the exception of the United Kingdom, where energy efficiency improved from 1960 to 1974). Since 1974 the energy efficiency in the production of GDP increased in Japan, Germany, and the United States but declined in the other four countries. In 1974 the average of TPES/$GDP for all G-7 countries was 410 and declined to 310 in 1991, for an improvement in energy efficiency of 24 percent. In 1974, TPES/$GDP was 570 in the United States and declined to 420, for a net improvement of about 22 percent. Thus, the United States started with a much lower energy efficiency than the average G-7 countries in 1974 and, despite its improvement in energy efficiency, ended up being less energy efficient than the average for the G-7 as a group in 1991.

Japan had the largest improvement in energy efficiency of all the G-7 countries. Japan started with a TPES/$GDP of 450 (above the G-7 average of 420) in 1974 and ended up with 145 (the lowest of any G-7 countries) in 1991, for a net improvement of 69 percent. Germany also had a good performance. Its TPES/$GDP in 1974 was 440 and declined to 250 (below the G-7 average of 310) by 1991, for a net improvement of 43 percent. France and Italy suffered decreases in energy efficiency from 1974 to 1991. Both countries started with a much lower TPES/$GDP than the average in 1974 and ended up with a TPES/$GDP of 270 in 1991, for a net worsening of energy efficiency of 29 percent. Italy started with the lowest TPES/$GDP of 120 in 1974 and ended up with a value of 230, for a net worsening of 92 percent. The energy efficiency in the United Kingdom in the production of its GDP also worsened from 1974 to 1991. The United Kingdom started with a TPES/$GDP of 300 (below the G-7 average) in 1974 and ended up with a TPES/$GDP of 310 (the same as for all G-7 countries as a group) in 1991, for a net worsening of 3 percent. Canada's energy efficiency also worsened between 1974 and 1991. Canada, which started with the TPES/$GDP of 450 (above the G-7 average) in 1974, ended up with TPES/$GDP of 460 in 1991, for net worsening of 2 percent.

The overall conclusion that can be reached regarding the energy efficiency in the production of GDP is that in 1974 the United States, Canada, Germany, and Japan had a TPES/$GDP higher than the average for the G-7 countries as a group. Japan, Germany, and the United States improved their energy efficiency from 1974 to 1991. However U.S. energy efficiency remained below the average for the G-7 countries as a group, while the energy efficiency of Japan and Germany rose to much above the average. The best performance in increasing energy efficiency was Japan. Canada, on the other hand, experienced a reduction in energy efficiency and became the least energy efficient among the G-7 countries, a position occupied by the United States from 1972 to 1978. Italy and France experienced large reductions in energy efficiency between 1974 and 1991, but having started with a TPES/$GDP much below the average for the G-7 countries as a group in 1974, remained below the average in 1991. Finally, the United Kingdom started below the average for the G-7 countries in energy efficiency in 1974, experienced a reduction in energy efficiency during the 1974–91 period, and ended up with an energy efficiency the same as for the G-7 countries as a group in 1991. The ranking in absolute energy efficiency in 1991, from the highest to the lowest, was Japan, Italy, Germany, France (below the G-7 average), the United Kingdom at the G-7 average, and the United States and Canada (above the G-7 average).

CONCLUSIONS

Japan is the most energy efficient and the most dependent on imported energy among the G-7 countries. Italy, Germany, and France are all highly dependent on imported energy, with Italy and Germany highly energy efficient in comparison to France, which is somewhat less energy efficient. The United Kingdom and Canada, on the other hand, are net exporters of petroleum and less energy efficient than Japan, Italy, Germany, and France. The United States is between the previous two groups of countries as far as its dependence on imported energy and remains less energy efficient than the average for the G-7 countries as a group. High dependency on imported energy thus seems to lead to high energy efficiency. That is, Japan, Italy, Germany, and France, the countries most dependent on imported energy, are also the most energy efficient. Canada and the United Kingdom, as exporters of energy, and the United States, which supplied more than three-quarters of its overall energy needs from domestic sources, are the least energy efficient among the G-7 countries.

Although the tendency of greater energy efficiency associated with higher dependency on imported energy seems natural, it also evidences a serious degree of uneconomic behavior in opportunity cost terms in the countries not dependent or less dependent on imported energy sources (Canada, the United Kingdom, and the United States). With a common international price of traded energy supplies, less dependency does not justify less efficiency because the latter leads to higher production costs and reduced international competitiveness in these nations. To put it differently, if the United States were as energy efficient as Japan or Germany, not only would the United States be less dependent on imported oil, but its international competitiveness would also be enhanced. This calls for policies to increase energy efficiency in the United States, the United Kingdom, and Canada as an important way to increase the international competitiveness of these nations.

NOTE

1. The G-7 countries include the United States, Japan, Germany, France, Italy, the United Kingdom, and Canada.

REFERENCES

Black, Stanley, W. "Learning from Adversity: Policy Responses to Two Oil Shocks." *Princeton Essay in International Finance*, No. 160 (December 1985).

Brown, Stephen P. A. and Keith R. Phillips. "U.S. Oil Demand and Conservation." *Contemporary Policy Issues* 9 (1991): 67–72.

Gately, Dermot. "OPEC: Retrospective and Prospects—1973–1990." *European Economic Review* 21 (1983): 313–321.

———. "Imperfect Price-Reversibility of U.S. Gasoline Demand: Asymmetric Responses to Price Increases and Declines." *Economic Research Report No. 91–55*, N.Y.U. Starr Center for Applied Economics, October 1991.

——— and Peter Rappaport. "The Adjustment to U.S. Oil Demand to the Price Increases of the 1970s." *The Energy Journal* 2 (1988): 93–107.

International Monetary Fund. *International Financial Statistics*. Washington, DC: IMF, various issues.

Organization for Economic Cooperation and Development. *Energy Balances of OECD Countries*. Paris: OECD: Various issues.

———. *World Economic Outlook*. Paris: OECD, May 1993.

Radetski, Marian. "Long-Run Factors in Oil Price Formation." In A. Winters and David Sapsford (eds.), *Primary Commodity Price: Economic Models and Policy*. New York: Cambridge University Press, 1989, pp. 157–179.

Salvatore, Dominick. "Oil Import Costs and Domestic Inflation in Industrial Countries." *Weltwirtschaftliches Archiv* 122 (1986): 281–291.,

———. "Petroleum Prices, Exchange Rates, and Domestic Inflation in Developing Countries." *Weltwirtschaftliches Archiv* 120 (1984): 580–589.

———. "Petroleum Prices and Economic Performances in the G-7 Countries." In B. S. Katz and Siamack Shojai (eds.), *Oil in the 1980s*. New York: Praeger, 1992.

——— and Greg Winczewski. "World Oil Prices and OECD Trade Balance." *Open Economies Review* 1 (1990): 89–106.

Chapter 12

Oil and the Economies of Oil Exporting Countries

Salah El Serafy

In late 1973 the price of crude oil quadrupled to about $12 a barrel after remaining low and even intermittently declining during the previous quarter-century. Prices had weakened on account of huge discoveries of petroleum deposits in the Middle East in the 1950s and 1960s, and because of increased market competition. In the post–World War II period, the international market has become dominated by an oligopoly of transnational oil companies, known as the "Majors," which operated the fields of the exporting countries under concessions negotiated individually with each of them. The formation of the Organization of Petroleum Exporting Countries in 1960 did not seem to increase the bargaining powers of the exporters negotiating the terms of the oil concessions that determined the quantities extracted and the royalties paid to them.[1]

The explosion of oil prices in 1973–74 gave rise to many interpretations as well as varying speculations about the future course of prices. As the newly established higher prices persisted, the dominant interpretation was that it was due to OPEC's monopoly power. OPEC came increasingly to be described as a cartel, an appellation that came naturally to oil market analysts.[2] OPEC, of course, had not triggered the original price rise, which was essentially due to panic prevailing in the uncertain and fragmented petroleum market of the day. It was the Arab boycott of shipments to the United States and the Netherlands for reasons related to the Middle East war that caused the uncertainty that quickly translated into higher prices. OPEC's daily exports in 1973 and 1974 were respectively 27.5 and 27.3 million barrels a day, well above the 24.1 mbd exported in 1972.[3]

During the 1970s and ever since then, OPEC's representatives would meet periodically amid great media publicity to consult on prices and extraction policies, and declare a set of prices that the market seemed to accept without any attempt by OPEC to impose quotas on exports or to share the market among its members. It can be argued that such behavior (i.e., declaring a price and letting the market determine the quantity bought) is consistent with a monopoly market form. But the absence of export quotas throughout the 1970s and until the spring of 1983 takes away much of the argument behind the notion of an OPEC cartel.[4]

Many analysts believed that prices much higher than the costs of extraction would eventually have to come down. The high prices would cause demand to contract and supply to expand. This is essentially what ultimately happened, but the time lag before the inevitable market adjustment proved to be considerably longer than expected. There were other analysts, however, who thought that the era of abundant fossil fuels was coming to an end. No more giant fields were being located, and the world had become addicted to petroleum in a fundamental way, with few substitutes in sight. This conformed with a pessimistic under-current in economic writings that ran back at least to Malthus. The same trend was receiving support from the Club of Rome and other like-minded groups, and became endorsed by the environmentalist movement. This trend was to lead to Harold Hotelling.

The Hotelling model, which had remained dormant for 40 years, suddenly became popular: as an exhaustible resource gets depleted and the markets be-come aware of its increasing scarcity, its net price, or marginal profit (net or extraction cost), rises exponentially at the current interest rate.[5] Thus many wild projections of ever-rising oil prices were made at the time, and the future ap-peared menacing as the power of the oil exporters soared. The oil exporters, it was feared, would end up as global rentiers, acquiring much of the assets of the industrial world in return for their essential commodity. This imparted the false message that they did not need to plan seriously for their future economic and social development. On the other hand there were many threats in the Western media of military attacks on the sources of oil to secure them for the oil con-sumers. This naturally created an atmosphere of insecurity among the exporters, and fundamentally affected their policies.

THE CLIMATE OF UNCERTAINTY

Practically all oil exporting countries declared at one time or another that they would use their oil earnings in the service of economic and social development. In retrospect, it was the rare oil exporting country that seriously pursued such a constructive route. Part of the reason lies in human weakness and the urge to satisfy pressing consumption needs, especially at the low standards of living prevailing in virtually all oil exporting countries. GNP per capita in 1972, it may be recalled, was $90 for Indonesia, $130 for Nigeria, $360 for Ecuador, $370 for Iraq, and $550 for Saudi Arabia.[6] But there were several additional factors. Many of the exporting countries were run by nonrepresentative ruling groups that sought to appropriate to themselves much of the oil revenue, with little regard for equity, and a few had sparse populations anyway. In such an atmosphere even public schemes to develop housing, schools, transport facilities, and industrial enterprises were used as a means to obtain illegal commissions and led to great waste and low productivity investments. Some oil exporters, sensitive to the threats by the oil importers of invasion or trade wars, resorted to pacifying the oil importers by cultivating special relationships with individual partners. Bilateral relationships were developed between the United States and Iran; the United States and Saudi Arabia; the United Kingdom and the Gulf Sheikhdoms; Italy and Libya; France and Iran. This secured large construction and other contracts for the oil importers, which worked as guarantees of oil accessibility. It also encouraged the investment in them of the financial surpluses of the exporters, thus increasing the interdependence between the economies of the two sides of the market. Although freezing financial assets in some of the industrial countries in reaction to later political disputes was to occur, this was done selectively and largely after the oil scarcity had begun to ease.

But perhaps the greatest waste of the exporters' surpluses was the huge defense contracts secured by the United States, France, the United Kingdom, Germany, and others that created an apparently never-ceasing outflow of petroleum exports to pay for often-complex defense systems that the exporters acquired but could not effectively operate.[7] The largest importers of arms in the 1970s and 1980s were the oil exporting countries, especially those in the Middle East.[8] In the period 1980–88 military imports by Iraq aggregated $67 billion; by Saudi Arabia $40 billion; by Libya $30 billion; and by Iran over $20 billion.[9] It is arguable that actual military conflicts could have been avoided or reduced with lower defense expenditures, and the course of economic and social development in many of the oil exporting countries might have been quite different if these resources had been used constructively.

SOME IMPORTANT DEVELOPMENTS

Before attempting to touch on the economic policies of the exporting countries, it would be useful to indicate a number of developments in the oil market during the past 20 years or so, with special reference to the position of OPEC. Many analysts now believe that OPEC has become irrelevant as a market power, though a few do not rule out a possible future resurgence.[10] OPEC's meetings no longer create much interest, and members' attempts at sharing a regulated export market are seen to be publicly flouted and ineffective. Prices seem to have come back in real terms to their long-term levels.

Writing recently on the course of oil prices during the past twenty years, *Petroleum Intelligence Weekly* (*PIW*) remarked that the nominal price of Mideast crude stood in December 1993 roughly at the same level as in December 1973. Correcting for inflation, however, current prices are about half what they were 20 years previously. *PIW* observed that, in constant 1993 prices, and despite periods of volatility, crude sold for about $10 a barrel for most of this century. "Only at the end of 1973, when nominal prices were raised to $11.65 a barrel for Mideast grades, did inflation-adjusted prices shoot up to around $30. Since 1986, real prices for Mideast light have hovered at around $15."[11]

The highest levels of prices (nominal as well as real) were reached in 1979–80, and again had a political cause: the Iranian revolution that ended the shah's regime. There was also a short burst associated with the 1991 Persian Gulf War. But the main reasons behind the return of prices to their "structural" levels are essentially economic. Higher prices triggered the search for oil that has been found in varying quantities in countries that had been dependent on imports. And the higher prices caused great economies in the use of energy, thus raising greatly the productivity of a barrel of oil. Petroleum (including gas) is still considered as a fairly clean source of energy as compared with coal and biomass and the untold environmental impact of nuclear energy wastes.

Because of the determined search for oil deposits worldwide, induced by the higher prices, and on account of improved technology used for oil field development and extraction, the world estimates of proven reserves, despite nearly a quarter-century of continued extraction, rose from 611 billion barrels in 1970 to 999 billion barrels at the end of 1993. Over the same period daily extraction rose from 44.9 million barrels to 59.6 million barrels, but the life expectancy of world oil reserves (at current extraction rates) fell from 61 years to 46 years. OPEC reserves rose from 71 to 77 percent of world reserves. OPEC extraction, however, had risen from about 19.7 million barrels to 24.7 million barrels over the same period, and the life expectancy of OPEC reserves lengthened from 61 to 86 years.[12] Importantly, the life expectancy of non-OPEC oil had declined to 18 years' supply. In other words, other things being equal, when the rest of the world had run out of its oil, say by 2010, the only remaining oil would be OPEC oil.

OPEC was to generate substantial surpluses on current account between 1975 and 1985, but has since been largely incurring deficits.[13] During this period, aid donated to the outside world was substantial, ranging between $10 and $15 billion a year from 1974 to 1981, and representing up to 5 percent of gross national product (GNP) in some years compared with a fraction of 1 percent for the traditional OECD donors.[14] Between 1980 and 1991, a period that witnessed the growing demand for funds by the oil exporters together with the price declines already described, eight members of OPEC for which statistics are available raised their total foreign indebtedness by $100 billion, reaching a total debt of $175 billion by 1992. The greatest debtors were Indonesia, Venezuela, and Nigeria, and some of the debtors were in difficult financial straits on account of debt servicing.[15]

FAILURE OF ECONOMIC ANALYSIS

Planning constructively for the use of oil surpluses to serve economic and social development was further handicapped by the uncertainty of future prices, the insecurity of investment markets abroad, and the limited availability of profitable opportunities for capital formation within the exporters' individual countries. Some of the so-called capital surplus oil exporters, particularly in the Middle East, embarked on large-scale power generation, water desalination, petrochemical industrial development, and other energy-intensive activities, including aluminum smelting, with little regard for economic calculations of costs and benefits, or sufficient attention to future marketing problems. Although some scattered investments were made by individuals, governments, and a number of Arab banks and development agencies in neighboring countries, and in various developing countries throughout the world, no consistent strategy was initiated to build up regional solidarity in order to secure food imports, or to develop large and more viable economic units that would rectify the factor imbalance of the exporting countries, particularly those in the Gulf area. The main force behind external investment was not for the purpose of integrating the oil economies with other developing countries, but with the powerful industrial countries that offered many inducements. The quotas of the oil exporters in such powerful institutions as the International Monetary Fund (IMF) and the World Bank were raised and the flow of aid from the oil exporters grew to very high levels.

There was one fundamental fault of economic analysis that underlay the economic policies pursued by the oil exporters in the period of their temporary affluence, and that analysts were slow to recognize. This was the illusion that oil revenues were pure rent, representing value added that could all be devoted to consumption, and not the proceeds from the sale of depletable assets. This exaggerated the calculated national incomes of the exporters, distorted their reckoned rates of growth, and inflated what foreign lenders regarded as collateral against which they were prepared to lend. This also gave false signals of security, which led to some of the highest birth rates recorded in human history. That oil proved in retrospect to be more abundant in a few countries, and hence globally, than previously perceived does not contradict the fact that for many individual countries the horizon of exhaustion was getting nearer, and the true level of income from their exhaustible resources was shrinking.[16]

FAILURE OF ECONOMIC POLICY

There are many common features to the reactions of the oil exporters to the sudden availability of foreign exchange brought about by the oil boom. Generally speaking they pursued high consumption, raised parastatal intervention in the economy, and indulged in huge infrastructural development schemes with little attention to directly productive ventures. They were generally lax on fiscal policy, and burdened the treasuries with many subsidies while neglecting to raise taxation. They may also have taken for granted that the boom would continue, so they tended to relax project viability criteria. Public expenditures in many cases exceeded the oil revenues so that domestic and foreign borrowing had to expand, which brought great trouble later on. Fiscal deficits did not always produce high inflation because the availability of foreign exchange to finance imports would keep consumer prices down. This, of course, did not apply to real estate and other nontradables, which boomed in reaction to public construction programs as well as to speculation. But the greatest common factor that defeated the declared policies of economic development and diversifying the economies away from dependence on petroleum was the Dutch disease phenomenon, which would have been alleviated by an active policy of foreign exchange adjustment that in many cases occurred much too late if at all. For some illustrations of actual experience, the cases of Gabon, Nigeria, and Indonesia are very briefly presented.[17]

Gabon, a small African country of 1.1 million people with a per capita income of $3,300 in 1990, presents a typical situation of an oil exporting country of a relatively high standard of living by developing country standards. Despite declared intentions, a decade and a half after the first price increase, the high expectations of development failed to materialize, and Gabon's dependence on oil, instead of declining, actually increased (from 32 percent of exports in 1972 to 90 percent in 1980 and 70 percent in 1984). Propelled by the oil windfalls, public spending sharply increased, exceeding the oil revenues, and Gabon resorted to borrowing. Foreign debt that had been nonexistent in 1970 rose to $1.51 billion by 1980, and reached $3.84 billion by 1991. More than two-thirds of public spending went to construction, urbanization, and transport. A trans-Gabon railroad, costing $2 billion, is said to have cost, through corruption and inefficiency, six times what it should have cost. Public enterprises multiplied and pervaded practically all sectors, were protected by high tariffs, and were inefficiently managed with little regard to economics and much attention to political expediency. These eventually became a drag on public finances. Between 1973 and 1985 the non-oil economy actually grew at half its growth rate before 1973. Throughout the boom years inflation presented little problem, but the small labor force, though supplemented by immigration, contributed to high wage levels, which further depressed international competitiveness. The major impediment to diversification, however, was the appreciation of the real exchange rate. When oil prices dropped sharply in 1986, exports declined by 60 percent, and the weakness of past economic policies became abundantly clear. Gabon then began a long painful process of structural adjustment, which still continues. Financial discipline, foreign economic support, and austerity will be necessary for several years to come, and per capita income is expected to fall as Gabon's population will be increasing faster than the economy can expand.

Nigeria presents another interesting case, though at a much lower level of income (per capita GNP of $120 in 1970). Nigeria's oil and gas reserves are considerable, with an end-1993 life expectancy for its oil of about 26 years. While two-thirds of employment was provided by agriculture, oil began in the 1970s to bring in 80 percent of foreign exchange receipts and 70 percent of government revenue. Nigeria's economic prospects brightened considerably with the oil boom. As in Gabon, large increases occurred in government expenditure, particularly for urbanization and construction. The real exchange rate soared as resources were siphoned away from the tradable to the nontradable sectors, thus undermining all efforts at diversification. Traditional agricultural exports shrank as a result, and oil exports rose from 58 percent of total exports in 1970 to 93 percent in 1975, to 95 percent in 1980, but declined somewhat later when oil prices began to decline. As in other exporting countries, domestic energy prices were kept low, thus encouraging consumption and discouraging energy efficiency, and various consumer subsidies added to the fiscal burden. The failures of economic policy became apparent after the weakening of prices in the early 1980s, and the government began an austerity program from about 1984, tightening administrative controls and resorting to import licensing. Non-oil GDP fell sharply as a result, and inflationary pressures increased. The government had to appeal to the IMF and the World Bank for help, and they prescribed a program of drastic structural adjustment and belt-tightening, including belated adjustments to the exchange rate. Per capita GNP, which had reached $1,000 in 1980, began a precipitous decline, taking it down to $490 in 1987 and $280 in 1990, comparable in real terms to the $120 of 1970. External debt had reached $35 billion by the early 1990s, and its servicing had become a real burden. Though the structural adjustment program brought in some debt relief through rescheduling, the debt-servicing problem reemerged later, and Nigeria, announcing that the policies associated with the adjustment program were not having the promised impact on the economy, has very recently abandoned the trade liberalization and deregulation measures of the program. With debt service arrears reaching $4.53 billion at the end of October 1993, Nigeria unilaterally declared limits on its service payments.

Indonesia is a significant case, because it offers an uncommon example of adopting a forthright set of economic policies that specifically addressed the phenomenon of the Dutch disease, and thus produced creditable economic results. This vast country of about 180 million people has a varied resource base with rich primary energy resources, timber, mineral deposits and a diversified system of agricultural commodity production and exports. Two-thirds of the population, however, live on the small crowded island of Java, but the oil wealth is spread widely, with beneficial effects on income distribution.

In 1970 Indonesia was primarily rural, with only an estimated 17 percent of its people living in urban areas. By conscious decision Indonesia avoided the urban bias of oil revenue spending in other exporting countries. An accident of history occurred in 1974 that fortunately ushered in an era of financial responsibility and fiscal discipline, and was to save Indonesia from many of the excesses experienced by other oil exporting countries. Pertamina, the national oil company, had assumed too much debt and got itself in financial difficulties. So it had to be rescued by the government, which used nearly half the oil windfalls in that year to repay the company's debt. Not only did this help "sterilize" part of the new financial flows, but it also made an imprint on the country's leaders and stamped financial conservatism on the country's economic management for a long time afterward. A determination was then made to keep government expenditures within the revenues derived from Indonesia's mineral sector, exceeding them only by the amount of foreign aid received, which continued to flow in by virtue of Indonesia's low level of income. A high saving, high investment development strategy was pursued and maintained until the present. In the five years 1973/74 to 1977/78 no less than half of the oil revenues were devoted to investment, and increases in consumption were kept low. Foreign indebtedness was also fairly constrained, amounting to $21 billion by 1980, or just under 30 percent of GDP.

A characteristic of Indonesia's investment program was that it eschewed large-scale projects until they were adequately researched, economically analyzed, and technically prepared. It focused on labor-intensive smaller projects and the development of infrastructure that served agriculture and industry. It paid high regard to equity considerations and avoided appreciable mistakes. Eventually this strategy was to yield a record of prolonged economic growth at fairly high rates. The terms of trade of Indonesia's other primary exports also improved, but by 1980 petroleum still accounted for three-quarters of export earnings and 70 percent of government revenues. Even the non-oil exports were dominated by primary commodities. But GNP per capita had reached $450.

Indonesia continued to progress despite the economic problems it faced in the 1980s. Serious macroeconomic imbalances were to follow from the oil price declines that caused oil revenues to fall sharply. Indonesia, however, had drastically devalued the rupiah in late 1978 in the mistaken belief that oil prices would weaken, whereas they soared on the eruption of the Iranian revolution. The devaluation, which in retrospect was timely, had not been inspired by any balance-of-payments difficulties, but by a deliberate policy to encourage non-petroleum exports and combat the Dutch disease. Throughout the 1980s Indonesia continued to adjust its policies to the weakening oil prices, and made serious attempts at structural adjustment and fighting inflation. It experienced a healthy and gradual decline in the share of agriculture in GDP and a creditable rise in manufacturing and manufactured exports. By 1991, however, its per capita GNP had reached $610, but external debt had grown to $74 billion (about two-thirds of GNP) and interest on the external debt was consuming 13 percent of export proceeds.

In a sample of oil exporting countries studied for adjustments of the real effective exchange rates in the period 1970–84, Indonesia led the group in carrying out remedial effective exchange rate devaluation that was exceedingly helpful to its development. Through a number of devaluations the rupiah, after appreciating a little in 1974–78, was brought down in 1984 to 91.5 percent of its level in 1970. Only Venezuela had a comparable record of successfully adjusting its exchange rate, and the worst victims of the Dutch disease in the sample (as measured by changes in the real effective exchange rate) were Nigeria, Iran, and Trinidad and Tobago.[18]

POSITIVE IMPACTS

It would be wrong to assume that the oil windfalls of the 1970s and early 1980s were a curse to the oil exporters, not just a mixed blessing. What went wrong was a failure to grasp a rare opportunity and turn it to great advantage. But there were mitigating reasons why this group of less-developed nations, lacking in institutions and human training and threatened with military attacks, did not take full advantage of their newly found prosperity. Ideally the exporters should have saved more, borrowed less, and invested more and better, in order to build up for a future made uncertain by their dependence (in the majority of cases) on one commodity. The oil revenues per head of population varied enormously from country to country. In the highest year of oil earnings, 1980, per capita revenue from oil accruing to OPEC members ranged from $88 for Indonesia to $19,500 for the United Arab Emirates.[19] At the lower end of the scale, Ecuador had a per capita oil revenue of $166, Nigeria $276, and Iran $347.

Taking advantage of their new wealth, the exporting countries managed to make great advances in social development as reflected in their social development indicators. Data are not complete and, if available, are not always reliable. Besides, the great influx of poorer-country labor in many of the sparsely populated oil exporting countries distorts the social indicators. However, significant advances were made in many of these countries in life expectancy, infant survival, and education and health—advances that would not have been possible without the oil earnings. Between 1970 and 1990 (or 1991) life expectancy at birth, measured in years, rose for Saudi Arabia from 52 to 65; for Ecuador from 65 to 70, for Nigeria from 44 to 52, and for Algeria from 53 to 66. The illiteracy rate also dropped in the same period: in Saudi Arabia from 49 to 38 percent; Ecuador from 18 to 14 percent; Nigeria from 58 to 49 percent; and Algeria from 50 to 45 percent. Remarkable improvements occurred in under-five mortality rates, calorie intake, and school enrollment. Total fertility rates (i.e., births per woman) also reflected advances in women's education and social status, falling from 6.3 to 3.6 in Ecuador; from 7.4 to 4.9 in Algeria; though in Saudi Arabia and Nigeria, despite falling, remaining quite high at 7.0 and 5.9, respectively.[20] In several exporting countries signs of progress abound, with modern airports, highways, well-equipped hospitals, airlines, universities, systems of communications, and government structures. But except in rare instances, alternatives to oil as a source of income and a sector that would provide employment have not been successfully developed.

CONCLUDING REMARKS

As mentioned before, in 1970 the world had about 37 years' supply of crude oil at the then-prevailing consumption rates. By the end of 1993 the life expectancy of the proved reserves of world oil had extended to 46 years, thanks to

new discoveries, improved energy efficiency, and improved technology that reduced development and extraction costs. Within the global context, however,
the group of exporters that make up OPEC now accounts for 77 percent of the
world's known oil stocks, and their oil has a life expectancy of 86 years. Non-
OPEC oil thus seems to have about 18 years before it is totally exhausted. If
this complex picture is correct, both optimism and pessimism about the future
are tenable. Viewed entirely from the perspective of the exporters, if no fundamental change such as a technological breakthrough in energy production
occurs, OPEC members may once more become the oil monopolists of tomorrow when prices, following the Hotelling trajectory, will begin to rise—perhaps
exponentially at current interest rates. The question may be asked if they are
likely to use their new oil earnings in serious pursuit of economic and social
development the next time around. Would they behave any better with their
future wealth than they did with their revenues in the 1970s and 1980s? Judging
from their own past experience, and from that of more advanced countries such
as Norway and the United Kingdom, the temptation is likely to remain strong
to indulge in yet higher consumption rather than exercise the restraint necessary
for them to build a more sustainable future. However, whether they exercise
restraint or not, some positive impacts are bound to be generated for their peo-
ples, and perhaps also for some of their neighbors and trading partners.

As the horizon of oil exhaustion gets nearer, however, the user cost contained
in oil revenues will progressively increase and the income content diminish, and
a greater part of these revenues will have to be devoted to productive investments specifically geared to the generation of income that would supplant the
dwindling income obtained from this wasting asset. How much the oil exporting
countries should set aside and invest in productive assets at home or abroad has
been indicated in the writings of this chapter's author.[21]

NOTES

1. Attracted by the high profits realized by the Majors, the Independents offered
better terms to the exporting countries, and their numbers increased from 53 in 1953 to
337 in 1969. See Jacques Cremer and Djavad Salehi-Isfahani, *Models of the Oil Market*,
(Chur, Switzerland: Hardwood Academic Publishers, 1991), p. 6, citing Neil H. Jacoby,
Multinational Oil: A Study In Industrial Dynamics (New York: Macmillan, 1974).

2. The Majors, it was recognized, ran a cartel that affected the prices of both crude
and products. As the power of the Majors declined with the nationalization of the oil
fields by the exporters, and the advent of the Independents (and probably also with the
dissolution of the empires to which many of the Majors belonged), OPEC seemed to fit
into the cartel role vacated by the Majors, though now, of course, as an exporters' cartel.

3. Data from OPEC, *Annual Statistical Bulletin* (Vienna: OPEC Secretariat, 1984).

4. See Salah El Serafy, "The Oil Price Revolution of 1973–74," *Journal of Energy
and Development* 4(2) (Spring 1979). There is, however the complicating factor that
Saudi Arabia took it upon itself occasionally to behave as a "swing" supplier, tightening
its extraction when the prices appeared to weaken. Such a role was later reversed as

Saudi Arabia resorted to flooding the market with expanded exports—a behavior that is more consistent with its long-term interest as the owner of abundant reserves.

5. Harold Hotelling, "The Economics of Exhaustible Resources," *Journal of Political Economy* 39 (1931). See also Robert Solow, "The Economics of Resources or the Resources of Economics" (The Richard T. Ely 1973 Lecture), *American Economic Review, Papers and Proceedings*, May 1974.

6. Data from World Bank *Atlas* (Washington, DC, 1974).

7. The Persian Gulf War of 1991 may also be seen in the same light. A conflict that could perhaps have been contained by other means was to be resolved at huge costs largely borne by the Middle Eastern exporters themselves, much of whose accumulated financial reserves became depleted, and who further felt the urge to borrow or mortgage future oil revenues to acquire yet more arms.

8. The conflicts between the Arabs and Israel, and possibly also between Iraq and Iran, could have been contained by diplomatic and other efforts, which would have reduced the arms exports of the oil importers, but also reduced their access to Middle East oil.

9. See *The Economist*, November 2, 1991, citing data from the U.S. Arms Control and Disarmament Agency.

10. See Edward L. Morse, "The Coming Oil Revolution," *Foreign Affairs*, Winter 1990/91, where another price rise is predicted in the 1990s as supply from non-OPEC sources declines.

11. *Petroleum Intelligence Weekly* 33, (1) (January 3, 1994).

12. Figures from the *Oil and Gas Journal*, various issues. OPEC 1970 data refer to countries that are now members of OPEC.

13. In the period 1975 to 1981 the "oil exporting countries" aggregated $300 billion of surpluses on current account, but developed deficits in the ten subsequent years adding up to about half of this amount. See IMF, *International Financial Statistics* (Year Book) (Washington, DC: IMF). OPEC, *Annual Statistical Bulletin* for 1984 shows data for OPEC revenues from oil (Table 33) that add up to $1,666 billion in the decade 1975–84.

14. See OECD, *Development Co-operation* (Paris: OECD, 1990), pp. 15, 160–162, and 243. In 1975, as a percentage of their respective GNPs, Qatar, United Arab Emirates, Saudi Arabia, and Kuwait gave concessional and untied assistance amounting to 14.17, 10.38, 7.60, and 6.91, and the Arab group as a whole gave 5.49 percent. Ibid., Section *F*. Table 45.

15. The eight countries are Algeria, Ecuador, Gabon, Indonesia, Iran, Nigeria, Trinidad and Tobago, and Venezuela. See World Bank, *World Debt Tables 1992–93* (Washington, DC), Volume 2 (Country Tables). Among OPEC members experiencing severe debt servicing problems are Nigeria and Algeria.

16. See Salah El Serafy, "Absorptive Capacity, The Demand for Revenues and the Supply of Petroleum," *Journal of Energy and Development*, Autumn 1981; and Salah El Serafy, "The Proper Calculation of Income from Depletable Natural Resources," in Y. J. Ahmad, S. El Serafy, and E. Lutz, *Environmental Accounting for Sustainable Development* (Washington, DC: World Bank, 1989).

17. Information is culled from various World Bank reports, including *Trends in Developing Countries* (Washington, DC, 1991), and Alan Gelb and Associates, *Oil Windfalls, Blessing or Curse?* (New York: Oxford University Press for the World Bank, 1988).

18. The sample comprised besides Indonesia, Algeria, Ecuador, Nigeria, Trinidad and

Tobago, Venezuela, and Iran, with the United States added for comparison. See Table 6-1 in Gelb et al. in ibid.

19. Saudi Arabia, with the highest revenue in absolute terms ($102 billion), had a per capita revenue in 1980 of over $11,000, Kuwait $12,800, Libya $7,500, and Gabon $2,600. Revenue data from OPEC, *Annual Statistical Bulletin*, 1984, and population data from World Bank *Atlas*, 1983.

20. Data from World Bank *Atlas*, various issues.

21. See, for instance, S. El Serafy, "The Proper Calculation of Income."

Chapter 13

The Sociopolitical Impact of the Oil Industry in Oil Exporting Countries

Carlos G. Elías

The price of oil more than tripled during the mid-1970s. The revenues generated by this increase were an opportunity for oil-rich less developed countries (LDCs) to accelerate the process of economic growth and political transformation. Although oil exporting LDCs grew considerably during the mid- to late 1970s, they did very little to diversify their economies. The dependence on oil revenues by these countries has jeopardized the growth of their economies at times when the price of oil remains weak.

It is reasonable to expect that this newfound wealth will increase demand for political participation and transformation. The objective of this chapter is to analyze the sociopolitical impact that oil exports had on oil exporting countries. The impact on Middle East oil exporting countries will be analyzed, and the case of Venezuela, a country that moved from economic expansion in the late 1970s to stagnation and political crises, will be covered.

OIL EXPORTS IN MIDDLE EAST COUNTRIES

Around 60 percent of the world's oil reserves are located in eight Middle East countries.[1] The revenues that oil brought to the region were used to finance big government projects. Oil revenues have increased the per capita income for oil exporters in the region. In order to obtain self-sustained growth, these countries have to invest in capital goods and human capital. One way to measure the level of human capital formation has been by looking at the levels of literacy. In this respect Middle East oil exporting countries score low as compared to other countries (this is especially true for women).[2] And this is despite a 10–15 percent government budget spent on education. In 1980 the literacy rate for male adults in Kuwait, Saudi Arabia, and United Arab Emirates was 72, 35, and 30 percent respectively. In the same year the same rates for adult females were 54, 12, and 19 percent (Richards and Waterbury 1990: 113). In 1990 the adult male and female literacy rates were 77 and 67 percent in Kuwait; 73 and 48 percent in Saudi Arabia; and 58 and 38 percent in the United Arab Emirates (UNICEF 1993).

According to Alan Richards and John Waterbury (1990), there are several factors for these low literacy rates: historically, colonial powers did little to educate Middle East natives; poor attitudes of peasants regarding education, especially for women; most countries are devoting few resources to adult education and concentrating on the education of the young population; money in education is not spent productively. Although history and attitudes are important, the resources spent on education in the Middle East are not spent efficiently enough.

Two major factors contribute to the inefficient expenditure of education funds. First, the separation of school by sex increases the cost of education. Second, and more important, most Middle East countries spent more at the university than at the elementary level, where these resources could be more productive.

Although the big revenues that oil generates in the Middle East place these countries among the world's richest with very high income per capita, this wealth is very unevenly distributed. The Physical Quality of Life Index (PQLI) has been developed to get a better understanding of the level of development of LDCs. In this index are included life expectancy, infant mortality, and literacy rates. Saudi Arabia, for example, is fifth in per capita income while tenth using the PQLI. This suggests uneven distribution of income (Bill and Springborg 1990).

It is very important to note that economic growth has not been followed by political transformation. Six of the eight countries with the biggest oil reserves have traditional conservative governments—the only exceptions are Iraq and Iran. An important question is why traditional governments have survived in the Middle East. The main explanation is that oil reserves are big enough to placate the demand for political reform. The population of these countries is small enough for the government to provide free housing, education, and medical care. In some countries the native population is very small: in Kuwait, for example, only 40 percent of the 1.6 million inhabitants were native-born.

This policy has reduced the demand for political reform but is not without cost or risk. In the case of Saudi Arabia, the government has been able to keep the status quo by keeping taxes very low and providing its citizens with social benefits such as health care and education. All this has been subsidized by the oil revenues that Saudi Arabia obtained during the boom years. With the oil boom over and the price of oil getting weaker, the government has run a budget deficit in the last ten years to finance spending. With this type of deficit, reserves of foreign currencies have fallen from $121 billion in 1984 to $51 billion in 1992 (Gerth et al. 1993). This could postpone economic crises, but not forever. When most of the oil wealth is gone, the government will have to increase taxes to reduce the budget deficit. This could lead to more demand for political liberalization.

Several factors could cause political problems in the near future for those countries (Bill and Springborg 1990: 372). The biggest political risk for the established political order is the gap that exists between economic modernization and political openness. This is especially true because of the growth of a professional middle class interested in more political power. The growth of Islamic fundamentalism is always a threat. The shortage of native labor that forces some of these countries to import a large part of their labor force could threaten the stability of the conservative governments in Middle East oil exporting countries. Still the most important problem that these countries face is the lack of diversification in their economies.

FROM ECONOMIC EXPANSION TO POLITICAL CRISIS: THE CASE OF VENEZUELA

Oil is the most important source of foreign exchange revenue in Venezuela. With the oil boom of the mid-1970s, the country experienced high economic growth and rapid transformation. Oil, however, was not enough to diversify the economy, and the reduction in the price of oil in the early 1980s was followed by economic stagnation and political crisis. In 1992 two coup attempts in less than ten months threatened the stability of one of the most politically stable countries in Latin America.

Although the first foreign concession of oil was granted during the presidency of Cipriano Castro (1899–1908), it was his successor, Juan Vicente Gómez (1908–35), who benefited the most from foreign investment in the Venezuelan oil industry. Investors reluctant to invest in Mexico, because of the Mexican revolution, turned their eyes to Venezuela. To regulate foreign concessions, two laws were enacted by then Development Minister Gumersindo Torres: the Mining Law of 1918, and the Petroleum Code. This helped to better monitor foreign companies' actions in Venezuela. Although Torres was considered a moderate who did not want to discourage foreign concessions, most foreign companies found his laws too restrictive. He was dismissed by Gómez in 1921. After this, foreign companies obtained an elimination of clauses that they did not like. Conditions for foreign companies were extremely good, including low taxes and no limit to the amount of land they could hold.

In the period 1922–45, Venezuela was the first exporter and the second producer of oil. The production of oil increased from 1 million barrels in 1921 to 323 million barrels in 1945 (Ewell 1984). Revenue from oil helped the country to finance public spending in roads and to pay the country's foreign debt. In 1930 Venezuela had no foreign debt. This prosperity increased the people's desire for political transformation. Between 1935 and 1945, two more military dictators became presidents: Eleazar López Contreras (1935–41) and Isaías Medina Angarita (1941–45). In 1945 military conspirators, who wanted more rapid modernization, took power and named a civilian president. Their choice was Rómulo Betancourt, president of the Acción Democrática (Democratic Action) party, who was Venezuela's president during the period 1945–48. In his agenda there was land reform and investigation of property obtained during dictatorship. The last item in his program did not please the military commanders that deposed him in 1948. The next ten years were years of military dictatorship. One of the leaders of the 1945 coup, Marcos Pérez Jiménez, became president in 1952 until he was deposed in 1958, and Venezuela returned to civilian rule for the next 35 years.

After 1958 the price of oil declined and that reduced Venezuela's revenues. For the first time since 1930, foreign debt began to rise. In spite of that, this period was one of social and political stability. Two major political agreements served as a basis for this stability: Workers-Employer Conciliatory Pact (Pacto de Avenimiento Obrero Patronal), and Pact of Punto Fijo.

The first was an agreement between unions and firms, as a basis for democratic consolidation. It provided job security to workers in exchange for labor restraint in wage demands; firms would support the democratic order, and a commission was set up to mediate in labor disputes. This commission had an equal share of workers and firms' representatives. The second was a political agreement between the two main political parties (Acción Democrática and COPEI) for collaboration and a share in the government.

The big opportunity for Venezuela came in the mid-1970s, when the price of oil increased dramatically, from approximately $2 in 1970 to more than $14 in 1974 and more than $29 by 1982. During the period 1972–77 its GDP grew at an annual rate of 7.8 percent. The oil boom came to an abrupt end in 1977. In 1977–78 GDP grew at a 3.2 percent rate, and from 1978 to 1985 it grew at -1 percent annual rate. With the end of the oil boom came an end to political cooperation. Labor strikes intensified and domestic capital, looking for a more stable environment, started to move abroad. By 1982 the private domestic investment had fallen to 7,023 bolivares compared with 19,092 bolivares in 1977 (McCoy 1988: p. 97; bolivares of 1968).

Several factors contributed to this stagnation: inflation, corruption, waste, foreign indebtedness, and oil dependence (Alexander 1988).

The inflation rate in Venezuela has never been too high. Under the assumption that oil revenues were too large for the economy to absorb, the government decided to buy foreign securities and in that way eliminate inflationary pressures of excessive aggregate demand. This was not completely successful, and oil revenues accelerated the inflation rate. To complicate things, this period was characterized by worldwide inflation, and this also contributed to Venezuela's inflation.

The revenues that oil generated were so abundant that little consideration was paid to the profitability of projects that were financed by the government. A lot of resources were wasted this way.

The country borrowed vast sums of money during the period, as if the increase in the price of oil was going to last forever. This foreign indebtedness put the country in a weak position when the price of oil started to fall.

A major obstacle was that Venezuela did not diversify enough to reduce its dependence on oil revenue. Although part of the government's program was to diversify the economy in order to reduce the dependence on oil, this was not very successful. Early attempts at import substitution failed and, by 1982, 94 percent of the export receipt came from oil (Randall 1987: 121).

After 1985 the Venezuelan economy started to show signs of life again. Between 1985 and 1988 GDP grew at a rate of 5.3 percent annually, although in 1988–89 it shrank by 8.6 percent. Carlos Andrés Pérez was elected president in 1988. In February 1989 he presented to Congress his economic reform package, which included removing quotas and tariffs and deregulation of interest rates. In January 1990 the government announced a reduction in maximum corporate taxes from 50 to 35 percent. In August 1991 it was announced that the price of gasoline would double by December 1992. The reforms induced violent opposition; riots followed the announcement of the president's package in March 1989. After an attempted coup in February 1992, the government decided to put some control on prices to ease the severe effects of reform in March 1992. This, however, did not avoid more riots in April and a second coup attempt in November 1992. After the coup attempt, due to a more uncertain political future, foreign investment plunged 94 percent, from $121.6 million in January 1992 to $9.2 million in March (*Wall Street Journal* 1992: A9). By June it was estimated that a third of the investments had returned. The unstable political climate can take a toll on the economic performance of Venezuela.

In December 1992 Pérez's Acción Democrática party threatened to withdraw support for him unless some measures of the austerity program were eased. His economic reform package was violently opposed in the country. Some analysts criticized the president's program as inadequate because it did not reduce sufficiently government intervention in the economy.

Political uncertainty is a real menace to Venezuela, especially after the impeachment of Pérez under corruption charges in 1993. After years of oil boom the Venezuelan economy does not look more diversified than before. In 1992 oil still generated 82 percent of the foreign exchange and 22 percent of GDP.

CONCLUSION

This chapter has examined the political implications of oil exports on oil exporting countries. Although these countries achieved high economic growth in the mid/late 1970s, their continuous dependence on oil revenue is a major liability for self-sustained growth. In most cases oil continues to be the major source of revenues. Not enough was done to diversify the economy, and weak oil prices have meant economic crises in Venezuela.

In the Middle East democratization has not gone hand in hand with economic growth. Some Middle East oil exporters have been able to keep in check demand for political reform by extensive benefits to the population. In the case of Saudi Arabia, this policy has generated budget deficits in the last ten years that have reduced the reserves of foreign exchange by more than 50 percent. The threat of political instability is present if the governments of oil exporting Middle East countries do not reduce the gap that exists between economic growth and democratization.

NOTES

1. These countries are Iraq, Iran, Oman, United Arab Emirates, Qatar, Bahrain, Saudi Arabia, and Kuwait.
2. As a group only Sub-Saharan Africa and South Asia have lower literacy rates than Middle East countries.

REFERENCES ·

Al-Ajmi, Fahed. "The Effect of Socio-political Events on OPEC's Market Share Stability." *Journal of Energy Development* 15 (2) (Autumn 1990).
Alexander, Robert J. "Venedemocracia and the Vagaries of the Energy Crisis." In Donald L. Herman (ed.), *Democracy in Latin America*. New York: Praeger, 1988.
Bill, James A. and Robert Springborg. *Politics in the Middle East*. New York: HarperCollins, 1990.
Ewell, Judith. *Venezuela: A Century of Change*. London: C. Hurst & Co., 1984.
Gerth, Jeff, Stephen Engelberg, and Tim Weiner. "Saudi Stability Hit by Heavy Spending over the Last Decade." *New York Times*, August 22, 1993, p. A1.
McCoy, Jennifer. "The State and Democratic Compromise in Venezuela." In Cal Clark and Jonathan Lemco (eds.), *State and Development*. Leiden: E. J. Brill, 1988.
"On the Wings of Cockroaches." *The Economist*, August 7, 1993, p. 39.
Owen, Roger. *State, Power and Politics in the Making of the Modern Middle East*. New York: Routledge, 1992.
Randall, Laura. *The Political Economy of Venezuela Oil*. New York: Praeger, 1987.
Richards, Alan and John Waterbury. *A Political Economy of the Middle East: State, Class and Economic Development*. Boulder, CO: Westview Press, 1990.
Samii, Massood V. and Masoud Ameri. "OPEC and the Oil Market: Short and Medium-Term Prospects." *Journal of Energy and Development* 16(1) (Spring 1990).
Shojai, Siamack. "Supply Shocks and the Economy of Selected OPEC Members." *Journal of Energy and Development* 2 (Autumn 1990).
UNICEF. *The State of World Children 1993*. New York: Oxford University Press, 1993.
Velázquez, Efrain J. "Devaluación, Ahorro Público y Actividad Económica." In Hans-Peter Nissen and Bernard Mommer (eds.), *¿Adios a la Bonanza? Crisis de la distribución del Ingreso en Venezuela*. Caracas: Nueva Sociedad, 1989.
Wall Street Journal, April 23, 1992, p. A9.
Waterbury, John. "The Growth of Public Sector Enterprise in the Middle East." In Haleh Estenbary and Al Udovitch (eds.), *The Economics Dimension of Middle Eastern History*. Princeton, NJ: Darwin Press, 1990.

PART III

ENERGY AND THE GLOBAL ENVIRONMENT

Chapter 14

Sources of Energy and the Environment

Asbjorn Torvanger

Of all human activities the extraction, conversion, and consumption of energy are among those having most influence over the environment. The influence can be in terms of air and water pollution, solid waste, global warming, and land depreciation. Associated with these environmental influences are consequences in terms of public health effects and increased corrosion of infrastructure, buildings, and works of art, and a possible reduced productivity in agriculture and forestry. The environmental effects depend on energy extraction, conversion efficiency, energy and use, fuel mix, and on the level of emission mitigation. There is some uncertainty associated with the physical and biological effects of energy production and use due to insufficient knowledge, natural variations, potential synergistic effects, and potential threshold contamination levels. For some energy production activities, like nuclear power production, there is some risk of accidents of extensive and serious consequences.

This chapter briefly considers the most important energy sources, their fuel cycle from production to end use, and the major factors determining the total environment impact. Then the environment impacts in terms of emission of pollutants and other effects of each energy source are discussed with reference to different types of environmental impacts, such as local impacts, acid deposits, and climate change. Priority is given to the description of various energy sources and their environmental impacts, whereas the treatment of mitigation options like energy efficiency improvement and environmental control technologies is cut short.

ENERGY SOURCES, FUEL CYCLES, AND TOTAL ENVIRONMENTAL IMPACT

Energy sources can be divided into exhaustible and renewable energy sources. The exhaustible energy sources are the fossil fuels—oil, coal, and natural gas—

and the nuclear energy source, uranium. The renewable energy sources are based on solar, geothermal, or gravitation energy (tidal power). The solar energy sources are hydroelectric, wind power, photovoltaic power, solar thermal, solar heating, biomass, and solar energy derived from the ocean, where the most important forms are wave energy and ocean thermal energy (heat pumps).

For each energy source there is a fuel cycle from exploration, to extraction, to conversion (e.g., electricity generation and oil refining), to transportation and distribution of energy, and to energy end use and consumption in sectors such as industry, transport, and buildings. To supply a given net use of energy, the necessary primary extraction depends on the efficiency for each of these fuel cycle steps. The lower the efficiency the more waste heat or unused material is released. Each fuel cycle step has some environmental impact through emissions and other influences. Some of the environmental impacts can be mitigated. Thus the total environmental impact from energy use depends on: (1) what and how much is produced, and where it is produced; (2) how goods and services are produced; and (3) how much of the impacts are mitigated.

Item 1 refers to the economic structure in terms of goods and services produced. There are different environmental impacts associated with different goods and services due to different production and consumption technologies and patterns, specifically with respect to energy requirements. The geographical distribution of production and consumption is of importance for the local environmental impacts.

Since the total environmental impact to a large extent depends on primary energy extraction, the efficiency through the fuel cycle to end use is important. For a given energy end use a low efficiency means a higher primary energy production and thus a larger environmental impact (item 2). The fuel mix (i.e., share of different energy sources) is another vital factor, since the environmental impact varies among different energy sources. A comprehensive study of the external costs of the coal fuel cycle has been initiated by the Commission of the European Community and the U.S. Department of Energy (see ETSU 1983; and Markandya and Rhodes 1992). The study will be expanded to include other main energy sources, including important renewables, and energy conservation.

Item 3 refers to mitigation of environmental effects through purification technologies and restoration activities like applying lime to lakes damaged by acid deposits. Some potential pollutants and waste materials can be recycled such that the environmental impact is reduced.

ENVIRONMENTAL IMPACTS OF DIFFERENT ENERGY SOURCES

Environmental impacts of some energy sources can be evaluated at three different levels. The first level relates to emission of pollutants to water and air, solid waste, radiation (from nuclear power facilities), and waste heat. The next level relates to the biological and physical consequences of these influences in terms of reduced forest growth, damage to other vegetation cover, reduced fish populations in lakes due to acid deposits, public health hazards, corrosion of materials, global warming, and land depreciation. At the third level the biological and physical consequences are evaluated and compared as part of the total consequences of different energy options, commonly by expressing everything in money terms. In this section the emissions, solid waste, radiation, and physical impacts related to energy use will be considered, whereas the public health, biological, physical, and climate consequences will be discussed in the final section of the chapter. On the valuation of environmental quality and the problems related to this there is a large literature that cannot be reviewed in the present context; see Maureen Cropper and Wallace Oates (1992) for a survey of contributions from economists.

Oil

The main environmental consequence from oil *extraction* is related to oil spills. The impact of oil spills depends on the oil quality, the volume and the speed of the spill (e.g., if there is a blowout from a production platform), and on the timing and location of the spill. In the case of offshore oil extraction, fish populations and sea birds are particularly vulnerable, but the experience is that such impact is local and limited in time. Oil shale is a fine-grained sedimentary rock containing layers of organic material. Oil can be extracted through heating, a process that gives rise to solid wastes, water contamination, air pollutants, and fugitive dust (see Argonne National Laboratory 1990). The extraction of oil and oil shale may lead to land subsidence, dependent on the overburden composition and thickness and the extraction technique. The impact of oil spills from transportation (e.g., oil tankers) and distribution are comparable to oil spills from extraction activities.

In the process of oil *refining* the main emissions are sulfur oxides, carbon monoxide, carbon dioxide, nitrogen oxides, hydrocarbons, and particulate matter. In addition there is some wastewater containing oil and water-soluble hydrocarbons.

The final step in the life cycle of oil is *combustion* for heat production, electricity generation in thermal power plants, or transformation to kinetic energy in engines and turbines in the industry and transport sectors. The main emissions related to combustion are carbon dioxide, carbon monoxide, sulfur oxides, nitrogen oxides, polynuclear aromatic hydrocarbons (PAH), and some heavy metals. These pollutants give rise to local impacts, in addition to acid deposits from sulfur oxides and nitrogen oxides, and global warming from carbon dioxide.

Coal

Coal is the most abundant fossil fuel at the global scale, and is available in different qualities, from anthracite (high carbon content) via bituminous coal to lignite (low carbon content). Coal is extracted from underground or surface mining. The quality of coal can be increased through a kind of refining process or preparation (''coal washing''). Coal is to a large extent transported on railroads and barges. There are some atmospheric emissions from diesel-powered mining equipment, thermal dryers, preparation activities, and transportation. These are primarily nitrogen oxides, sulfur compounds, hydrocarbons, and carbon dioxide (see Argonne National Laboratory 1990). Methane, other mine gases, and coal dust can lead to explosions. Surface mining causes disruption of large areas and landscape changes, and release of fugitive dusts. Another consequence of coal mining is water quality degradation due to water drainage from mines, leaching and erosion of solid wastes, and modifications of aquifers. Underground mining may lead to land subsidence. Furthermore, sites are needed for solid waste disposal. These emissions can lead to dust problems and reduced visibility, damage to vegetation, and human health consequences (a review of environmental impact assessment for coal is given by Jones [1992]).

In a conventional coal-fired power plant, electricity is generated through combustion of coal in a boiler, which produces high-pressure steam that propels a turbine, which thereafter drives a generator. The thermal efficiency (the fraction of the energy converted to electricity) is typically 35 percent in most developed countries (WRI 1990). During the combustion process particulate matter (solid and liquid) is emitted to the atmosphere together with sulfur dioxide, nitrogen oxide, carbon dioxide, carbon monoxide, PAH, and some heavy metals. Discharges to water are mainly associated with cooling water and ash handling. These emissions and thermal pollution can have a significant impact on aquatic ecosystems. Systems for controlling emissions to air and water, as well as solid waste, are auxiliary to a modern power plant. Sulfur dioxide can be removed through a stack scrubber where the gas reacts with limestone or lime to produce calcium sulfite or sulfate (Argonne National Laboratory 1990). Through a second main desulfurization method sulfur is regenerated as a by-product and the reactant is recycled to the scrubber. Large amounts of ash and scrubber sludge can cause a waste disposal problem. The site size of a power plant in the 500 megawatts electric (MWe) is typically between 500 and 1,000 acres (Argonne National Laboratory 1990).

A newer coal technology is based on *fluidized-bed* combustion, where fuel burns in a bed of particles that are suspended and rapidly moved by an upward flow of air and combustion gases. Three advantages compared to a conventional boil are higher thermal efficiency, removal of sulfur dioxide during combustion, and reduced level of nitrogen oxides. Coal gasification and coal liquefaction are alternative technologies. The products of the latter, however, are generally more toxic than crude oil and shale oil.

A higher overall thermal efficiency can be achieved through combined cycle power plants, up to 44 percent (WRI 1990). Hot-combustion gas turbines and steam turbines are then combined to generate electricity. In addition to a lower primary energy use causing less emissions, this technology allows emissions to be reduced compared to the conventional boiler technology. In cogeneration systems (i.e., combined heat and power systems) electricity is generated and direct heat provided for residential and commercial heating. The overall efficiency (electricity and heat) can be up to 85 percent (WRI 1990).

Coal-burning magnetohydrodynamic (MHD) electricity generation is likely to be available in the future, where electric power is generated by passing an electrical conducting fluid (coal combustion products) through a magnetic field without any moving mechanical parts. The advantages of this technology would be higher thermal efficiency and less release of pollutants than conventional coal technologies (Kessler 1991).

Natural Gas

Gas leakages may occur during extraction activities and transport through pipelines or on liquified natural gas ships. In the latter case the natural gas is liquid at a temperature of $-161°C$. Extraction of gas may lead to land subsidence. Gas leakages are a fire hazard and in some concentrations there is a danger of explosion. Before the gas is distributed, water, carbon dioxide, higher hydrocarbons, and hydrogen sulfide are removed.

During combustion of natural gas the emissions are substantially smaller than for coal and oil. For nitrogen oxides the release to air is about half of that for coal and oil combustion (Pleym et al. 1992). The emissions of carbon dioxide are about 60 percent of coal-related emissions and 70 percent of oil-related emissions.

In fuel cells electricity is generated from the chemical reaction of a fuel, such as natural gas or coal gas, and an oxidant, such as air or pure oxygen (see Schora and Cámara 1991; and Argonne National Laboratory 1990). This technology has many advantages compared to conventional fossil fuel electricity generation technologies. The energy efficiency is relatively high and emission levels of nitrogen oxides, sulfur dioxide, and particulates are low. One reason for the low emissions is the use of relatively clean fuels.

Nuclear Energy

Most commercial power reactors producing electricity are light-water reactors (LWRs), which use ordinary water as the heat-transfer medium and as a moderator for the nuclear reaction. The fuel is uranium, which is enriched to increase the concentration of the fissionable isotope uranium-235. There is some release of radioactive materials from uranium ore milling and enrichment facilities. The breeder reactor is an alternative nuclear technology where excess neutrons from the fission process are employed to convert a radioactive material to a fissile fuel and thus obtain a net production of fissile fuel. Fusion power plants may be available in the future, and are expected to be much safer than fission reactors.

Nuclear power plants produce radioactive isotopes, and small amounts of these are leaked during normal operation through the cooling system of the plant and as radioactive gases and particles through ventilation systems and control systems for radioactive waste. Of the numerous fission products one is most concerned for the long-lived isotopes tritium, carbon-14, krypton-85, and iodine-129, which pose the largest public health hazards (Argonne National Laboratory 1990; Pleym et al. 1992). The threat to human health is negligible under normal operation, but there is a small risk of major accidents of large consequences, as for example the Chernobyl accident of 1986.

The main types of radioactive waste are high-level waste (spent fuel and high-level waste from reprocessing), uranium mill tailings (sand and fine-grained material with low concentration of radioactive isotopes), and low-level waste (all other types of radioactive waste). Some of the high-level radioactive wastes can be reprocessed but the rest require long-term storage. The release of radioactive materials from the reprocessing plants during normal operation is larger than from the power plants. Geologic repositories are considered to be the best alternative for permanent disposal. There is some risk of release of radioactive materials from accidents related to waste transport, handling, and reprocessing.

Hydroelectric

Hydroelectric power plants are relatively clean in terms of environmental impacts, but they cause microclimatic, hydrological, biological, and landscape effects. Most of these effects are related to formation of artificial lakes (reservoirs) and resulting change in river flow and hydrological regime. Vegetation, fish populations, and other species are negatively affected by the hydrological and climatic changes. The aesthetic value of the landscape may be reduced owing to reservoirs and power lines. Furthermore, resettlement of local inhabitants may be required, and a risk of flooding the downstream population arises because of the possibility of a collapse of reservoir walls. The environmental impacts are reduced for small-scale hydropower plants.

Transmission of electricity requires high-voltage lines, whether produced by hydropower, thermal power, or nuclear power. Due to cost considerations these are commonly overhead transmission lines and not underground cables (see Belmans and Geysen 1992). In Western Europe the highest voltage level is around 400 kilovolts (kV), whereas 750 kV lines are installed in North America. From present knowledge the electromagnetic field surrounding the lines does not appear to pose any health risk to people living nearby. However, some audible noise is generated by the lines.

Solar Energy Derived from the Ocean

These technologies are not well developed today, but a few small-scale pilot projects exist.

Wave energy is based on two main technologies for electricity generation, either wave-focusing moving water into a reservoir at the shore, where the water flows back through a turbine, or buoys with swinging water columns pumping air through a turbine. The area requirements for wave energy plants are large, and there will be restrictions on ship traffic, fishing, and other use. There will be some influence on fish populations, vegetation, and marine life in general.

The future potential of *Ocean Thermal Energy Conversion* (OTEC) is probably large. The idea is to exploit the large temperature gradient that exists in much of the world's oceans. OTEC systems are realistic only in tropic waters, since a temperature difference of at least 20°C is needed. In a closed-cycle system warm water is used to evaporate a suitable working fluid running a turbine, after which the fluid is recondensed in cold water. In the open-cycle system the ocean water itself is used as working fluid (see Fisher 1990). Full-scale OTEC plants could harm tropic biota, disrupt ocean currents, and influence the climate. There could be harmful emissions of the working fluid. If chlorofluorocarbons are employed, emissions cause stratospheric ozone depletion and, because chlorofluorocarbons are greenhouse gases, increased global warming.

In a smaller scale ocean thermal energy is available close to the shore through *heat pumps*, employing a similar working fluid as in OTEC. This thermal energy is suitable for heating buildings. Other thermal energy sources for heat pumps are waste water, soil, underground water, and bedrock.

Wind Energy

Wind energy is captured through a turbine design that converts the kinetic energy to electricity with the help of a generator. The most common type has a horizontal axis and three blades (see Fisher 1990). The energy-producing potential is very sensitive to the wind quality of the site (i.e., speed and reliability). The best wind energy technology at the best sites is competitive with fossil-fired power plants. Wind energy is likely to be more area-intensive than solar energy, but the land between the turbines can be used for growing crops and cattle grazing. Wind energy sites influence the landscape aesthetics and some noise is generated (see Stevenson 1993). A small impact on the local ecosystem, in particular birds, can be expected.

PHOTOVOLTAICS, SOLAR THERMAL, AND SOLAR HEATING

Sunlight is directly converted to electricity by *photovoltaic cells*. The cells are made of a thin semiconductor material (mostly silicon) doped with a specific amount of impurities. This technology has developed substantially in later years in terms of cost reduction and solar energy conversion efficiency, and future prospects are even better (WRI 1990). The best photovoltaic cells are able to convert 14 percent of the solar energy to electricity under field conditions (see Fisher 1990). Photovoltaics are employed in small scale in various consumer products, such as calculators and garden lighting, and also for lighting and charging systems for cottages and boats. Large-scale power stations require large areas and cause some environmental impacts. However, at 14 percent efficiency and a 25 percent capacity factor, only 0.38 percent of the land area of the United States is required to supply the entire electricity load of the United States (Fisher 1990). There are some toxic materials involved in manufacturing photovoltaic cells, which may be a health hazard for workers.

Solar thermal technologies can be employed in large scale to capture solar energy as heat or to produce steam for electricity generation. Parabolic dishes, parabolic troughs, or flat mirrors employ tracking systems to focus the light on a receiver. The thermal efficiency can be up to 75 percent, whereas the electricity generation efficiency is up to 32 percent (Fisher 1990). Solar thermal plants require some land and have some visual impact on the landscape. If solar collectors are overheated they may release toxic and corrosive gases. A solar technology suitable in smaller scale is *solar space heating* of buildings and *solar water heating*. Passive systems use only convective forces generated by temperature differences to transport the heat transfer fluid, which is commonly water or air. In an active system the fluid is moved by a pump or fan. The solar energy is trapped as heat in flat plate collectors containing a black absorber, or through concentrating parabolic troughs or dishes. Solar technologies are also available for space cooling. An alternative technology is solar ponds, where solar energy is collected by water or another fluid and stored in a mass of the same fluid. Passive solar heating systems are often cost-effective, especially if they are integrated in new buildings. The environmental impact of decentralized solar heating is small, but there is a potential risk from leakage of toxic heat transfer fluids to domestic water supply (Fisher 1990).

Biomass

Biomass energy is derived from vegetation or animal wastes. Fuelwood combustion is the simplest and most common thermochemical process for producing energy from biomass. Animal wastes and crop residues can be directly combusted or used for gas production. Another biomass energy source is municipal solid waste. Energy crops such as sugarcane, oil palm and fast-growing tree plantations can be converted to fuels like ethanol, methanol, and various oils. Peat resources can be dried and burned. During biomass combustion carbon dioxide is released to the atmosphere. If the biomass stock is kept constant through reforestation and the soil is not eroded, the same volume of carbon dioxide is sequestered in the new biomass. The environmental impacts of large-scale peat extraction are significant, since the vegetation has to be stripped to remove the peat layer and the regeneration time is many hundred years. An advantage of using animal waste and municipal solid waste for combustion or as a gas resource is reduced emissions of the greenhouse gas methane. Other pollutants released to the atmosphere are particulates (i.e., polycyclic organic matter), nitrogen oxides, PAH and other hydrocarbons, and carbon monoxide (Argonne National Laboratory 1990). Uncontrolled residual emissions may reduce ambient air quality in local communities and be a public health hazard. Wood-burning stoves employing newer technologies are available that reduce fuel consumption and release of air pollutants.

Geothermal Energy

Geothermal energy is based on the heat that is contained within the crust of the earth. This heat is generated from nuclear fusion processes under very high pressures and temperatures at the center of the earth. At suitable sites (of high geothermal gradient) wells are drilled into a hot formation and heat extracted in the form of steam and/or hot water, which is employed to drive an electricity generator (see DiPippo 1991). Hot dry rock is a less mature technology with large potential, where heat is extracted from unusually hot regions of the earth's crust by way of drilling two wells and pumping water through (see Brown, Potter, and Myers 1991). At some sites hot water at lower temperatures is available close to the surface for district heating and heating of greenhouses (Thurston 1993). The environmental impacts from geothermal energy systems are relatively small. Some carbon dioxide, hydrogen sulfide, and mercury is released from the geofluid if it is not reinjected into the reservoir. Release of toxic brine (i.e., geothermal fluid) can pose a threat to local vegetation and groundwater. The land requirements and visual impact on the landscape of geothermal plants are less than for competing power plants (DiPippo 1991). Some cases of land subsidence due to loss of geothermal pressure have been reported.

Tidal Power

In tidal power plants the gravitational energy from the attraction of the sun and moon on the oceans is exploited. Huge masses of water are moved as a result of the Earth's axial rotation and the gravitational forces. Toward the coast at some locations the tidal difference can be greater than six meters due to shelving of the sea bed and the funnelling of estuaries (see Carter 1993). The flooding tide is allowed to fill a basin naturally, after which the water is trapped behind a dam and released through turbines to generate electricity when the water ebbs away. Potential sites for tidal power plants are restricted owing to the distribution of tides, in Europe to the United Kingdom and France, and to the Bay of Fundy in Canada. There may be some minor environmental impact from tidal power on fish and other marine life, since coastal currents are affected.

CLASSIFICATION OF ENVIRONMENTAL IMPACTS

Environmental impacts may be classified according to geographical scale. At the local scale there are emissions of gases and particulate matter to air (atmosphere), release of pollutants to water (hydrosphere), and waste deposits (lithosphere). Furthermore there can be environmental impacts from excessive use of water (e.g., in geothermal power plants) and geologic impacts (such as land subsidence due to underground extraction of fossil fuels). At the regional scale (up to a few hundred kilometers) to the continental scale (up to 2,000–3,000 kilometers) the air and water quality may be affected through emissions of gases and particulate matter, in particular through acid deposits. Finally, at the global scale the atmosphere may be affected through the release of greenhouse gases causing global warming and stratospheric ozone depletion. We emphasize emissions to the atmosphere since these are considered to cause the most serious environmental impacts from extraction, conversion, distribution, and consumption of energy.

Local Impacts

Several of the gases released to the atmosphere from energy conversion and consumption activities may have detrimental health effects on the population. Sulfur oxides, nitrogen oxides, carbon monoxide, and particulates may induce pulmonary diseases such as asthma and allergies. Polynuclear aromatic hydrocarbons and other hydrocarbons are suspected to be carcinogens. Photochemical smog is generated by solar radiation acting on nitrogen oxides and hydrocarbons (from vehicle exhaust) in urban areas and contain reactive gases (like ozone) causing eye irritation and impaired lung function. Sulfur oxides, nitrogen oxides, and photochemical smog have negative impacts on vegetation and crops. These anthrophogenic emissions are probably one of the factors that can explain the damage to forest areas in Central Europe first detected in the 1980s (Pleym et al. 1992).

Local and regional climates (and possibly global climate) are influenced by thermal pollution from power plants and urban industrial areas, and through changes in the characteristics of the land (and ocean) surface (see Jäger 1983). One example of the latter could be large-scale development of solar thermal plants. Thermal pollution is related to energy conversion and uses releasing heat—for example, through cooling systems, which is a part of power plants. The most well-known example is ''urban heat islands.'' Such climate changes will influence local ecosystems.

Facilities for extraction, production, conversion, and distribution of energy have some physical impact on the landscape. These facilities occupy land and the aesthetic value may be reduced because of mines, power plants, water reservoirs, and power lines.

Acid Deposits

Emissions of sulfur oxides and nitrogen oxides (and probably some particulates) can cause acidification of lakes and soil from local to regional scale. The acid deposits place severe stress on many ecosystems—fauna, soil, and vegetation. Well-known examples are the reduced size and diversity of fish populations in Scandinavian lakes, the northeastern United States, and southeastern Canada (Graedel and Crutzen 1989).

An additional damage from acid deposits is corrosion of outdoor equipment, buildings, and works of art. Photochemical smog has a corrosive effect on rubber and plastics, as well as a deleterious effect on human health.

Climate Change

Carbon dioxide is responsible for about half of the global warming potential of all greenhouse gases in the atmosphere. The main source is combustion of fossil fuels; an additional source is emissions due to deforestation and reduced biomass stock, partly caused by biomass fuel combustion (such as firewood) and inadequate reforestation. There is also some warming contribution from nitrous oxide, where one of the sources is combustion of fossil fuels. Houghton et al. (1990 and 1992) present model estimates showing an increase in global average temperature from 2.2°C to 4.8°C from preindustrial time (taken to be 1765) to year 2070, with a best estimate of 3.3°C. A global warming at this scale could have large consequences for natural ecosystems and human activities. There are, however, considerable uncertainties with respect to the speed and scale of regional warming, and to the geologic (i.e. Antarctic ice cap melting and sea level rise), environmental, and economic consequences. One important feature is the speed of warming, since plants and animals have some ability to adapt to a changing climate as long as the rate of change is not too high.

Sulfur particulates from coal and oil combustion are likely to have a cooling influence on the Northern Hemisphere, since they reflect solar radiation and may affect the optical properties of clouds, and may thus have held global warming down somewhat (Houghton et al. 1992).

REFERENCES

Argonne National Laboratory. *Environmental Consequences of, and Control Processes for, Energy Technologies*. Pollution Technological Review No. 181. Noyes Data Corporation, New Jersey, 1990.

Belmans, Ronnie J. M. and Willy J. D. Geysen. "Environmental Implications of High Voltage Overhead Lines." In World Energy Council, *Energy and the Environment*, No. 1.1, 15th Congress, Madrid, 1992.

Brown, D. W., R. M. Potter, and C. W. Myers. "Hot Dry Rock Geothermal Energy— An Emerging Resource with Large Worldwide Potential." In Jefferson W. Tester, David O. Wood, and Nancy A. Ferrari (eds.), *Energy and the Environment in the 21st Century*. Cambridge, MA: MIT Press, 1991.

Carter, Shaun E. F. "Prospects for Tidal Power in the Year 2000." In Bruce Cross (ed.), *European Directory of Renewable Energy Suppliers and Services 1993*. London: James & James Science Publishers, 1993.

Cropper, Maureen L. and Wallace E. Oates. "Environmental Economics: A Survey." *Journal of Economic Literature* 30 (2) (1992): 675–740.

DiPippo, Ronald. "Geothermal Energy: Electricity Production and Environmental Impact, A Worldwide Perspective." In Jefferson W. Tester, David O. Wood, and Nancy A. Ferrari (eds.), *Energy and the Environment in the 21st Century.* Cambridge, MA: MIT Press, 1991.

Energy Technology Support Unit (ETSU). *Assessment of the External Costs of the Coal Fuel Cycle.* CEC/U.S. Joint Study on Fuel Cycle Costs, Prepared for the DG XII of the Commission of the European Community. Draft, February 1993.

Fisher, Diane (ed.). "Options for Reducing Greenhouse Gas Emissions." Draft. Stockholm: Stockholm Environment Institute, 1990.

Graedel, Thomas E. and Paul J. Crutzen. "The Changing Atmosphere." *Scientific American,* September 1989.

Houghton, J. T., G. J. Jenkins, and J. J. Ephraums (eds.). *Climate Change—The IPCC Scientific Assessment.* Intergovernmental Panel on Climate Change (IPCC). Cambridge: Cambridge University Press, 1990.

Houghton, J. T., B. A. Callander, and S. K. Varney (eds.). *Climate Change 1992: The Supplementary Report to the IPCC Scientific Assessment.* Intergovernmental Panel on Climate Change (IPCC). Cambridge: Cambridge University Press, 1992.

Jäger, Jill. *Climate and Energy Systems: A Review of Their Interactions.* New York: John Wiley, 1983.

Jones, Tim. "Environmental Impact Assessment for Coal." In World Energy Council, *Energy and the Environment,* No. 1.1, 15th Congress, Madrid, 1992.

Kessler, Robert. "Economic, Environmental, and Engineering Aspects of Magnetohydrodynamic Power Generation." In Jefferson W. Tester, David O. Wood, and Nancy A. Ferrari (eds.), *Energy and the Environment in the 21st Century.* Cambridge, MA: MIT Press, 1991.

Markandya, A. and B. Rhodes. *Economic Valuation—External Costs of Fuel Cycles: An Impact Pathway Approach,* EC/U.S. Fuel Cycle Study, June 1992.

Pleym, Harald et al. *Miljøstudier,* 3rd ed. Bekkestua, Norway: NKI Forlaget, 1992.

Schora, Frank C. and Elias H. Cámara (1991). "Fuel Cells: Power for the Future." In Jefferson W. Tester, David O. Wood, and Nancy A. Ferrari (eds.), *Energy and the Environment in the 21st Century.* Cambridge, MA: MIT Press, 1991.

Stevenson, Ruth. "Environmental Aspects of Wind Farms." In Bruce Cross (ed.), *European Directory of Renewable Energy Suppliers and Services 1993.* London: James & James Science Publishers, 1993.

Thurston, Robert. "Towards the 21st Century with the World's Largest Energy Resource." In Bruce Cross (ed.), *European Directory of Renewable Energy Suppliers and Services 1993.* London: James & James Science Publishers, 1993.

World Resources Institute (WRI). *World Resources 1990–91.* In collaboration with the United Nations Environment Programme and the United Nations Development Programme. New York: Oxford University Press, 1990.

Chapter 15

Environmental Imperatives and Renewable Sources of Energy

Clive L. Spash and Andrew Young

Energy in accessible forms is central to modern-day existence with industrial economies based upon the use of fossil fuels in ever-increasing quantities. The United Kingdom is a typical example of this dependence, with 95 percent of final energy consumption derived from fossil fuels (Department of Energy 1992). The insecurity of foreign oil supplies (exemplified by OPEC price rises, the Iranian revolution, and the invasion of Kuwait by Iraq) and growing awareness of the social costs of fossil fuel use have encouraged the development of alternative energy sources. This second incentive is analyzed here.

The chapter divides energy sources into fossil fuels and nuclear power, as the conventional sources, and renewable and geothermal energy, as the alternatives. While conventional and geothermal sources use energy capital (i.e., a finite stock), so reducing future options, renewable energy sources employ energy income (i.e., the stock remains constant). At present utilizing capital appears to be most efficient; however, the true cost of fossil fuel use is misrepresented by market prices. For example, fossil fuel combustion produces emissions that degrade the environment and impose costs on society—for example, through poorer health. Thus, pricing is inaccurate and excessive energy use occurs from polluting sources. The hypothesis we wish to investigate here is that renewable energy sources are falsely seen as too expensive because their external benefits to society, such as energy capital maintenance and lower pollution, are ignored. We review the environmental impacts of each energy source, and use this to draw out key features of the debate over the potential for fossil fuel substitution by renewable energy sources.

CONVENTIONAL ENERGY SOURCES

Oil, Coal, and Natural Gas

A considerable amount of resources are used in the exploration for and extraction of oil and gas. Oil and gas wells cause visual, noise, and ecological impacts and rely on extensive transportation, storage, and refining sectors. Environmental impacts from coal extraction vary with the choice of open-cast versus closed-pit mining. Both can cause acid mine drainage affecting local water supplies and the ecosystems they feed. In the case of the open-cast mines a major aesthetic impact occurs and the site may never be returned to its former condition (despite attempts at reconstruction). During oil extraction there is the risk of accidents, such as subsidence of spent fields, rig disasters (e.g., Piper Alpha in the North Sea) and oil spills. Transport accidents have received considerable attention due to oil tanker spills, such as the *Amoco Cadiz*, *Exxon Valdez*, and *Braer*. In the case of the *Exxon Valdez*, damages ran into millions of dollars and the spill partially destroyed a habitat of international importance.

Fossil fuel combustion releases gases that affect health, cause acid rain, and contribute to the greenhouse effect. Acid deposition is the result of sulfur oxides (SO_x) and nitrogen oxides (NO_x) becoming weak acids, and falling to the ground as particulates (dry deposition) and acidic rain (wet deposition). Dry deposition can lead to respiratory illness in humans and acidify water and soils. Regionally acid deposition can be transported over large distances affecting whole continents. For example, the air pollution damage to West German and Scandinavian forests and lakes has been attributed to acid deposition originating from the United Kingdom and Eastern Europe (*Acid News* 1992: 10–12). Similarly, acid deposition in Canada is attributed to fossil fuel combustion in central and eastern United States. Most important among the greenhouse gases are carbon dioxide (CO_2), methane, and nitrous oxide N_2O), which contribute 50, 11, and 6 percent, respectively, to climate forcing (Spash and Hanley 1993). The ratios of CO_2 per unit of energy are 5 for coal, 4 for oil, and 3 for gas (Thurlow 1990). Emissions of greenhouse gases prior to 1985 have already committed the earth to a warming between 0.9°C and 2.4°C, of which 0.5 has already been experienced (Ciborowski 1989). This may cause the instability of atmospheric systems resulting in sea level rise, loss of agricultural productivity, and reductions in biodiversity. The costs are globally distributed and will be pushed onto future generations (Spash 1994).

Other environmental impacts include thermal pollution, the aesthetics of the power plant, and land use. Thermal pollution can be measured by the ratio of thermal power rejected to the total electrical output produced. This gives a ratio of 1.7, 1.6, and 3.0 for coal, oil, and gas fired power stations, respectively, and 2.5 for nuclear (Dipippo 1991: 804). Control of thermal pollution requires coolant water, which can adversely affect the ecology of water courses upon release.

Nuclear Power

Environmental impacts from nuclear power range from the mining of uranium through nuclear accidents and contamination to the disposal of wastes and decommissioning power stations. The issue of nuclear accidents has loomed large since the Chernobyl reactor partial meltdown, which released radiation around the globe. The problem of where to store nuclear waste remains unsolved and raises the issue of intergenerational ethics (Routley and Routley 1980). The decommissioning process still awaits practical experience as governments prefer to keep old stations open rather than face up to the problems posed by the disposal of thousands of tons of materials contaminated with low levels of radiation.

ALTERNATIVE ENERGY SOURCES

The energy flow absorbed by planet Earth in just one year is 100 times the world's proven fossil fuel reserves (Flood 1991). Given current technology, the potential energy that could be recovered is: solar 1,000 TkW (tera kilowatts or 10^{12} kilowatts) wind 10 TkW, wave 0.5–1.0 TkW, hydroelectric 1.5–2.0 TkW, tidal 0.1 TkW, and biomass 30 TkW (Jackson 1992). Present world energy demand is approximately 10 TkW. The energy technologies analyzed here are the renewables: solar, wind, ocean, hydroelectric, and biomass; and nonrenewable geothermal energy.

Solar Energy

There are three solar technologies: passive solar, thermal conversion, and photovoltaic. In a good solar climate (such as Southern California) the average energy available will be 5–6 KWh/m²/day (kilowatt hours per meter squared per day), while in poorer areas (such as Northern Europe) the mean is 2–3 KWh/m²/day (Charters 1991: 738).

Passive Solar

Passive solar can be an almost benign method of extracting energy relying on building design. Factors to be considered include site selection, building orientation, insulation, and thermal mass for storage. In many temperate and tropical regions zero energy structures can be designed, requiring no energy input other than solar for both space and water heating (Charters 1991: 739). Reduced air exchange from insulation may cause the buildup of gases such as carbon monoxide, radon, or formaldehyde leading to health risks, but this can be prevented by improved ventilation. The manufacture of fillers for cavity walls (polystyrene and mineral wool), and the use of glass fiber and metal foil for insulating roofs could have some environmental impacts.

Thermal Conversion

Thermal conversion refers to the concentration of sunlight using parabolic mirrors to reflect onto a central receiver. Turbidity affects the diffusion of radiation, reducing the efficiency of focusing on the central receiver, making clear skies preferable—such as in deserts where 80 percent of radiation is direct. Successful conversion occurs when working fluids are supplied to a turbine at temperatures above 175°C (OECD 1988: 27). Currently the largest such plant is 354 MW (megawatts) at Luz, California, with contracts for another 320 MW (Charters 1991). Air pollution could occur due to an accident involving the by-products of the heat transfer systems (NO_x, sodium monoxide and peroxide). Water pollution via planned or accidental release will vary with the type of system but could include oil, corrosion inhibitors, bactericides, and glycols (OECD 1988: 28). In both cases the quantities are small but could cause significant local impacts. Washing the mirrors would use large quantities of water, which could be problematic if the oil-based detergent or heated water is released into the environment. Some effects on local climate may occur, such as wind deflection and reduced albedo.

Photovoltaic

Photovoltaic methods of energy extraction directly convert light into electricity using silicon solar cells. Environmental concerns arise as a result of the introduction of exotic materials, such as gallium arsenide, which are used to increase cell efficiency. Careful handling is required during the refining, fabrication, and decommissioning of cells and when chemicals are being transported (Jackson 1992: 873). The fabrication of photovoltaic cells requires large quantities of gases such as arsine or diobrane, which are among a list of 17 highly toxic and potentially lethal chemicals identified by the OECD (1988). While such chemicals are already used in industry with a good safety record, the risk of accidents will rise with the scale of fabrication.

Wind Power

Wind power has proved to be one of the most successful renewable energy sources. The engineering design is relatively simple, the raw materials are fairly common, and the waste problem is minimal. In California 1,500 MW of capacity has been installed using 1,600 terawatt (TW) stations with medium-size machines (250–300 KW) standing 50 meters high (Clarke 1991: 743). Wind turbines have proved to be viable in the 75–300 KW range in both Europe and the United States (Dawber 1992). The principal impact is visual, but the effect is largely limited to a local area. The need for stable and adequate wind flows means the most economic sites are inland elevated areas or exposed coastal areas, which are both sensitive to visual intrusion. Noise may be a problem but is usually restricted to a zone of 300 meters around the station. A California study showed that only 4 percent of people living within two miles of a large wind turbine development at San Gorgino Pass were disturbed by the noise (Pasquatti and Butler 1987). Other concerns that have been raised but seem minimal are health risks (see Clarke 1991: 751), electromagnetic interference, and bird kills. Electromagnetic interference may occur with some aircraft navigation systems within 1 to 5 kilometers, while a booster station can counter radio and television interference (OECD 1988). At Altamont Pass, California, bird strikes have been recorded, but monitoring at a test site in the United Kingdom led the Royal Society for the Protection of Birds (RSPB) to conclude there was no impact on any birdlife (Clarke 1991). Claims that large land areas will be employed have ignored the potential for multiple land use. For example, in Velling Maersk, Denmark, tillage is allowed up to the tower base so that only 3.2 percent of the land is used by the wind plant, and in Altamont Pass no more than 5 percent of leased land is removed from grazing (Gipe 1991: 764). In addition, by reducing wind speeds soil erosion can be reduced in some areas.

Ocean Energy Systems

There are four ocean energy systems: On- and off-shore wave, ocean thermal electrical conversion (OTEC), and tidal barrages.

On-shore and Off-shore Wave Energy

The potential for the extraction of wave energy is considerable and predictable. Andrew Young (1993) has estimated that in-shore wave power at three Scottish islands could supply 35 percent of Scotland's current demand. The potential for on-shore energy can be enhanced by natural or man-made gullies and there are operational stations in Scotland (100 KW) and Norway. Off-shore stations have been tried using several types of technology—buoys, Salter's ducks, and rafts. The U.K. government funded research into a 2 gigawatt (GW) off-shore station during the 1970s and 1980s but withdrew support as economic feasibility drew near. Without practical experience, environmental impacts are highly speculative but seem minimal. The visual impacts are small as on-shore facilities are sited in gullies, while off-shore facilities are usually far from any population centers. The removal of energy in large quantities from marine ecosystems will have some impacts as shorelines have high-energy input-output ecologies. Silt could build up along coastlines, changing habitats with uncertain effects on aquatic life. Hydraulic fluid could leak from off-shore units. Health and safety risks may occur during maintenance of off-shore facilities. Potential benefits include the provision of habitat for fish and, via a dampening of wave power, reduced wear and tear on coastal structures and facilities, such as coastal defenses.

OTEC

OTEC requires a temperature gradient of at least 20°C to get sufficient energy—for example, the gradient between the hot surface water (27°C) of the tropical seas and the cold bottom water (2°C) 1,000 meters below (Odum 1988: 86). A 50 KW demonstration project is currently running in Hawaii, but without a comprehensive environmental impact analysis. The impacts will be dependent upon site characteristics, the scale of the station, and the energy extraction technique (open or closed systems). In open systems cold nutrient rinse water is released back into the sea, changing water temperature and salinity, which can alter circulation patterns and create cold water sinks. This could affect plankton and thus fish and aquatic life. In addition, coral reefs might be damaged as they are sensitive to thermal and nutrient pollution. Closed systems try to mitigate such impacts by preventing the rerelease of rinse water. Pollution emissions from OTEC could arise owing to the discharge of working fluids and bioaids, and the potential release of CO_2 from deep water sites. Other concerns include the production, use, and decommissioning of the bioaids and their accidental release. Beneficial by-products of OTEC are pure water and nutrients. In Hawaii the generation station has sold nutrient-rich waters to farmers.

Tidal Barrages

Tidal power harnesses the gravitational pull of the moon and sun using a barrage across an estuary to extract the power release when water passes through a vertical distance (the "head"). The turn of each tide generates electricity via the use of turbines, providing a highly predictable amount of energy. The technology is well-developed—a 240 MW station has been operating for 20 years at La Rance, France. Such stations totally alter the estuary and the overall ecosystem affects, while mixed, tend to be negative. The water table is liable to rise as a result of holding tides longer, although this can contrast with a decrease in flooding. As the velocity of tidal currents is reduced, the water's power to erode and transport sediments changes. This causes sediments (which largely govern estuarine ecology) on the on-shore side to "freeze," where they would normally be mobile, and decreases turbidity. This can provide a more stable environment for organisms living in muddy deposits, which in turn leads to higher invertebrate populations benefiting wading birds. Meanwhile, on the off-shore side, erosion of sedimentary banks will destroy habitats irreversibly (a problem that prevented a barrage across the Severn, in England). Potentially there could be a buildup of pollutants leading to toxicity and eutrophication, although this would be dependent upon chemical and nutrient inputs to the site. One unavoidable change is decreasing salinity upstream causing the domination of fresh water species, while the brackish water zone is impoverished and moves downstream. The reduced salinity will affect breeding zones for crustacea and shellfish with resulting economic impacts on fishermen. Where an estuary is a major fish run or on the migratory path of birds, impacts can be international.

Hydroelectric Dams

Hydropower extracts the ambient flow of solar power expressed as the evaporation of water and its release on higher ground. Dams vary widely in size, affecting the environmental impacts—for example, the 10,000 MW La Grande River development at James Bay in Canada versus 100 KW at Lyemouth Gorge, U.K. Mega projects threaten widespread impacts—for example, proposed dams in the Himalayas of Nepal (Chisapani Gorge) would lower sedimentary yields and runoff for the whole subcontinent, besides making 70,000 people homeless (*The Independent* 1991).

The environmental damages are various. The dam creates a reservoir behind which the land (often fertile valley bottoms) is inundated with water, precluding it from other uses. The standing water in the reservoir causes sedimentation, while clearer water leaves the dam, reducing oil replenishment and increasing erosion downstream. Thermal stratification, especially in deep reservoirs, can lead to the formation of ammonia and hydrogen sulfide, which are toxic to marine life. Water passing through the turbine will be heated and on release can lead to a reduction in insect life (e.g., the mayfly), which is a building block of ecosystem structure. The creation of large reservoirs will also affect migratory patterns of larger mammals, such as reindeer in Canada. The change from riverine to lacustrine (river to lake) environment changes water flow, nutrient content, temperature, oxygen content, and sedimentation. As a result spawning fish like salmon may fail to pass through larger lakes, thereby dying or turning back. Fish migration will be restricted by the creation of the dam requiring fish ladders where feasible. Other species may be harder to protect, such as the snail darter, a protected bird, threatened by Telic Dam in Tennessee (OECD 1988: 78). Health and safety concerns arise because dams often create favorable conditions for disease-carrying agents—an increased frequency of malaria and bilharzia at the Selingua Dam in Mali (Sims 1991). The potential failure of large dams poses the risk of disastrous flooding and there can be a temporary increase in seismic activity because of the construction of large reservoirs like the one at La Grande.

On the beneficial side, a well-constructed and implemented dam can lead to better water management, as shown by the Danube in Austria. The water body created by a dam does provide recreational opportunities and can be an attraction for tourists. Effects on the microclimate near the dam can also be beneficial. Large water bodies ameliorate temperatures and decrease convection-reducing cloud cover, thus benefiting agriculture by preventing freezing (Sims 1991: 779).

Biomass

The discussion of biomass is complicated by the wide range of production choices that can be made to achieve the same energy output. In general terms biomass can be broken down into two categories: energy plantations, and cleanup biomass. The latter category can be further split into biomass from farming residues, and waste from industrial and noncommercial processes. The energy product from biomass can be provided in several different forms: electricity, liquid fuel, or gas.

Energy Plantations

The impact of a large switch into biomass depends upon the previous land use and the type of plantation, such as monoculture conifer plantations, short rotation coppice, or natural woodland. Where the land was under intensive agriculture a reduction in fertilizer use can be expected (Rowan 1991: 80), as well as improvements in soil structure, nutrient retention, and nitrate leaching. However, the routine application of chemicals from the air to protect monocultures seriously affects insect life. Afforestation of some soil types can also be negative (by drying out peat bogs) while in other areas it can be used for water management (by preventing floods). If the use prior to biomass production was grassland, bird habitat may be reduced. Monoculture conifer plantations reduce biodiversity, although this may be ameliorated by careful siting and interspersing other tree species. Generally, the greater the age structure and species diversity the richer the habitat. Monocultures provide only canopy feeders and often result in irreversible loss of species that were previously present (Moss 1978).

The choice of trees and felling methods are important determinants of environmental impacts. Conifers can acidify soils and mobilize heavy metals, such as aluminum, which kill fish and cause irreversible damage to water courses. During planting and felling the use of large machines results in soil compaction and erosion. Clear felling exacerbates this situation by exposing mineral soils to leaching and extremes of climate, reducing the level of organic matter under short rotation coppice and monoculture plantations. When clear felling occurs there will be an obvious visual impact as the land is scarred. Selective felling (silviculture) can avoid these impacts.

End-use decisions will also determine the extent of social costs. Drying wood can greatly increase fuel efficiency, but bark decomposition while drying can allow tannic acid to leach into water courses. Unregulated wood combustion causes more air pollution by weight per thermal unit than oil and coal (IEA 1989: 1298). Air pollution from domestic wood burning can be avoided by regulating stove and fuel types. A major advantage is that net CO_2 release is zero over the rotation of a plantation. Thermal pollution can be avoided by using low-grade heat for community water heating as in Denmark. Solid waste, low in toxins, can be used as a fertilizer.

Clean-up Biomass

Farming residues can be classified as waste from current activities that are normally dumped. In the United Kingdom there is a surplus of 5 to 7 million tons of straw and 1,400,000 tons of poultry waste per year. Denmark has 54 straw-fired district heating systems of 3–5 MW (Department of Energy 1991). The United Kingdom has a 30 MW station using 25,000 tons of straw annually and two projects using straw and poultry litter. There are significant environmental advantages in terms of reducing pollution associated with waste disposal (e.g., nitrate leaching from manure). The levels of NO_x and SO_x are small fractions of those from coal-fired stations. The emissions are low in particulates and have a quarter of the CO_2 and equivalent greenhouse gases of coal-fired plants. The main by-product is nitrogen-free ash, which is an environmentally friendly fertilizer (Department of Energy 1993: 10–12). Human waste products from hospitals, industry, and sewage stations can also be used for the generation of energy. There is a 975 KW sewage station at Finham, U.K. The economic incentive is provided by avoiding disposal costs (in London municipal waste disposal costs £10 per ton). However, if the biomass waste is contaminated, emissions after combustion can contain high levels of toxic substances, including heavy metals and dioxins (Department of Energy 1993: 6).

Geothermal Energy

Geothermal energy is extracted from the accessible heat in the outer 15 kilometers of the Earth's crust. Three broad categories are hydrothermal, reservoirs of steam or water; geopressurized, reservoirs of brine; and hot dry rock, often too deep for tapping but viable where molten rock has broken through the Earth's crust. At the end of 1990 installed geothermal capacity worldwide was 6,071 MW from 330 individual turbines with 47 percent in the United States (DiPippo 1991: 799). In the United States the potential is for some 25,000 MW of (electrical) energy, but this will last for only 40 years because the heat reservoirs will become exhausted.

Air pollution will occur in relatively small quantities. Carbon dioxide is always the principal gas released but the quantities are only 10 percent of those from oil for an equivalent amount of energy. Other gases include hydrogen sulfide, H_2S, a toxic foul-smelling gas. However, most geothermal areas are already burdened by such gases and therefore nearby vegetation should already be resistant. Although wastes can contain a whole cocktail of chemicals, dependent upon rock composition, water pollution is minimized by reinjection into the ground, which is common practice. Reinjection can cost $10–20 per KW with a corresponding decrease in output of 10–20 percent; resulting in a $85–$90 per KW loss in annual revenue on a 50 MW station. When venting steam from the plant, noise can reach 114 decibels at a range of 8 meters (comparable to a jet plane at 120–130 decibels). Subsidence and seismic activity can occur. At Wairakei, New Zealand, the ground level has dropped 7.5 meters in some places and continues at 0.4 meters per year. While subsidence is localized it can fracture pipelines and requires monitoring.

ALTERNATIVE ENERGY SOURCES VERSUS FOSSIL FUELS

In order to draw a general picture from the evidence presented so far we can consider only those environmental impacts that seem most important to the substitution debate. That is, we wish to discern the relative merits of alternative energy sources from the way in which they affect the environment. More specifically we consider the following impacts: land use, physical changes, air pollution, aesthetics, and health and safety.

Land Use

Generally, renewable energy sources appear to cover a greater land area than fossil fuels. Photovoltaics require 66,000 m^2/MW compared to 40,000 m^2/MW for coal derived from a strip mine over 30 years (DiPippo 1991). Wind power uses a larger area but allows continued use of 95 percent or more of the land in other activities (Gipe 1991: 764). However, over their life-cycle fossil fuels can use large areas—oil requires land for wells, drilling, refining, storage, terminals, generating plants, and transportation systems. Certainly passive solar will release land from current energy production, thus providing net gains. Biomass can also be designed for multiple use and dams create recreational opportunities. The relative merits of opportunities lost and gained is central to alternative energy in contrast to fossil fuels, where land use is exclusive.

Physical Changes

In the case of fossil fuels, impacts can be numerous and widespread: oil spills at sea, strip mining, slag heaps, dead trees due to acid rain, and so on. In the case of renewable energy sources there are often profound and irreversible physical changes, but these are normally limited spatially. Damming a river valley produces irreversible change throughout the water course, causing revised flows, thermal pollution, clear water poison, and lower oxygen content. Biomass also totally alters the environment but can provide benefits such as reduced soil erosion, lower nitrates in water courses, and increased biodiversity. The net outcome of such a development is site specific, but unique areas can be destroyed. Wind, solar, and geothermal appear the most benign physically. The only wider spatial effects of alternative energy sources are if the area has a unique ecology (endangered species) or if the areas are particularly sensitive (such as estuaries where migrating birds feed), in which case there can be international costs.

Air Pollution

The large-scale release of chemicals associated with fossil fuels (previously stored within the biosphere) damages terrestrial and aquatic ecosystems at local, regional, and global scales. Regional impacts include acidification of water and soils and the release of aluminum to water courses, which leads to tree damage, fish deaths, and reduced biodiversity. As a direct cost, the estimates lie in the range of 0.17–4.5 pence/KWh, without the costs of health and global warming, estimated at a further 2–4 p/KWh (Twidell and Brice 1992). SO_x and NO_x can be removed from smokestacks, but this process produces gypsum salts as solid waste. Disposal of these wastes can result in leaching, causing significant local or regional acidification. Lime used in some control systems is mined, which will create its own environmental costs.

Renewable energy sources would reduce air pollution compared to fossil fuels, although biomass can create significant emissions. Energy plantation biomass has zero net CO_2 emissions over a complete rotation period and the benefit of storing more free CO_2 within the cycle as use increases, while controlled combustion releases NO_x in smaller quantities than fossil fuels. Energy from organic waste appears to reduce pollution compared to other disposal methods. The trade-off in terms of emissions is dependent on fuel type and combustion method, but is similar to energy crops and definitely less than fossil fuels. Incinerating waste probably has negative impacts in the long run through discouraging recycling, while creating toxic emissions. Geothermal has relatively low CO_2 emissions, so there are temporal benefits and other emissions are localized. Photovoltaics create some risk of emissions during the production of solar panels.

Aesthetics

Visual intrusion is a matter of the perception of people toward a specific structure. This issue has been raised most often with regard to wind power, which tends to be spread out, with structures standing up to 50 meters high. However, in a California study a "Not In My Backyard" (NIMBY) index was created on the basis of visual intrusion and acceptability. The findings show wind was rated as more acceptable than either biomass or fossil fuels, with the latter being most unacceptable of the three (Clarke 1991). As far as other renewable energy sources are concerned, visual intrusion is usually limited. While the change can be drastic with the construction of a dam, the scale of the effect is a function of the size of the development. The extent to which renewable energies can be expected to impact visually is heavily site dependent. Thus, if the demand for energy from renewable sources grows we can expect more sensitive sites to be employed. The push for larger dams or wind generators on exposed sites in open moorland and national parks will result in a greater impact, as has occurred with the drive to find fossil fuels in such areas. The movement to small-scale local generation of electricity, which some renewables offer, would remove the need for national grid lines that cause a major visual intrusion, such as in the United Kingdom.

Health and Safety

Risks to workers in oil fields and coal mines are often internalized through higher wages and compensation from accidents such as Piper Alpha. Therefore we might expect that any risks resulting from the production of renewable energy sources—such as exotic materials involved in the production of photovoltaics—would be treated similarly. This excludes effects borne by society in general. In the case of fossil fuels these include the incidents of respiratory disease, cancer, asthma, and ozone smogs. The costs are borne either by the individual or the state through medical bills and lost production. As noted above, biomass combustion will release similar gases to fossil fuels but with controlled combustion in small net quantities. However, other renewable energy sources are less prone to cause externalities of this sort. Thus, one of the major benefits of renewable energy sources is in terms of human health.

CONCLUSIONS

It terms of generating costs, renewable energy is generally more expensive than fossil fuels. Including the social costs of fossil fuels in their price would dramatically change this picture (Jackson 1992). Olar Hohmeyer (1990) has calculated the social costs of generation for the Federal Republic of Germany and shows how wind power has positive benefits over conventional sources. Research and development expenditures on alternative energy sources have been minuscule relative to nuclear power, where the returns have been poor. The implication is that research in the area of renewable energy generation would seem to offer great potential returns for society. However, the costs associated with alternative energy sources will increase and benefits will decrease with greater substitution for fossil fuels. That is, the more valuable ecological areas dependent upon particular energy flows will be disrupted or destroyed. The remaining natural areas will therefore become more highly valued. As emissions from fossil fuels decline, the social costs per KWh will fall so that renewable energy prevents fewer less important externalities.

Air pollution from fossil fuel combustion is one of its most serious environmental impacts. Emissions disperse widely, degrading the environment indirectly via chemical changes, such as acidification which kills trees and fish. Cause-effect relationships are hard to discern because damages are separated from the emitter (e.g., CO_2 released 100 years ago contributing to global warming now). At the same time fossil fuels are a finite resource so that their depletion can reduce the opportunities and capabilities of future generations.

The replacement of fossil fuels by renewable energy sources creates a different set of impacts. The social costs of renewable energy sources tend to occur at a specific site and are normally highly visible. Thus the argument over fossil fuels versus renewable energy sources tends to be an argument over global versus local impacts on the environment. Social benefits of renewable energy can include decreased pollution, maintenance of depleted fossil fuel reserves, flood control, greater national security, higher employment, and reduced investment in overcapacity. Over their life-cycle, from extraction to disposal and end use, renewable energy sources have the potential to give significant benefits over current fossil fuel use. However, the specific sites involved in the development of renewable energy sources is a key to their social cost.

In summary, we can generalize that fossil fuels tend to have dispersed (temporal and spatial) chemical impacts, while renewable energy sources tend to have more local physical ones. The principal advantage of renewable energy is the lower level of environmental impact. However, renewable energy sources do create their own set of externalities that need to be acknowledged in order to avoid the type of backlash of public opinion nuclear power has created. The impact of renewables can be expected to increase with their scale of use, such as exotics in photovoltaics, sensitive sites for wind and wave energy, fertilizer use in energy plantations. The choice between fossil fuels and renewable energy appears to turn on the decision of whether to accept definite changes today in local ecosystems or uncertain changes tomorrow in regional and global systems.

REFERENCES

Acid News. December 5, 1992.

Charters, William W. S. "Solar Energy Current Status and Future Prospects." *Energy Policy* 19(8) (October, 1991): 738–741.

Ciborowski, Peter. "Sources, Sinks, Trends and Opportunities." In Dean E. Abrahamson (ed.), *The Challenge of Global Warming.* Washington, DC: Island Press, 1989.

Clarke, Alexi. "Wind Energy: Progress and Potential." *Energy Policy* 19(8) (October 1991): 742–755.

Dawber, Keith. "Harnessing the Wind in Otago (and in the rest of the world)." *The Otago Graduate*, Otago University, New Zealand, 1992, pp. 12–13.

Department of Energy, United Kingdom. "Poultry Power: An Offbeat Source of Energy." *Review Issue* 20 (March 1993): 10–12.

———. *Energy Trends.* London: Department of Energy, 1992.

———. "What Next for Straw?" *Review Issue* 17 (Autumn, 1991): 18–20.

DiPippo, Ronald. "Geothermal Energy, Electrical and Environmental Impact." *Energy Policy* 19(8) (October, 1991): 798–807.

Flood, N. *Energy Without End.* Washington, DC: Friends of the Earth, 1991.

Gipe, Paul. "Wind Energy Comes of Age: California and Denmark." *Energy Policy* 19 (8) (October, 1991): 756–767.

Hohmeyer, Olav. "Social Costs of Electricity Generation: Wind and Photovoltaic versus Fossil and Nuclear." *Contemporary Policy Issues* 8 (July 1990): 1–29.

IEA. *Energy and the Environment: Policy Overview.* Paris: OECD, 1989.

Independent, The. "Power of the Himalayas." December 1, 1991, p. 64.

Jackson, Tim. "Renewable Energy." *Energy Policy*, September 1992, pp. 861–888.

Moss, D. "Songbird Populations in Forest Plantations." *Quarterly Journal of Forestry*, 72 (1978): 288–292.

Odum, Howard T. *Energy, Environment and Public Policy: A Guide to the Analysis of Systems.* UNEP Regional Seas Reports and Studies No. 95, 1988.

OECD. *The Compass Project: Environmental Impacts of Renewable Energy.* Paris: OECD, 1988.

Pasquatti, Martin and E. Butler. "Public Reaction to Wind Development in California." *International Journal of Ambient Energy* 8(2) (August 1987).

Routley, R. and V. Routley. "Nuclear Energy and Obligations to the Future." In E. Partridge (ed.), *Responsibilities to Future Generations.* New York: Prometheus Books, 1980.

Rowan, Leslie. "An Analysis of the Potential of Wood for Energy in the U.K." B. S. dissertation, University of Stirling, Scotland, 1991.

Sims, Geoffery P. "Hydroelectric Energy." *Energy Policy* 19(8) (October 1991): 776–786.

Spash, Clive. L. "Double CO_2 and Beyond." *Ecological Economics*, forthcoming, 1994.

Spash, Clive L. and Nick Hanley. "Cost-Benefit Analysis and the Greenhouse Effect." Economics Department Working Paper, University of Stirling, U.K., 1993.

Thurlaw, G. (ed.). *Technological Responses to the Greenhouse Effect*. Watt Committee Report. Ser. No. 23, 1990.

Twidell, John and Robert Brice. "Strategies for Implementing Renewable Energy: Lessons from Europe." *Energy Policy* (May 1992).

Young, Andrew. "Inshore Wave Power for Electricity Generation in Island Communities." Unpublished manuscript, Economics Department, University of Stirling, 1993, p. 142.

Chapter 16

Global Oil Spills, the Environment, and Oil Pollution Legislation in the United States

Kusum W. Ketkar

On March 12, 1990, the *Exxon Valdez*, an oil tanker, spilled 11 million gallons of crude oil in the pristine waters of Prince William Sound, Alaska (Grumbles 1990). In reaction to the incident and public outcry, the U.S. Congress and the Bush administration finally passed, with overwhelming majority, the Oil Pollution Act (OPA).

The distinguishing characteristics of OPA 90 are that it requires all entities engaged in the production, storage, transportation, and distribution of petroleum and petroleum products to undertake preventive and safety measures to reduce the probability of accidental oil spills, as well as improve their preparedness to contain accidental spills in U.S. waters. It also imposes stiffer financial penalties and provides funding for additional navigational aids for high-risk waterways. OPA 90 represents a departure from the past, since traditionally the International Maritime Organization (IMO), a watchdog agency, has issued regulations to control the discharge of pollutants and waste, including ballast water, by the maritime industry into world's oceans. Even though the U.S. government has unilaterally issued regulations under OPA 90, the impact of these regulations is felt worldwide, due to the global nature of the oil and maritime industries. Furthermore, approximately 50 percent of the current U.S. demand for petroleum and petroleum products is met by imports. These imports represent more than 30 percent of the world's crude oil and products that are transported by sea annually worldwide. Most of these products are shipped to various U.S. ports in foreign-flagged tank ships (National Research Council 1991).

The objective of this chapter is to critically evaluate the cost-effectiveness of OPA 90 as a deterrent to accidental oil spills in U.S. waters, and to develop a case for market-based incentives designed to reduce the probability of accidental spills.

OIL SPILLS AND MARINE RESOURCES

The IMO estimates that worldwide accidental input of hydrocarbons by tankers into the marine environment is only about 12.1 percent of the total input, whereas input of hydrocarbons on account of municipal and industrial wastes and street runoffs contribute three times as much. Furthermore, tankers discharged more than twice the hydrocarbons into the world marine environment during operations than accidental spills did in 1990 (U.S. Coast Guard 1990). Out of 0.57 million tons of oil that entered the marine environment as a result of accidental and operational losses, only 0.11 million tons, or 20 percent, were due to accidental spills, while 0.25 million tons were bilge and fuel oil (National Research Council 1991). Lloyd's Register (1990) reported that, overall, accidental spills remain random occurrences, and that less than 6 percent of worldwide marine accidents result in spills. It also reports that since the mid-1970s there have been far fewer spills in U.S. waters compared to the rest of the world. Total number of reported oil spills by tank ships and tank barges into U.S. waters fell from an annual average of approximately 1,640 spills in the 1970s to 868 in the 1980s, a decrease of 47 percent. It is the smaller spills, those of less than 10,000 gallons, however, that have fallen substantially, not the medium and large spills. The average number of medium and large spills did fall from an annual average of 21 in the 1970s to 17 in the 1980s. The average input into the U.S. marine environment by tank vessels carrying oil as cargo rose marginally by 9 percent from an average spill of 0.017 million tons in the 1970s to 0.019 million tons in the 1980s. From 1980 to 1984, tank vessels spilled an average of 0.0136 million tons of oil, while from 1985 to 1990 the average spill size almost doubled, reaching 0.0215 million tons (U.S. Coast Guard 1973–1990). This observed increase in the volume of accidental oil spills was accompanied by a steady increase in the import of crude oil and petroleum products and its movements in U.S. waters. Imports of oil and products rose by 38 percent from 286 million tons in 1985 to 395 million tons by 1990, but oil movements in U.S. coastal waters rose by only 7 percent, since domestic production has failed to keep up with the domestic demand for petroleum products. By the end of the decade, imports contributed over 45 percent of domestic consumption of petroleum products compared to 33 percent in 1984. The origin of these imports also became more diversified; however, the Middle East remained the most important exporter of oil to the United States. The United States imported 395 million tons of petroleum and petroleum products in 1990, of which 70 percent came from the Middle East, the North Sea, Africa, or Latin America. This increase in imports has resulted in an increase in tanker traffic, which, consequently, has greatly heightened the potential risk of large accidental oil spills in U.S. coastal waters. One reason is that over 80 percent of the crude oil from the Middle East, Far East, and North Sea is brought to the United States in supertankers that range in capacity from 90 to over 300,000 deadweight (DWT) tons. A second reason is that shallow coastal waters along the eastern seaboard and along the Gulf Coast necessitate the lightering of supertanker cargo onto smaller vessels in open waters. Lightering activity increases the risk of oil spills because of the resultant increased congestion during both lightering in open waters and unloading operations at the dock. For instance, it is the medium-sized tankers, those between 10,000 and 50,000 gross ton capacity, that spilled 50 percent of the oil, while the remaining 50 percent was spilled by large tankers. However, large tankers were responsible for just 2 percent of all the oil spills during the 1980s.

According to S. A. Gerlach (1975) over 75 percent of tanker accidents worldwide are caused by human error. Analysis of pollution incidents from the Marine Safety Information Service data files of the Coast Guard shows that human error is responsible for about 50 to 60 percent of tanker casualties in U.S. waters. Furthermore, the total volume of oil spilled due to human error is larger than that spilled from any other cause, such as collisions, groundings, or fires and explosions. The second most frequent cause of oil spills in U.S. waters is groundings. Globally, collisions and groundings occur with almost the same frequency. Marine casualties caused by collisions and groundings of tank vessels input approximately 30 percent of the total oil into the world marine environment. In the United States, 45 percent of the total oil input from marine casualties is a result of groundings and only 25 percent is due to collisions. Over 60 percent of the total oil is spilled in shallow water bodies like bays and harbors. Thus, tank vessels transiting water bodies like New York Harbor and the Gulf Coast face higher risk of casualties and oil pollution because of heavy traffic and shallow-water ports.

ENVIRONMENTAL IMPACT OF OIL SPILLS

When an oil pollution incident occurs during transit, a large volume of oil is likely to be spilled in a short period of time. During cargo transfer operations, however, vessels may discharge small quantities of oil for such reasons as tank overflow. The environmental impact of an oil spill depends on a number of factors, including the dosage of oil and duration of exposure, the type of oil and the area involved (coastal, estuarine, or open water), the water temperature, the wind speed, the season, the sensitivity and type of ecosystem, and the history of exposure to oil and other pollutants. And it is also known that between one-third and two-thirds of the oil spilled evaporates in a short period of time. The soluble components of the remaining oil degrade in water, the nonsoluble components tend to form "mousse" or tar balls, while a residual fraction of crude oil, in particular, settles into the sediment at the bottom of the ocean floor. For example, refined products such as gasoline or fuel oil have a greater concentration of toxic substances than does crude oil, but they evaporate more quickly. The visual impact of a refined product spill is of shorter duration than that of crude oil. Refined products have less likelihood of shoreline impact but they are likely to have greater ecological impact because of their toxicity. The Congressional Research Services (Mielke 1990) examined scientific investigations that followed six major spills of the 1970s and early 1980s to determine the short- and long-term impacts of these spills—*Amoco Cadiz*, a Liberian-registered tanker spill off the coast of France; *Argo Merchant*, a Liberian-registered tanker spill of No. 6 residual fuel on the Nantucket Shoals off Massachusetts; blowout at Platform A, Santa Barbara Channel; blowout at Ixtoc I exploratory well in the Bay of Mexico; collision between *Burmah Agate*, a Liberian-registered tanker, and *Mimosa*, a Liberian freighter, resulting in a spill of 250,000 barrels of crude oil off the coast of Texas; and *Alvenus*, a British-registered tanker spill of crude oil in Calcasieu River Channel entrance in Louisiana. The Congressional Research Service report concluded that "each event [spill] received extensive media coverage at the time. In fact, the environmental damage and socio-economic consequences were relatively modest, and of relatively short duration." The ecological impact of oil trapped in intertidal and subtidal zones, estuarine and fresh water communities is heaviest, and the effects appear to last from a few months up to 20 years. These areas are biologically important as they support juvenile fish, vegetation, sea otters, sea mammals, and other lower species, which are a principal source of food for fish (Mielke 1990). On January 12, 1993, tanker *Braer* ran aground off the coast of England near the Shetland Islands and spewed 25 million gallons of crude into the sea—twice as much as the *Exxon Valdez*. One month after the spill, however, only 1,549 birds were found dead, compared with 36,000 in Alaska after the *Exxon Valdez* spill, and the shoreline had been washed by wind and waves (Reuters 1993). During the Gulf War in 1991, 250 million gallons of oil were spilled into the Persian Gulf. After visiting the affected area, the Coast Guard found minimal damage to the coastline. However, the long-term biological and ecological impacts of this spill are not as yet known (Farmanfarmaian 1991). In 1985 the National Research Council also concluded that the most damaging effects of petroleum are the oiling and tarring of beaches, the endangering of sea bird species, and the modification of benthic communities along polluted coastline. The scientific evidence so far has failed to confirm that hydrocarbons are dangerous to either the food chain or human health (National Research Council 1985). The *Exxon Valdez* Oil Spill Trustee Council report also concluded after a three-year study that Prince William Sound has recovered and that the ecosystem recovered more quickly on uncleaned beaches than those that were cleaned (*New York Times* 1992). There seems to be a general consensus among marine biologists that pressurized, hot water washing of the shoreline did more damage to the marine life and pushed more oil into the sediment. Exxon spent $2.5 billion to clean up the spilled oil. In addition, the company also agreed in October 1991 to settle court cases resulting from the spill by paying $900 million over 11 years to restore Prince William Sound, $100 million in restitution—half to the State of Alaska and half to the federal government—and a $25 million fine (Holloway 1991). So far, most of the money out of the Trust Fund has been spent on assessment studies and on payments to lawyers, government, and interest groups and not on the restoration of damaged natural resources.

ECONOMIC IMPACT OF OPA 90 ON THE OIL AND MARITIME INDUSTRIES

As mentioned earlier, 11 million gallons of crude oil spill in Prince William Sound gave OPA 90 to the U.S. public. The basic thrust of OPA 90 is based on "the polluter pays" principle. This law provides for the cleanup of spills and compensation for public and private damages. It requires new tank ships and barges operating in U.S. waters to be constructed with double hulls and existing single-hull vessels to be phased out by the year 2015. It also strengthens manning standards, crew-licensing procedures, vessel design requirements, and navigation systems. OPA 90 also requires the Coast Guard to improve the quality of its advisory services for tankers, dry cargo, and other vessels in U.S. waters by installing and operating Vessel Traffic Service (VTS) and additional navigational aids at congested ports. The Coast Guard must also improve its spill response capabilities by stationing and maintaining specialized equipment at 19 different sites along the U.S. coastline. Tank vessels carrying oil as cargo are also required to develop spill response plans. OPA 90 established an oil spill cleanup trust fund of up to $1 billion. This fund is to be financed by a 5-cent per barrel fee on domestic and imported oil. The act also places liability for oil removal cost and damages, including those damages to natural resources, on the responsible party. Finally, it amends the Clean Water Act to strengthen civil and criminal enforcement provisions. The act left open the possibility for state governments to pass stiffer laws that override OPA 90 authority. Most of the coastal states have passed Oil Spill Liability Laws that impose no upper limit on the liability of oil transporters with respect to cleanup costs and damages to natural resources and third parties (Meade and LaPointe 1983).

OPA 90 proposes various manning initiatives that aim at ensuring that vessels' crews are well qualified (e.g., by strengthening licensing requirements for merchant marines), alert (by mandating maximum hours of work within a specified period or testing for alcohol or drug abuse), and sufficient to handle responsibilities (by requiring two officers on the bridge during transits of critical waters). The compliance cost of these measures would be small while effectiveness in reducing casualties and oil pollution could be considerable. However, it would be difficult to enforce proper alertness and staffing aboard a vessel away from the shoreline and even more difficult to impose licensing and testing for alcohol and drug abuse requirements on foreign flagships, outside U.S. jurisdiction.

Operational measures like VTS, pilotage requirements, communications equipment, tug escort requirements, or transmitting requirements in certain waters in the dark or under severe weather are aimed at reducing the likelihood of casualties because of human error, equipment failure, or natural disasters. These measures should help reduce casualties due to lack of familiarity with local waters and weather conditions.

Construction requirements are aimed at reducing the outflow of oil in the event that a tanker's hull is ruptured because of a collision or grounding casualty. The United States can impose changes in the design of tank ships irrespective of their country of registry and can expect compliance from vessel operators engaged in oil trade in the U.S. market. However, compliance costs of double hull requirement will be high because this measure forces the maritime industry to replace those vessels trading in U.S. waters with new tank vessels by 2015 and in the interim modify existing tank vessels to reduce the probability of oil outflow in the event of a casualty.

Finally, improvement in vessel response capability is expected to reduce environmental damage following an accidental discharge. Vessel operators are required to provide for quick containment and recovery of the oil from the marine or coastal environment. Compliance would require tank vessels—U.S. and for-eign-flagged—and shore facilities to maintain detailed oil spill response plans and ensure adequate shore-based spill response equipment capabilities. The compliance costs of these requirements will be large.

The relative economic impact of OPA 90 is expected to be heavier on the international industry compared to the domestic industry. The U.S. registered coastal tanker and barge industries are small. The U.S. tanker fleet consists of only 147 tankers with total cargo capacity of 13 million tons, while the tank barge industry operates 3,450 barges with cargo capacity of 11 million tons. Under the provisions of the Jones Act, only U.S.-owned and -operated vessels can transport domestically produced cargo in the U.S. coastal and inland waters. The domestic tanker and barge fleet, therefore, moves Alaskan crude to refineries and tank barges distribute products to coastal communities. The international tanker fleet, on the other hand, consists of over 2,900 tankers. In 1990 over 1,400 different tankers out of the international fleet made port calls to deliver crude oil and refined products to the United States. It is also observed that while both international and coastwise vessels accounted for about 40 percent of the number of incidents (60 percent of the incidents were in inland waters), international tankers were responsible for about 80 percent of total spill volume in U.S. waters from 1972 to 1990 (Volpe National Transportation System Center 1992). Analysis of marine casualties and oil pollution data by tanker registry and age suggest that older and foreign tankers spill more oil in U.S. waters than domestic tankers. Meade and LaPointe (1983) found that Liberian registries experienced marine casualties three times as often as those of Italian and Japanese tank vessels, and that age and registry have significant influence on tanker casualties. It is to be noted, however, that among the foreign registries, Liberian tankers most frequently call on U.S.-based oil and shipping companies. Thus, on the surface it may seem that foreign flag tankers spill more oil in U.S. waters, but in reality it is the U.S.-owned, but Liberian-registered, tankers that are to be held responsible for the spills (Volpe National Transportation Systems Center 1992).

The international tanker industry is owned and operated by major oil companies like Shell, Exxon, and Chevron; independent oil companies; independent tanker operators; and government-owned companies. Major oil companies own and operate 17 percent of the international tanker fleet and independents operate 65 percent. The U.S. international tanker fleet is also small, controlling only 4 percent of the world's gross tanker tonnage. High crew costs, stringent regulations, and high liability limits seem to have driven the U.S.-based major oil companies like Chevron, Texaco, Mobil, Esso, as well as independent tanker operators like Stoltz and others to register their tankers in foreign countries like Liberia, Panama, and the Bahamas and to register each tanker as an independent entity. The Coast Guard estimates that over 40 percent of the U.S.-controlled tanker fleet is under foreign registry.

The unilateral issue of regulations by the U.S. Congress has introduced artificial distortions in the world oil trades. It has given rise to a two-tier market: the United States and the rest of the world. The immediate effect of OPA 90 has been to shift younger, better maintained tankers to the U.S. waters at the cost of other markets. OPA 90's impact on the markets extends from differentials in freight rates, insurance premiums, liability limits and financial certification, tanker design and construction, crew size and its qualifications, to spill response equipment and strategy. It is difficult to accurately quantify long-term financial impact of OPA 90 on the oil and the international tanker industry, since it would greatly depend upon the degree to which the industry chooses to separate the two markets. The compliance costs would be minimal if the industry chooses to fully dedicate the tanker fleet to the United States. These costs will be maximum if the current triangular trading pattern is maintained. For instance, if the international tanker fleet is fully dedicated to the United States, then the *additional* construction cost (above the cost of single-hull tankers) of the 995 double-hull tankers needed to meet the U.S. demand for crude and products by 2015 is estimated to be $11 billion at 1991 prices. The *additional* construction cost of the nondedicated double-hull tanker fleet is estimated to be $35 billion at 1991 prices. The additional cost of building a dedicated fleet of 346 double-hull coastal tankers and barges in U.S. shipyards will be substantially higher because of the high labor costs compared to construction costs of Japanese and Korean shipyards. The additional construction cost of the double-hulled coastal fleet is estimated to be $2 billion. The additional cost of construction of inland double-hull tank barges is estimated at $8 million. Because of pressure from coastal communities, the inland tank barge industry has already replaced over 60 percent of its inland single-hull tank barges with double-hull barges.

The transportation of imported oil with a fully dedicated fleet will increase costs by $1.35 billion annually and the cost of coastal movements with a fully dedicated fleet will increase by only $158 million per year. Fully 90 percent of this incremental cost will be borne by the international tanker industry. Transportation costs include voyage cost, insurance premium for hull and machinery, Protection and Indemnity (P&I) clubs, annualized capital cost, repair and maintenance, manning costs, and so on. These cost estimates assume 25 years as useful for an international tanker fleet and 30 years for a coastal fleet. It is further assumed that imports of crude oil and products will more than double, rising from 489 million tons in 1990 to 999 million tons by 2015. The shipments of Alaskan crude are expected to decline, leading to a decrease in demand for coastal tankers from 288 million tons in 1990 to 237 million tons by 2015, a reduction of 18 percent.

Double-hull tankers, however, will be limited in their ability to control outflow of oil in the event of a casualty. These tankers may be effective in controlling oil outflow in the event of low energy collisions and/or groundings but not in the event of either a high energy collision and/or grounding or a fire or explosion. Naval architects have warned that the double-hull tankers may be more susceptible to fires and explosions and may be more difficult to repair if damaged (Temple, Barker, and Sloane 1991). Another costly regulation under OPA 90 is vessel response plans. Implementation of this regulation includes the cost of developing plans, plan maintenance and revision, vessel response plan drills, the cost of shore-based spill response equipment, and Coast Guard costs. Total cost of this regulation is $2.3 billion (in 1991 prices), of which $899 million is to be spent for the preparedness for catastrophic response capability. It should be noted that ability to reach the location of a spill event in a timely fashion depends not only on the availability of spill response equipment and training but also time of day, season, location, weather, waves, and wind speed. And furthermore, given the current state of technology, no more than 20 percent of the spilled oil can be recovered even if the response is timely.

Finally, manyfold increases in liability limits and civil and criminal penalties have led to skyrocketing of insurance premiums for tanker operators engaged in oil trades in U.S. waters. According to industry estimates, this increase in insurance premiums cost the industry upward of $1 billion. The cleanup costs and compensation for damages to natural resources since *Exxon Valdez* has resulted in record losses for the world's largest marine insurer, Lloyd's of London. The cleanup costs and damage awards for oil spills in U.S. waters since *Exxon Valdez* have exceeded by a factor of 10 to 15 over similar spills in the rest of the world.

CONCLUSIONS

Skeptics such as the former assistant secretary of the Department of Interior argue that all oil spills are not reported and even if they are, the volume of oil spilled is underreported. According to Max N. Edwards (1969), "there are no teeth in the prohibition against dumping in certain zones because the reporting of violations is on the honor system. Unfortunately, the pangs of a sea captain's conscience are not adequate deterrent to oil pollution." This statement holds true even today. Probably more oil is spilled during offshore lightering operations than is officially reported. Reporting of large and catastrophic spills of more than 100,000 gallons has improved markedly since the 1960s, but accurate reporting and recording of small and medium spills remain a challenge for the Coast Guard.

Oil spills induced by marine casualties input relatively small volumes of hydrocarbons in U.S. waters, but media coverage of oiled beaches, birds, and sea mammals has raised public sensitivity toward these spills. OPA 90 was Congress's response to environmentalists and the public's concerns regarding the safety of marine environment. New standards imposed by OPA 90 are costly, with limited impact on marine pollution from tanker casualties, and they seem to have ignored more economical measures to combat marine pollution and oil-spill problems. According to the American Chemical Society, the most effective weapon against large oil spills should involve exploring solar energy, bacteria, and mechanical agents like glass beads and not costly equipment. In the words of marine toxicologist Riki Ott, "animals killed in big spills get the attention because they look so awful, but it is the toxic compounds of shipboard waste, when dissolved in sea water, that have truly long term and insidious effects on our marine food chain the world over" (Coughlin 1991).

REFERENCES

Coughlin, William P. "Illegal Disposal of Toxic Wastes from Ships Seen Global Occurrence." *Commerce Journal*, March 5, 1991.

Edwards, Max N. "Oil Pollution and the Law." In Stanley E. Deglar (ed.), *Oil Pollution: Problems and Policies*. Washington, DC: Bureau of National Affairs, 1969.

Farmanfarmaian, Verdi. "Comment on Oil Spill in the Persian Gulf." In *Iran, the Middle East, and the Decade of the 1990's*. Proceedings of a one-day conference held at Montclair State College, October 25, 1991.

Gerlach, S. A. *Marine Pollution*. Berlin: Springer-Verlag, 1975.

Grumbles, Benjamin G. "Federal Oil Spill Legislation in the Wake of Exxon Valdez." *Marine Technology Society Journal* 24(4) (December 1990): 5–11.

Holloway, Marguerite. "Soiled Shores." *Scientific American*, October 1991.

Lloyd's Register of Shipping. *Oil Tankers and the Environment Planning for the Future*. June 1990.

Meade, Norman and Thomas LaPointe. "Multivariate Analysis of Worldwide Tanker Casualties." Oil Spill Conference, March 1983.

Mielke, James E. *Oil in the Ocean: The Short and Long Term Impacts of a Spill*. Congressional Research Service Report for U.S. Congress, July 24, 1990.

National Research Council. *Oil in the Sea: Inputs, Fates, and Effects*. Washington, DC: National Academy Press, 1985, p. 442.

———. *Tanker Design: Prevention by Design*. Washington, DC: National Academy Press, 1991.

New York Times. "Valdez Spill Toll Is Now Called Far Worse." April 1992.

Plume, Janet. "Insurances Financing Begin to Dry Up for U.S. Oil Carriers." *Journal of Commerce*, August 20, 1991.

Reuters. "Sea Appears to Swallow 85,000-Ton Oil Spill." *Star Ledger* (Newark, NJ), February 3, 1993.

Temple, Barker and Sloane. *Interim Regulatory Impact Analysis for the Oil Pollution Act of 1990, Titles IV & V*. Prepared for the U.S. Coast Guard, October 1991.

U.S. Coast Guard. *Marine Safety Information Service (MSIS) Database 1973–1990*. Washington, DC, 1990.

Volpe National Transportation Systems Center. *Regulatory Impact Analysis for Vessel Response Plans*. Prepared for the U.S. Coast Guard, 1992.

Chapter 17

The Impact of Environmental Controls on Petroleum Exploration, Development, and Extraction

Diana Denison, Thomas D. Crocker, and Genevieve Briand

Globally, but especially in the wealthier parts of the world, media, political, and citizen worries mount annually about the impact of petroleum exploration, development, and extraction upon natural environments. In roughly declining order the worries focus upon the fouling of ground, surface, and marine waters through spills and toxin and salt invasions; compromises of the ecological integrity of wildlife and wilderness habitats through drilling and transportation-induced fragmentation; and air pollution through storage facility leaks, gas flaring, and accidental combustion. Any attempt to evaluate the significance of these environmental worries for the fates of global oil markets must recognize that five key linked influences shape their intensity: (1) petroleum production and trade patterns; (2) the technological, financial, and management practices used in production and trade; (3) the effects of these practices upon waste loadings in natural environmental assets; (4) the impact of these loadings upon the natural assets' productivities; and (5) the weight these loadings and productivity and trade changes exercise upon individual and collective behaviors and the values they express. This chapter considers the influences that environmental controls are likely to exercise upon petroleum production and international trade patterns.

In purely economic efficiency terms, these five influences upon citizens' worries about petroleum production are worthy of policy and thus regulatory attention only when the system of voluntary exchanges known familiarly as the "market" fails to cause petroleum producers to act as if they will bear all the costs of their activities. These costs include those that production activities and pollution flows impose upon the present and those that resource depletion and accumulated pollution stocks impose upon the future.

In petroleum production, as in many other sectors where production activities can degrade and disrupt natural assets, the values that citizens attach to these assets loom large. The quantity of petroleum produced and the technological, financial, and management practices that produce it contribute to citizens' perceptions of waste loadings and consequent natural asset productivity effects. In turn, these perceptions determine the individual and collective expressed values that decide the extent to which petroleum markets are to be trusted. Even if petroleum producers' current contributions to physical measures of environmental waste loadings and natural asset productivity effects are unchanged, increasing future wealth and population will pressure them to reduce quantities produced and to alter production and trade patterns. Quantities produced and production and trade practices used can be changed voluntarily or they can be collectively mandated. This chapter discusses the impact upon the time patterns and volumes of petroleum exploration, development, and extraction when voluntary acts are undertaken and collective mandates are enforced to protect environmental assets by altering petroleum production quantities, practices, and trade patterns.

VOLUNTARY ACTS AND COLLECTIVE MANDATES

Petroleum production activities that do not post direct risks to environmental assets are exceptional. The rock examinations, geological mappings, and aerial photographic surveys used in exploration qualify. Otherwise the shallow holes and detonations used in seismological exploration tear up land surfaces. Well drilling disturbs land surfaces and requires the continual injection of lubricants into the bore. Corrosion inhibitors, scale preventers, paraffin solvents, acidizers, and many other chemicals are intermittently applied. After use, ways must be found to dispose of these lubricants, other exhausted chemicals, and any cuttings, along with contaminated water produced with the petroleum. Deep drilling encounters high pressure and heat, which may cause blowouts and crude oil spills. Drilling, pumping, and transport operations can be noisy and unsightly, and the internal combustion engines often used as power sources produce air pollution. The fluids and chemicals employed in secondary and tertiary recovery might be transformed, accumulated, and transported by natural processes to produce water, soil, and air pollution. Finally, even when individual site operations are benign, cumulative operations among sites can distress wildlife by blocking migration corridors and altering feeding and reproduction strategies.

Intense public and media scrutiny and the felt obligations of employees and even stockholders have caused petroleum producers to become ever more sensitive to the impacts of their activities upon environmental assets. In instances where voluntary compliance is thought to be unlikely, public authorities in oil producing regions around the world have promulgated a vast array of regulatory schemes intended to lessen the environmental consequences of petroleum exploration, production, and extraction.[1]

The regulations forced upon petroleum producers are intended to provide them with incentives to reduce the likelihood of harming environmental assets (self-protection) or to reduce the liabilities the producers will suffer when harm does occur and is recognized (self-insurance). For self-protection purposes the command-and-control or quantity rationing schemes much maligned in other settings continue to dominate environmental asset allocation exercises. The control planning authority states the allowable level of the offending pollutant that can be produced and often specifies the technological means by which each producer is to attain this level. A system of fines and other sanctions enforces the central commands. Informational demands placed upon the central authority are severe and such schemes are readily susceptible to abuses of power.

Pollution taxes, a form of price rationing much favored among economists in the 1960s and 1970s, are rarely accepted in unadorned form by policymakers. Even though pollution taxes encourage least-cost compliance while encouraging innovations in the technologies of pollution prevention and control, their current frequency of use still approaches zero. A pollution tax scheme would have the policymaker charge the value of that impact to the producer whose activities negatively impact an environmental asset. This value, the situation-specific determination of which would keep armies of economists fully employed, includes the money equivalents of losses in noncommercial as well as commercial values.

Price rationing has been treated with greater policymaking respect in a self-insurance context. Petroleum producers are motivated to self-insure when they expect to be liable for any realized negative impacts that individual owners of environmental assets recognize. Owner recognition must occur for valuation efforts to be started and owners would want the efforts applied only to those features of the asset having values they can or want to capture. Thus, contrary to the central authority that employs economist armies to tote up noncommercial as well as commercial values, owners might consider only commercial values. They might sue the oil producer for the loss their oil spills impose upon the agricultural productivity of their land but disregard the losses that passersby suffer from the unsightliness of oil-covered land. Petroleum producers are therefore motivated to self-insure only to the extent to which they expect to be liable for the realized negative impacts of their activities upon the environmental assets of others. Expected profits for producers are their net revenues less expected liabilities and less the costs of preventing potential liabilities from being realized. These costs of prevention constitute self-insurance. In response to a liability assignment, producers must therefore select the amount of petroleum to be produced and the level of self-insurance to be adopted. Though this self-insurance does away with public monitoring costs and reduces—probably greatly—public enforcement and value determination costs, it can and often does cause some scarce features of an environmental asset to be treated as free.

Because of the perceived faults of both the self-protection and the self-insurance forms of price rationing, economists have recently been announcing the virtues of a combination of price and quantity rationing known as "tradeable permits" (Crocker 1966; Montgomery 1971). This scheme has the public policymakers set the allowable level of the offending pollutant but lets producers select the means by which they will achieve these allowable levels. They clearly have incentives to find a least-cost means to achieve these levels as well as to invest in developing innovations to reduce costs further. In addition, monitoring and enforcing compliance is less costly than with the earlier reviewed schemes, because the prevention and control technologies they employ do not have to be observed. Most importantly, the continuous value determination process that unadorned pollution taxes require and the dangers of the power abuses inherent in strict quantity rationing are set aside. Allowable pollution levels, which will now be viewed by producers as an invariant and finite stock to which they must adapt all of their activities, can be set such that noncommercial as well as commercial values are represented. Though the tradeable permit scheme is beginning to be viewed approvingly by many public environmental policymakers, it has not yet been systematically applied in any petroleum production setting. Strict quantity rationing schemes continue to prevail near universally. They increase the petroleum producers' costs.

AN ANALYTICAL FRAMEWORK

The analytical and empirical grasps of the impact of various exogenous factors on petroleum supply have become increasingly robust in the past two decades, though little formal attention has been devoted to environmental controls.[2] Following H. S. Burness (1976) and P. S. Dasgupta et al. (1983), a general statement of the decision problem for the petroleum firm in a world of heterogeneous environmental controls and homogeneous resources and with a known finite reserve is

$$Max \int_{t=0}^{T} [pR \quad C(R) - K(R,Q,)] \; e^{-rt} \; dt \tag{1}$$

subject to $\dot{S}3 = -ds/dt = R(t) \geq 0$, with $S \geq 0$ for all dates t, and with $S_0 = S(0)$ given. T is the date on which extraction ceases, p is the exogenous price for extracted petroleum with $\dot{p} < r$,[3] R is the rate of extraction, S_0 is the initial petroleum reserve, S is the remaining petroleum reserve, Q is a scalar measure of the severity of pollution control, $C(\cdot)$ is the cost of extraction with $dC/dR = C' > 0$, and $K(\cdot)$ is the cost of pollution control compliance with $\partial K/\partial R \geq 0$ and $\partial K/\partial Q \geq 0$. The time discounting term is e^{-rt}, where $r > 0$ is the producer's rate of discount and e is the base of the natural logarithms. All terms but p within the brackets are functions of t. The form of K varies with the pollution control scheme. $C(\cdot) + K(\cdot)$ is jointly convex in R and Q. A thorough Ricardian version of equation (1) in which cumulative extraction affects extraction costs would have S enter $C(\cdot)$ and $K(\cdot)$ as arguments.

The present-value Hamiltonian is

$$H(\cdot) = [(p - \lambda)R - C(R) - K(R,Q)] \, e^{-rt}, \tag{2}$$

where λ is the costate or adjoint variable representing user cost—the opportunity cost of the future extraction foregone by a marginal unit of current extraction. By the maximum principle, necessary first-order conditions include

$$p - (\lambda + C' + \partial K/\partial R) = 0, \tag{3}$$

$$\lambda = (r\lambda + \partial K/\partial Q) = 0 \tag{4}$$

Equation (3) is the ever-familiar price equals marginal cost condition, where in this case cost includes user costs as well as extraction costs and pollution control costs. The manner in which user cost evolves is given by equation (4). At T the Hamiltonian must vanish, which implies

$$p = \lambda + (C/R) + (K/R), \tag{5}$$

given that T is finite. When equation (5) is combined with equation (3) in order to eliminate λ, it follows that the terminal condition at time T is

$$(C/R) + (K/R) = C' + \partial K/\partial R. \tag{6}$$

Equation (6) says that maximization of the discounted present value of extraction requires that in the terminal period average extraction costs be equal to marginal extraction costs. After considerable algebraic manipulation the conditions in equations (4), (5), and (6) can be used to derive equation (7).[4] Given that the firm decides to extract, equation (7)

$$R = \frac{r(p - C' - \partial K/\partial R - \partial K/\partial Q) - (\partial^2 K/\partial R \partial Q)R}{- (C'' + \partial^2 K/\partial R^2)} \tag{7}$$

generally implies that the rate of extraction declines over time since all the terms in the numerator on the righthand side of equation (7) are positive and the denominator is negative if, reasonably, the marginal costs of extraction, C', and marginal compliance costs, $\partial^2 K/\partial R^2$, are increasing in the extraction rate. The impacts of pollution control compliance costs, $K(\cdot)$, upon the extraction path, its duration, and upon user costs or Hotelling (1931) scarcity rents are now easily discerned.

From equation (7), any increase in marginal compliance costs, $\partial K/\partial Q$, which is constant over time, will slow the rate of extraction since the positive magnitude of the numerator falls. Intuitively, the producer is motivated to delay these compliance costs and thus reduce their present value. The slowed down rate of current extraction reduces marginal extraction and compliance costs in future periods, thus increasing rents in future periods and, from equation (6), motivating the producer to stretch the time interval over which extraction occurs.

Some producers' compliance costs may not vary with their production level but may rather be a condition for undertaking production. For example, producers may have to install lined holding pits or produce water treatment equipment with high upfront capital costs and very low operating costs. In equation (1), fixed-cost effects like these can be captured by subtracting a constant term from the righthand side. This term will increase the rate of extraction and will thereby compress the extraction interval. The rate of extraction increases because of the producers' incentive to move their revenue-generating activities closer to the time when they must make the outlays necessary to have any of these activities occur.

Exploration is a means of accumulating a reserve stock of the petroleum resource. Decisions about exploration can be included in equation (1) by making S_o endogenous and adding a stochastic term representing discovery costs (Lasserre 1984). The solution of the problem would then show that additional reserves reduce future extraction and development costs, since the user costs associated with a given amount of extraction fall. Exploration is thus worthwhile to the extent that the present value of expected future marginal cost reduction exceeds current marginal discovery costs. Obviously, exploration activities will be reduced by increases in the fixed and variable compliance costs associated with pollution control for such activities. Less obviously, the discovery cost increase will increase extraction costs because of the lower user costs that will now not be realized. Consequently, a pollution-control-induced increase in discovery costs will slow the rate of extraction, reduce current period rents on known reserves, and extend the time interval over which extraction occurs.

EMPIRICAL MEASURES

Careful empirical efforts fully grounded in economic theory that consider the impact of environmental controls upon petroleum production do not yet exist.[5] However, some empirical literature is available about the impact of severance and other taxes upon petroleum production. Because these taxes also increase petroleum production costs, available empirical results regarding them may be directly transferred to the environmental control impact issue.

Severance taxes, which are a percentage applied to the value of the extracted petroleum, increase marginal extraction costs. $K(\cdot)$ in equation (1) could just as readily have been labeled a severance tax cost function as an environmental compliance cost function. Similarly, a constant term to be added to equation (1) to represent fixed costs of environmental compliance can also be interpreted as a property tax that producers must pay to retain a legally enforceable claim to their petroleum reserve stock.

The more notable of recent empirical studies of the impact of severance and property taxes upon petroleum include R. T. Deacon (1993), C. A. Favero (1992), J. M. Griffin and J. R. Moroney (1985), and M. K. Yucel (1989). Qualitatively the empirical results these studies obtain conform to theoretical predictions. Both severance taxes and property taxes reduce rents. They also cause exploration activity to shrink, thereby reducing reserves. Severance taxes are generally shown to lengthen extraction intervals while property taxes contract them. The empirical evidence is that severance taxes slow extraction rates and property taxes accelerate them. Therefore if fixed costs dominate petroleum producers' costs of complying with environmental controls, reduced rents, and exploration and increased extraction rates with compressed time intervals for extraction from individual fields will appear. Ultimately the reduction in accumulated reserves must translate into falling extraction rates. Alternatively, if compliance costs vary with extraction rates, these rates will decline and extraction intervals will lengthen as exploration activity slows and rents decrease.

Whether compliance costs be primarily fixed or variable, the magnitudes of their impacts upon extraction rates and exploration activity are potentially substantial. Griffin and Moroney (1985) econometrically estimate that a 1 percent severance tax increase from a base 4.5 percent rate would reduce Texas crude oil production over a 20-year horizon by 0.31 percent, net industry oil revenues by 1.37 percent, exploration wells by 0.84 percent, new oil pool discoveries by 0.42 percent, and enhanced oil recovery production by 1.06 percent. Deacon's (1993) simulation study was structured to assure that severance taxes and property taxes would each generate present values of tax revenues equal to 15 percent of the gross revenue earned in an untaxed regime. Severance taxes caused U.S. crude oil production to fall by 6.5 percent over a 61-year horizon. Property taxes result in a 4.8 percent drop in crude oil production over the same horizon. In a simulation study calibrated to Texas' Permian Basin region, Yucel (1989) concludes that severance taxes lead both competitive and monopolistic oil industries to reduce production and exploration. The reductions were more pronounced in the competitive case. Favero (1992), using a combination of econometric and simulation techniques, estimates that a 45 to 75 percent United Kingdom severance tax with several complicated accounting allowances would reduce the shadow price of oil remaining in the ground by nearly an order of magnitude.

INTERNATIONAL TRADE EFFECTS OF ENVIRONMENTAL CONTROLS

The previous empirical examples and the analytical discussion that preceded them were confined to an oil industry operating within one political jurisdiction. However, the oil industry is worldwide and domestic environmental controls can affect the international competitiveness of the domestic oil industry and those domestic industries for which oil is an input (Yergin 1991). We will illustrate the type of thinking required to grasp how domestic environmental controls can affect international trade patterns and the domestic supply of oil.

Pething (1976), B. A. Forster (1977), and J. D. Merrifield (1988), among others, use the Heckscher-Olin framework to address the effects of environmental policies on terms of trade, pollution levels, and production. In a two- or three-resource-factor world, each country in the framework is endowed with a different relatively abundant resource. The country specializes in the industry that uses intensively the factor it has in abundance. Product prices are exogenously determined and, following trade, the factor price ratios are equalized among countries (Takayama 1972).

Consider a two-product, three-factor economy with labor, L, mobile and real capital, K, and energy (oil), E, industry-specific. Real capital and energy or natural capital can be complements (Daly and Cobb 1989). With the two technologies,

$$Y_1 = f_1 (L_1, E), \tag{8}$$

and

$$Y_2 = f_2 (L_2, K), \tag{9}$$

let the North specialize in real capital-intensive industries and the South specialize in energy-intensive industries. Full employment is assumed.

Each country maximizes gross national product requiring that the marginal value product of each resource factor equals its factor price in each country. Domestic environmental controls upon petroleum production alter, as previous sections have shown, these factor prices and production levels. Prior to trade, factor price ratios in each country differ. With trade, they equilibrate. If environmental controls in the South cause the variable costs of producing the energy-intensive good to rise, labor will migrate from South to North as the relative cost of the real capital-intensive good declines. Alternatively, if environmental controls induce increases in fixed costs, labor will migrate from North to South as the relative cost of producing the energy-intensive good declines. In short, today's global oil economy does not allow the economic repercussions resulting from one country's environmental controls to be confined to that country. It follows that environmental controls on domestic petroleum industries may sometimes be directed more at international strategic economic and political issues than at the protection of domestic natural environmental assets (Mäler 1989; Hoel 1991). Certainly any evaluation of domestic environmental controls should consider the international trade repercussions.

CONCLUSION

Environmental controls, whether they are enforced during extraction or are required compensations after environmental damages have occurred, alter the cost structure of the petroleum industry. This, in turn, changes the rate at which resources are extracted. If a firm is faced with compliance costs that are based on the level of production, current extraction will be reduced. When environmental costs are fixed independent of production rates, current extraction will increase to cover the added costs.

As the economy evolves to a global one, it is necessary to consider international implications of environmental regulations. Traditional international trade models allow one to trace the impact of such controls on national competitiveness. Unilateral environmental regulations can increase domestic production costs, decreasing the "relative abundance" of petroleum in that country. This results in reduced exports of energy-intensive goods and a decrease in the demand for petroleum as a factor of production.

Both on national and international levels, increased environmental protection compliance expenses per unit extracted will tend to reduce current production of petroleum. In a single industry model, the loss in current production is moved to the future. With the addition of a second industry, production is shifted to the industries using nonenergy factors intensively, reducing the energy intensity of the economy. In an international framework, the reduced energy use domestically is shifted overseas where the foreign country's comparative advantage in energy-intensive production increases.

NOTES

1. In the United States, the more important of these for petroleum production are the Clean Air Act (CAA), the Clean Water Act (CWA), the Safe Drinking Water Act (SDWA), the National Pollutant Discharge Elimination System (NPDES), the Resource Conservation and Recovery Act (RCRA), the Comprehensive Environmental Response, Compensation and Liability Act (CERCLA), the Federal Land Policy and Management Act (FLPMA), and the National Environmental Policy Act (NEPA).

The CAA sets national ambient standards for sulfur dioxide, nitrogen oxides, and volatile organic compounds, and empowers state and federal regulatory agencies to specify technological, economic, and legal means to meet them.

The CWA specifies effluent guidelines and specifies appropriate technologies to achieve them.

The SDWA sets national primary drinking water standards and requires permits for subsurface injections that might pollute groundwater. Technological controls to be used may be specified in the permit.

The NPDES requires that any point source of water pollution obtain from federal or state environmental authorities a permit to discharge. The permit may specify the technological controls to be used.

The CERCLA requires current and past owners of officially designated existing hazardous sites to clean them up.

The FLPMA sets procedures for withdrawing federal lands from leasing for petroleum production.

The NEPA requires that environmental impact statements (studies) be done prior to petroleum leasing on federal lands.

2. See Forster (1977), M. Cropper (1980), and T. Lewis (1981) for highly general analytical frameworks that treat interactions between energy use and the environment.

K. R. Stollery (1985) appears to have been the first to model the impact of environmental controls on the time path of extraction for a competitive industry.

3. An assumption of exogenously determined prices is consistent either with a competitively organized industry or one that centers upon a dominant firm or cartel with a competitive fringe.

4. The manipulation involves totally differentiating equation (3) with respect to t and using equations (4) and (5) to get rid of λ and $\dot{\lambda}$.

5. D. Jin and T. A. Grigalunas (1993) is an exception. In their study of the costs to the U.S. offshore oil industry of complying with representative but stringent environmental regulations, they estimate that after-tax net present values can be reduced by 51 percent for "small" fields and by 11 percent for "large" fields. These authors imply (p. 92) that compliance costs vary much less than proportionately with the size of the field—that is, that the size of the reserve exercises little influence upon compliance costs. The absence of a stock size argument in the compliance cost function, $K(\cdot)$, in equation (1) should thus not seriously compromise the formulation.

REFERENCES

Burness, H. Stuart. "The Taxation of Non-renewable Natural Resources." *Journal of Environmental Economics and Management* 3 (1976): 289–311.

Crocker, Thomas D. "The Structuring of Atmospheric Pollution Control Systems." In H. Wolozin (ed.), *The Economics of Air Pollution*. New York: W. W. Norton, 1966, 61–86.

Cropper, Maureen. "Pollution Aspects of Nuclear Energy Use." *Journal of Environmental Economics and Management* 7 (1980): 334–352.

Daly, Herman E. and James B. Cobb, Jr. *For the Common Good*. Boston: Beacon Press, 1989.

Dasgupta, Partha S., Geoffrey M. Heal, and Joseph E. Stiglitz. "The Taxation of Exhaustible Resources." In George A. Hughes and Geoffrey M. Heal (eds.), *Public Policy and the Tax System*. London: George Allen and Unwin, 1983.

Deacon, Robert T. "Taxation, Depletion, and Welfare: A Simulation Study of the U.S. Petroleum Resource." *Journal of Environmental Economics and Management* 24 (1993): 159–186.

Favero, Carlo A. "Taxation and the Optimization of Oil Exploration and Production: The U.S. Continental Shelf." *Oxford Economic Papers* 44 (1992): 187–208.

Forster, Bruce A. "Optimal Energy Use in a Polluted Environment." *Journal of Environmental Economics and Management* 7 (1977): 305–313.

———. "Pollution Control in a Two-Sector Dynamic General Equilibrium Model." *Journal of Environmental Economics and Management* 20 (1991): 55–70.

Griffin, James M. and John R. Moroney. *The Impact of Severance Taxes: Results from an Econometric Model of the Texas Oil and Gas Industry*. A report to the Texas Mid Continent Oil and Gas Association. College Station, TX: Department of Economics, Texas A&M University, 1985.

Hoel, Michael. "Global Environmental Problems: The Effects of Unilateral Actions Taken by One Country." *Journal of Environmental Economics and Management* 20 (1991): 55–70.

Hotelling, Harold. "The Economics of Exhaustible Resources." *Journal of Political Economy* 39 (1931): 137–175.

Jin, Di and Thomas A. Grigalunas. "Environmental Compliance and Energy Exploration and Production: Application to Offshore Oil and Gas." *Land Economics* 69 (1993): 82–97.

Lasserre, Pierre. "Reserves and Land Prices with Exploration under Uncertainty." *Journal of Environmental Economics and Management* 11 (1984): 191–201.

Lewis, Tracy. "Energy vs. the Environment." *Journal of Environmental Economics and Management* 8 (1981): 59–71.

Mäler, Karl G., "The Acid Rain Game." In H. Folmer and E. van Ierland (eds.), *Valuation Methods and Policy Making in Environmental Economics*. Amsterdam: Elsevier, 1989.

Merrifield, John D. "The Impact of Selected Abatement Strategies on Transnational Pollution, the Terms of Trade, and Factor Rewards: A General Equilibrium Approach." *Journal of Environmental Economics and Management* 15 (1988): 259–284.

Montgomery, William D. "Markets in Licenses and Efficient Pollution Control Programs." *Journal of Economic Theory* 5 (1971): 143–151.

Pething, Rudolph. "Pollution, Welfare, and Environmental Policy in the Theory of Comparative Advantage." *Environmental Economics and Management* 2 (1976): 160–169.

Stollery, Kenneth R. "Environmental Controls in Extractive Industries." *Land Economics* 62 (1985): 136–144.

Takayama, A. *International Economics*. New York: Holt, Rinehart and Winston, 1972.

Yergin, David. *The Prize: The Epic Quest for Oil, Money, and Power*. New York: Simon and Schuster, 1991.

Yucel, Mine K. "Severance Taxes and Market Structure in an Exhaustible Resource Industry." *Journal of Environmental Economics and Management* 16 (1989): 134–148.

Chapter 18

Corn-Derived Ethanol as a Liquid Fuel

Wallace E. Tyner

There has been considerable interest in the agricultural sector in using corn to make ethanol fuel. Ethanol is seen as a means of increasing the demand and, consequently, price of corn. The corn growers and alcohol producers have been successful in obtaining substantial subsidies from federal and state governments for alcohol production. Today ethanol subsidies are about the same as the whole-sale spot gasoline price per gallon (meaning a 100 percent subsidy).

Even with these high subsidies, interest in ethanol fuels had waned a bit until the passage of the 1990 Clean Air Act. That act mandates a substantial change in the motor vehicle fuels used in the United States over the next decade to reduce the amount of auto-based air pollution. In particular, it mandates that gasoline, in general, have a higher oxygen content. Ethanol has a high oxygen content, and its potential use as a gasoline oxygenate has stimulated a renewed interest in ethanol production and use. Some analysts and advocates have predicted rapid rises in the price of ethanol due to its value as an oxygenate and as an octane enhancer.

Various organizations have produced forecasts indicating ethanol production could double, quadruple, or expand even more by the end of the decade. Current (1993) ethanol production capacity is about 1 billion gallons per year. This 1 billion gallons of ethanol uses about 390 million bushels of corn. Some ethanol producers have indicated they intend to expand production. Some oil companies have indicated they intend to use ethanol; others plan to use different oxygenates.

This chapter reviews the key issues or drivers that will in the future determine the extent to which ethanol is used as a petroleum fuel or oxygenate. The drivers that will determine the demand for ethanol as an oxygenate are as follows: federal and state subsidies on ethanol production and use; interpretation and rule making on the 1990 Clean Air Act; competition from other oxygenates, principally MTBE; regional supply/demand patterns for oxygenates; future oil prices; and by-product prices and export potential. Each of these is discussed below.

FEDERAL AND STATE ETHANOL SUBSIDIES

The current federal ethanol subsidy amounts to 54 cents per gallon of ethanol. Under current law, this subsidy is set to expire in the year 2000. In addition, several state governments offer subsidies of as much as 20 cents/gallon, usually for ethanol produced in the state.

The U.S. Gulf spot gasoline wholesale price recently has been ranging between 40 and 60 cents/gallon. The Midwest ethanol price generally ranges 55–60 cents/gallon above the wholesale gasoline price. Recent Midwest ethanol prices have ranged between $0.95 and $1.25/gallon. Almost all of the difference between ethanol and gasoline price is accounted for by federal and state gasoline subsidies. This fact implies that ethanol is used (and priced) in the market at present as a gasoline extender. It does not receive a premium in Midwest markets either as an octane enhancer or as an oxygenate.

The ethanol price is 10 to 20 cents/gallon higher in certain Western cities (Albuquerque, Denver, Boise, Seattle), at least in winter months. However, most of this difference is accounted for by the 10–12 cents/gallon transport cost from the Midwestern production region to the West. Because of its solvent and corrosive characteristics, ethanol cannot be transported by pipeline. It must be transported by truck, rail, or ship, which increases the transport cost over gasoline/MTBE (methyl tertiary butyl ether). The rest of the difference is accounted for by oxygenate demand in those regions, as will be explained later.

THE 1990 CLEAN AIR ACT

The 1990 Clean Air Act contains requirements for gasoline changes designed to reduce carbon monoxide (CO) and ozone. The CO rules took effect in October 1992, and the ozone regulations will come into effect in 1995. The gasoline changes to meet CO rules are applicable during the four winter months in 41 cities, which is the lowest demand period for gasoline. During that period gasoline must contain 2.7 percent oxygen. Standard gasoline contains no oxygen, and ethanol contains 35 percent oxygen, so a 10 percent ethanol blend meets and exceeds the CO oxygen requirements. Most of the nonattainment cities are on the East and West Coasts or in the South. Most of the ethanol is produced in the Midwest. To be used in meeting the winter months' clean air rules, ethanol would have to be transported to the demand regions.

The ozone rules require reformulated gasoline to be used year-round in nine nonattainment cities. Reformulated gasoline must contain 2 percent oxygen and meet other requirements. One of the other requirements relates to evaporative emissions. Ethanol or ethanol/gasoline blends result in higher evaporative emissions than gasoline. California rules essentially eliminate the possibility of using ethanol to meet ozone standards. If the Environmental Protection Agency and other states followed the California lead, ethanol would not play a major role in reformulated gasoline.

In late 1993 President Clinton announced a compromise implementation of the Clean Air Act regulations that would maintain the air quality standards in the act but require that 30 percent of the oxygenates used in the nine ozone nonattainment cities come from renewable sources. The renewable fuel would be ethanol from corn, since no other alternative is available. This compromise essentially means that ethanol would have to be converted into ETBE (ethyl tertiary butyl ether) to be used because ethanol/gasoline blends cannot meet the evaporative emission standards in summer.

COMPETITION FROM MTBE

MTBE is another oxygenate and octane enhancer available to oil companies. It is produced from methanol, which is produced from natural gas or coal. MTBE production capacity is growing at a very rapid rate at present all over the world. Demand for MTBE will grow very rapidly in the United States and Europe over this decade.

MTBE contains 18 percent oxygen, so a 15 percent blend could meet the CO oxygen standards. MTBE blends can be transported by pipeline, so transportation cost is much lower than for ethanol. MTBE vapor pressure is lower than ethanol (blending RVP [Reid vapor pressure] equals 8 compared to 17 for ethanol), so it can be used in reformulated gasoline to meet ozone standards.

MTBE has been selling in the 60–90 cent/gallon price range. At that relative price, MTBE will be the oxygenate of choice in the South and Gulf Coast areas. It will capture a major share of the East Coast market as well because of the ready availability of pipelines. There will be more potential for ethanol to compete with MTBE in some Southwestern and Western states. Ethanol will likely capture a large share of the Midwestern oxygenate market, but that market is smaller than the others.

REGIONAL SUPPLY/DEMAND ISSUES

The previous sections have delineated some of the regional supply/demand issues. The major point is that most of the supply of ethanol is in the Midwest, where the corn is produced, and most of the demand for oxygenates is outside the Midwest. Either the corn must be shipped to other regions, and ethanol produced there, or ethanol must be produced in the Midwest and shipped to those regions. Ethanol in the Midwest is now being priced and used as a fuel extender, which is enabled by the federal and state subsidies.

FUTURE OIL PRICES

As indicated earlier, ethanol price is determined by gasoline price (which is determined by oil price) and government subsidies. Ethanol prices historically have moved very closely with oil prices. If oil prices were to increase or decrease significantly, that could have a major impact on the demand for ethanol. The economics of ethanol production are driven by gasoline (oil) prices, corn prices, and by-product prices. At current subsidy levels and price of corn at $2.50 per bushel, oil price needs to be about $24/barrel to make ethanol expansion attractive. In recent years, oil has ranged from $14 to $20/barrel. Futures prices out to 1997 go no higher than $20/barrel. Our expectation is that oil prices will not rise in real terms over the decade. Hence, unless some of our base assumptions change or the subsidies are increased even further, ethanol capacity expansion will not be attractive.

ETHANOL BY-PRODUCTS

Ethanol is produced by either wet milling or dry milling processes. The wet milling process yields corn oil, corn gluten meal, and corn gluten feed as by-products. The dry milling process yields distillers' dried grains and solubles (DDGS) and carbon dioxide. About three-fourths of U.S. ethanol is produced via the wet milling process. Hence, most of the by-products are gluten meal and gluten feed. Most of the glutens are exported to Europe, because they enter without duties and command a higher price on the European market than they would here.

In 1991 the European Community challenged the duty-free entry of gluten on two grounds. The first basis of the challenge was that gluten feed is a corn product and not a corn substitute. Corn products fall into a different category and would pay an import tax. The second ground was that the by-products are effectively subsidized because of the high U.S. subsidy on ethanol. Most of the gluten by-products come from manufacture of corn sweeteners. However, the Europeans fear that an expanded ethanol industry would dump substantially more gluten by-products on their markets.

If the United States were to lose the European market for the by-products, that would make ethanol manufacture less economically attractive. The 1991 dispute was resolved, at least temporarily, in the U.S. favor. However, the issue is still alive. The General Agreement on Tariffs and Trade action resulted in no change in status for gluten in the future. One possible outcome would be that current levels would continue to come in duty free, but any increases would be taxed. That outcome would put a damper on ethanol production expansion. In any event, the European market for by-products is clearly an important driver of the expansion possibilities for ethanol.

IMPLICATIONS FOR THE FUTURE

It is likely that ethanol production will grow beyond the current capacity level of 1 billion gallons over the decade. The increase in ethanol demand due to the Clean Air Act compromise will range between 300 million and 1 billion gallons. Hence, we could see a doubling of ethanol capacity by the end of the decade. The U.S. Department of Agriculture (USDA) (in *Ethanol and Agriculture*, May 1993) has estimated the impacts on agriculture of an increase in ethanol production of 1 billion gallons. According to their estimates, corn production would increase 3.4 percent, and corn price would increase 0.5 percent, which amounts to about 1.25 cents/bushel. Corn price does not increase very much because the United States has idle land in an Acreage Retirement Program that could be brought back into production as the demand for corn increases. However, soybean production would fall 0.9 percent, and soybean price would decline 1.1 percent, which amounts to about 7 cents/bushel. Counting both crop and livestock compacts, farm income is expected to increase 0.3 percent due to the increase in alcohol production of 1 billion gallons. If the increase is less than 1 billion gallons, all these impacts would be reduced.

The bottom line is that doubling ethanol production from 1 to 2 billion gallons has a very minor impact on agricultural producers and prices of agricultural products. The billion gallons of ethanol would entail an ethanol subsidy cost of $540 million from the U.S. Treasury. The impact of that subsidy would be a reduction of $540 million per year going into the Highway Trust Fund used for construction and maintenance of highways.

We also can examine these impacts from the perspective of 100 acres of cropland used for corn or soybean production. Using typical Midwest yields of 130 bushels per acre for corn and 40 for soybeans, we find that income on the acreage used for corn increases $162.50. If the acreage is used for soybeans, income decreases by $280. The subsidy cost for the ethanol from 100 acres of corn is about $275 (130 bu./ac. × 100 ac. ÷ 2.55 gal./bu. × .054 $/gal.). The subsidy cost is greater than the corn price increase even without considering the income decrease from soybeans.

Some ethanol advocates have discussed the possibility of ethanol production growing to 5 billion gallons by the end of this decade, but it is unlikely that this level of ethanol production will come about. That level would signify an increased demand for corn of 1.5 billion bushels. That magnitude of increase would bring about a large corn price increase (USDA estimates 7.6 percent), which, in turn, would put pressure on the economic viability of ethanol production. This higher level of ethanol production likely could not be achieved at the current subsidy levels. Only higher oil prices would permit ethanol to be viable without a higher subsidy. Corn exports would fall because of the corn price increase. Net farm income would rise somewhat at the expense of higher consumer prices.

The bottom line is that unless there are significant changes in the critical drivers discussed above, ethanol production will grow over the decade due to the increased demand for oxygenates, but it will grow at a much slower rate than envisioned by many groups. It is likely to grow to about 1.5–1.7 billion gallons by the end of the decade. Growth in that range will have a modest impact on agriculture and on the liquid fuel and oxygenate markets.

PART IV

ENERGY, NATIONAL SECURITY, AND PUBLIC POLICY DEBATE

Chapter 19

Oil and National Security: An Assessment of Externalities and Policies

Douglas R. Bohi and Michael A. Toman

It is frequently argued that oil imports involve costs and risks to society that are not recognized by buyers and sellers of oil. These additional costs, called externalities, imply that the market price of oil is too low and that the volume of consumption and imports is too high. The recommendation that usually follows is to place a tax on oil imports or on oil consumption to correct the price for these excluded costs.

This chapter critically examines the potential sources of the externalities and assesses their implications for energy policy. We conclude that there are limited externalities that warrant consideration for possible government intervention, and that their quantitative significance is very much in doubt. Consequently, little government action can be justified solely because of energy security considerations.

In keeping with most of the literature on the subject, we consider two broad sources of externalities: those associated with the quality of oil imports, and those associated with the volatility of the price of oil. The issues related to the quantity of oil imports involve excess price and volume of imports and the indirect consequences of these payments for inflation and the international value of the dollar. We also consider the military costs of maintaining access to foreign sources of oil in this category. The issues related to the volatility of the price of oil refer to the economic costs of adjusting to oil price fluctuations. In contrast to the generally longer term nature of the first set of issues, the problems of adjusting to oil price fluctuations are inherently short term in character. The reason is that gradual changes in oil prices are unlikely to generate externalities because markets have the ability to adjust over time without serious efficiency problems, and because externalities associated with rapid price changes will dissipate over time.

POTENTIAL EXTERNALITIES RELATED TO THE QUANTITY OF OIL IMPORTS

We consider the following reasons why the oil market may not function efficiently: market power on the part of buyers or sellers of oil, indirect effects on inflation and the dollar exchange rate, and military costs in the Middle East.

OPEC Market Power

There can be no doubt that the members of OPEC are *capable* of influencing the market price of oil if they should choose to exercise their market power. It is also easy to show that OPEC has not behaved (so far) as a classic market-sharing, price-setting cartel. There is, however, disagreement about the degree of market control that OPEC has exerted. P. MacAvoy (1982) takes issue with the conventional wisdom that observed petroleum prices and quantities reflect significant exercises of seller market power, arguing that the price explosions of the 1970s primarily reflected individual political events and demand-side responses, not concerted OPEC decisions. MacAvoy attempts to support his argument about market scarcity with a very simple simulation model showing that price increases much like those observed in the 1970s would have emerged even under an extrapolation of OPEC behavior from the 1960s, a period of less collusion than that which occurred in the 1970s. Unfortunately, attempts to statistically estimate coefficients in the model fare very poorly, and even with judgmentally specified parameters the model is not too successful in tracking actual market outcomes through the 1970s. Thus, while MacAvoy's assertions about market influences may be plausible conjectures, they receive fairly little empirical support in his study.

David Teece (1982) presents an argument in favor of market power based on the so-called target revenue theory. According to this view, once petroleum prices rise to the point where additional revenues no longer could be comfortably absorbed by the exporting country, further price increases would cause a reduction of supply. Revenue absorption levels, in turn, are complex functions of national development objectives, the size of national oil reserves, the returns of foreign investment of oil proceeds, and political risks. With a backward-bending supply curve, prices that have fortuitously risen above the marginal cost of reserve production and replacement—the standard for price behavior in a competitive market (Bohi and Toman 1984)—may remain so even without collusive output restrictions, because individual suppliers have no incentive to expand output and put downward pressure on the price. Producer rivalry would emerge only as revenues are eroded over time by demand stagnation and growth of non-OPEC supply. Teece presents a substantial amount of factual and anecdotal evidence, which he interprets as explaining observed petroleum market behavior during the 1970s.

In a series of papers, M. A. Adelman (1980, 1986, 1990) presents the more widely accepted view that OPEC has exercised market power, though he readily acknowledges that it has functioned only as a "clumsy cartel." The core of Adelman's argument is a set of calculations attempting to measure the marginal cost of producing and replacing reserves, which is the standard for a competitive price as noted above. From his calculations Adelman concludes that the gap between the world oil price and the marginal cost of oil supply in OPEC is too large to be explained by competitive market forces. This approach presumes that individual OPEC members can be characterized as seeking to maximize the present value of financial wealth. As Teece suggests, a variety of economic and noneconomic factors may reduce exports' propensities to hold petrodollar balances. In addition, Adelman considers all of the difference between the oil price and his measure of marginal supply cost to be monopoly profit. He does not give much weight to the possibility that the gaps could also represent scarcity rents. For example, OPEC countries may not have been in a position to rapidly expand output after the first oil price increase because of deliverability constraints.

Another study of OPEC market power by J. M. Griffin (1985) econometrically tests several categories of hypotheses about the behavior of individual oil producing countries inside and outside of OPEC. Griffin's principal conclusion (reinforced in a follow-up study by C. T. Jones [1990]) is that OPEC seems to most closely resemble a partial market-sharing cartel: individual member outputs are sensitive to other countries' shares, but the output responses to changes in price are not strictly proportional. In contrast, output decisions in a group of non-OPEC countries appear to be competitively determined by prices. Griffin rejects the property rights theory, while his findings concerning the target-revenue explanation of OPEC behavior are generally unfavorable. While Griffin's results are provocative, they have some weaknesses that point to the need for further investigation. For example, the market-sharing cartel model cannot be rejected for many non-OPEC oil producing countries either.

One must conclude at a minimum that the state of knowledge about OPEC and the world oil market is incomplete. This view is bolstered by comparisons of findings from different oil market models (Energy Modeling Forum 1982; Gately 1986), which highlight the sensitivity of outcomes to assumptions about oil supply and demand, energy-economy interactions, OPEC incentives, and the level of aggregation. For example, none of the models in the Energy Modeling Forum study were very successful in simulating the market over the period 1980–85.

Uncertainties and suspicions about OPEC's dominance are enhanced by an informal look at the data. Direct evidence of the exercise of market power by OPEC would be present if there were reductions in supply in 1973–74 and 1979 when the two price shocks occurred. Indirect evidence of market power would be present if the price of oil failed to decline after 1980 when world oil demand was declining. Experience in each of these cases does not support the view that OPEC has exercised a significant degree of market power.

U.S. Monopsony Power

The United States as a whole may possess monopsony power in the world oil market, even though individual buyers do not. If oil import demand could be coordinated it might be possible to drive down the world price of oil by restricting import demand, benefiting all oil users in the United States (and elsewhere).

Monopsony power in this way typically is thought to involve only pecuniary externalities, where rents may be redistributed from producers to consumers. Indeed, such possibilities are ubiquitous in efficient markets, where increasing supply costs cause a bidding up of prices with increasing demand. However, when the rent redistribution involves rent transfers from exporting to importing countries, these wealth transfers may be attractive to policymakers even if the market is efficient from a global perspective.

Nevertheless, it does not necessarily follow that a potential monopsony position should be exploited. In the absence of market power exercised by oil exporters, the only rationale for exploiting monopsony is neighbor-beggaring. This may be feasible looked at in isolation, particularly since exporters incapable of exercising market power would have little capacity to retaliate. However, behavior of this type would sacrifice U.S. leadership in maintaining free trade and could have significant implications in other markets.

The exercise of monopsony power could be justified if OPEC exercises sufficient market power to make the exploitation of buying power more than marginally profitable. In this case, however, OPEC will also possess the power necessary to retaliate against import restrictions by raising the world price of oil. Retaliation will not result in higher OPEC profits if a profit-maximizing monopoly price has been established already. Retaliation simply reduces revenues and will be contrary to OPEC's interests. In contrast, however, if OPEC is not already earning monopoly profits, then retaliation can be profitable and OPEC is more likely to undertake such a response. Ironically, efforts to exercise monopsony power may galvanize OPEC into a more cohesive entity and increase its capacity for exercising monopoly power.[1]

It also remains to be seen whether coordinated demand restrictions by the United States could substantially affect world oil prices without retaliation. The ability of the United States to unilaterally affect world oil prices is limited, since U.S. oil demand is only about 30 percent of world oil use, and imports are only 40–50 percent of U.S. demand. Any drop in oil prices from a decline in U.S. demand will be partially offset by increases in other countries' demands. Even proponents of an active oil import control policy, such as H. G. Broadman and W. W. Hogan (1986, 1988), conclude that the direct value to the United States of unilateral import restrictions to reduce world oil prices is only a small fraction (4–8 percent) of the price unless the base price of oil is low and a very substantial import control program is deployed.[2]

An important corollary to this discussion is that import tariffs and quotas are not likely to be wise choices as policies intended to address externalities related to OPEC market power. These policies are highly visible beggar-thy-neighbor actions. A better way to mitigate export market power, as will be argued further later, is through energy research and development that expands the range of substitutes for OPEC oil and indirectly reduces OPEC market power.[3]

Indirect Costs of Market Power

Even without the presence of monopsony power or the exercise of market power by oil exporters, transfers of wealth for oil imports could have secondary effects on the economy that are not reflected in the price of oil and thus constitute an externality. We consider two possible spillover effects: the effect on the international exchange value of the dollar and the connection between oil prices and domestic inflation.

The argument that higher oil prices translate into depreciation of the dollar seems intuitively appealing. An increase in the price of oil means (assuming oil demand is price-inelastic) that total payments for oil will rise and (assuming all other trade is fixed) the current account will move toward deficit. A current account deficit leads to an overall balance-of-payments deficit (assuming no change in capital flows), which in turn implies an excess supply of dollars in foreign exchange markets. Consequently, the international value of the dollar will fall and all U.S. imports will be more costly—the United States must export more goods to buy the same amount of imports. While this is a pecuniary effect, it could be viewed as relevant to U.S. national welfare in the same way that U.S. interests are related to monopsony power: limits on U.S. oil imports could curb the cost. However, while the argument may have appeal, the necessary sequence of assumptions is not likely to hold.

The conclusion of two complementary approaches to the analysis of the balance-of-payments effects on prices, and the behavior of exchange rates after each oil price shock, is that it is inappropriate to attribute an exchange rate externality to oil imports. One analytical approach is concerned with real terms-of-trade effects of higher oil prices, as in Nancy P. Marion and Lars Svensson (1986), which refers to the amount of imports a given unit of exports will command in the international market. A rise in the price of oil means that the United States must export more goods to buy the same amount of oil, but Marion and Svensson demonstrate that the overall terms-of-trade effect of higher oil prices can be positive or negative for any individual oil importing country, depending on special circumstances for each country.

The second analytical approach by Paul Krugman (1983) looks at the effect of oil prices on the monetary exchange rate, and shows again that the relationship between a country's exchange rate (or, for that matter, its current account position) and the price of oil is ambiguous in general. All oil importing countries will experience an initial current account deficit when the price of oil rises, but the effect on exchange rates among oil importing countries will depend on the willingness of the oil exporting countries to hold different foreign currencies (that is, on relative capital flows). If oil exporters prefer to hold more dollars than other currencies, for example, the dollar exchange rate will rise. Over time, the exporting countries will spend their foreign currencies on goods or assets, and the countries of preference for these expenditures will experience currency appreciation.

An empirical study of exchange rate behavior by Bharat Trehan (1986) finds weak support for the view that higher oil prices lead to an appreciation of the dollar contrary to the externality argument. A more defensible conclusion, in view of the weak statistical results, is that the price of oil is a poor predictor of the dollar exchange rate, either positively or negatively.

We turn next to the connection between oil prices and inflation. Higher oil prices will no doubt raise all prices somewhat, but unless oil prices continue to rise there is no ongoing inflationary process in the long term, only a one-time increase in the price level (though that increase may take time to dissipate). Similarly, a rise in oil prices will aggravate an inflationary process that is already in motion, but higher oil prices are not the cause of that inflationary process. The distinction between inflation and a rise in price levels and between cause and effect is important in establishing whether higher oil prices give rise to a need for a deflationary policy response.

To attribute an inflationary side effect to increases in oil prices, the increase must be in the rate of growth of oil prices, not merely in the level of oil prices. Our understanding of world oil markets is not complete enough to rule out the possibility of a boost in oil price growth rates. However, a rise in growth rates is inconsistent with the predictions of resource supply theory and with the record of actual oil prices. Resource supply theory as described in Douglas Bohi and Michael Toman (1984) predicts that increased producer market power will likely result in a rise in the initial price level, and that the price thereafter will likely grow more slowly over time compared to the price in a competitive market.

Another possibility is that an ongoing bout of inflation can result from an overzealous monetary authority who is seeking to accommodate a rise in oil prices. The monetary authority could err in estimating what is required to adjust to a higher level of oil prices, thereby setting in motion an inflationary spiral that requires a deflationary jolt to stop. However, inflation scenarios that rely on planning errors by the monetary authorities can be triggered by any number of events; to focus policy on the triggering event rather than the cause of the problem seems misguided at best. In short, any connection between oil prices and inflation seems dubious and would reflect at most a policy failure, not a market failure.

Military Expenditures and Oil Import Costs

It is sometimes argued that substantial military expenditures such as in the Middle East add a substantial premium to the social cost of oil imports. This argument rests on several logical and practical flaws. First, military expenditures are a cost of mitigating energy insecurity rather than a cost of insecurity itself. The cost of insecurity should tell us how much we would be willing to spend on mitigation; if the former is taken to be the same as the latter, then whatever we spend would be considered worth the cost. In addition, these expenditures are made to serve a variety of other national security interests, so it is incorrect to interpret all of these expenditures as a cost of pursuing energy security. Indeed, since the expenditures are a common cost for many purposes, any assignment of cost shares among different purposes is arbitrary.

The arithmetic of assigning a premium to oil imports based on military expenditures also suffers from shortcomings. Spreading these costs over only U.S. imports is questionable for at least two reasons. First, if energy security is primarily a question of adjusting to price shocks, where the damages depend on total oil consumption or even total energy consumption (see below), then the unit cost of seeking to stabilize the market through military activity should reflect this larger denominator. Second, and more important, the U.S. undertakes a military presence in the Middle East on behalf of many allies, not just for its own narrow self-interest. It is incorrect to assign all these costs to U.S. oil or energy use without recognizing the existence of benefits to the United States that transcend its position in the oil market. These considerations, together with the observation that military expenditures serve multiple purposes, sharply reduce the apparent "military expenditures premium."

POTENTIAL EXTERNALITIES RELATED TO PRICE VARIABILITY

Externalities may arise from difficulties experienced by the domestic economy in adjusting to rapid fluctuations in world oil prices due to a shift in world oil supply or demand. Moreover, given substitution possibilities between petroleum and other energy sources, Knut Mork (1985) shows that oil price shocks are capable of causing a simultaneous disruption in all energy markets. The overall energy shock could have additional macroeconomic consequences.

Energy price shocks can have both long-term and short-term effects on the economy, though only the short-term effects will likely involve externalities. Long-term adjustments will take place in the amount of energy-related investment and in the rate of innovation. These adjustments could have significant effects on the level of productivity in the economy over time.[4] However, these adjustment costs will be fully internalized in private decisions and there is no a priori reason to believe the costs could be avoided by correcting a market failure. Thus the following discussion of price-related externalities, drawn from Bohi (1989), deals exclusively with the problems of adjusting to a sudden change in energy prices.

The most important short-term adjustment problem concerns the possibility that real wages will not adjust to maintain employment when energy prices suddenly rise. A rise in energy prices will reduce the use of energy and (when energy and labor services are complementary inputs in production) will lower the marginal productivity of labor. Lower productivity implies an increase in the cost of labor, which employers will seek to reduce. If wages cannot be reduced (for institutional reasons such as periodic labor contracts), employers have no choice but to reduce the amount of employment. The decline in employment is an indirect effect of higher energy prices that lowers total output of the economy.

A second possible indirect effect of an energy price shock is a reduction in capital services because of premature obsolescence of energy-using capital stocks. A sudden increase in energy prices will make some energy-inefficient capital goods superfluous, either because of competition with more efficient capital goods or because the demand for more expensive energy-intensive end products declines. A decline in capital services implies a reduction in productive capability throughout the economy, and thus a reduction in potential output.

Employment and output losses may be further aggravated by difficulties in reallocating factors in response to changes in the mix of final demand brought about by changes in product prices. For example, commodity price rigidities could cause inefficient inventory accumulations in some sectors and unwanted reductions in others. Another source of commodity price rigidity is public utility regulation in the natural gas and electricity industries. Since prices are set administratively in these industries and will not easily adjust to changes in market conditions, energy supplies will not necessarily flow to their highest valued uses, and productivity can be adversely affected.

These macroeconomic adjustment problems are fundamentally different in character from the problems associated with oil imports discussed previously. The problem of excess wealth transfer for imports depends on the *level* of energy prices and the volume of energy *imports*, whereas the macroeconomic adjustment problems depend on the size of the *change* in energy prices and the volume of energy *consumption*. In addition, the wealth transfer problem operates at a fundamentally national scale, whereas the oil price adjustment problems could vary significantly from region to region depending on the causes of the disturbance, the flexibility of local energy production and consumption, and the effects of energy prices on local labor markets and capital utilization.

EMPIRICAL INFORMATION

Empirical studies of the macroeconomic effects of energy price shocks do not try to distinguish between the potential externalities described previously and the loss of gross output. The distinction is important because the loss of GNP that occurs when more resources are required to pay for energy is not an externality. Moreover, whether the increased cost refers to higher payments for oil imports or the further diversion of resources away from other activities and into domestic energy production, these responses by the private sector to higher prices represent costs that are internalized in private decisions. In reviewing the macroeconomic studies, therefore, the best we can do is to try to draw inferences about the empirical significance of the externality component from measures of the gross macroeconomic costs.

Perhaps surprisingly, the evidence about the gross costs at the national level is mixed. The coincidence of timing of the two oil price increases and two recessions during the 1970s leads many observers to believe that the effects of energy price shocks on the economy are large.[5] This view is best represented by an extensive simulation analysis conducted by the Energy Modeling Forum and published in B. Hickman, H. Huntington, and J. Sweeney (1987).[6] The study compares estimates of the effects of various oil shock scenarios on U.S. GNP calculated by a group of 14 macroeconometric models, including standard large-scale models used by forecasting and consulting companies. While there is considerable variation among the findings among individual models, there is a consensus that the calculated GNP losses are substantial.[7]

The authors of the EMF study take pains to enumerate caveats that must be considered when interpreting their results. They indicate that the individual model results vary significantly because of differences among the models with respect to the relationship between GNP and the overall price level, and with respect to the link between oil prices and the general price level. Nevertheless, most of the models have the same basic mechanism for the transmission of energy shocks. Increased energy costs cause firms to increase their price mark-ups, and higher prices depress aggregate spending. The reduction in aggregate spending reduces the demand for labor, but wages cannot fall fast enough to trim labor costs in line with reduced demand. Consequently, employment declines.

The main source of skepticism about the results of these models is that the equations of the models employ parameters estimated from limited experience with price shocks over the 1950–80 period. During this period real oil prices were stable or falling except for the two brief explosions during the 1970s. Thus, the conclusions of the models regarding the relationship between oil price increases and GNP will be determined by the experience with the two recessions that followed the 1970s price shocks, although this experience may not be representative of the true energy-economy relationship. As noted below, the recessions experienced in some countries could be explained by factors other than energy prices, such as differences in macroeconomic stabilization policies. It is possible, in other words, that the econometric models are confusing the effects of deflationary macroeconomic policies with those of changes in oil prices.

Another reason for skepticism in blaming energy prices for the recessions of the 1970s is that the price collapse of 1986 did not cause an economic boom in the United States and other industrial countries. The absence of a positive boost to GNP in the major industrial countries suggests again that the experience of the 1970s gives a misleading impression of the energy-economy relationship. Additional corroboration is provided by comparing the conclusions of J. D.

Hamilton (1983) with Mork (1989). Hamilton looks at correlations between energy prices and GNP before 1981 and concludes that higher energy prices cause recessions, while Mork finds that the same statistical methods applied to data extended through 1986 give a different impression.

Doubts about the meaningfulness of statistical results based on aggregate economic variables led Bohi (1989, 1991) to examine disaggregated industry data for the United States, Germany, Japan, and the United Kingdom for explanations of the experiences of these countries during the 1973–74 and 1979–80 shocks. The results of this analysis suggest that energy prices may have had little to do with the macroeconomic problems of the 1970s. To begin with, one might expect more similarity in the way different sectors of the economy were affected, both across the two recessions and across the four countries, if the common cause was energy prices. Within each country, the industries hit hardest are quite dissimilar from one recession to the next and, for each recession, the industries hit hardest are dissimilar across the four countries.

Another set of statistical tests examined the relative economic performance of different sectors to see if the effects of the shocks are more pronounced among the more energy-intensive sectors. The tests reveal no significant negative correlations between energy intensity and changes in output, employment, or capital formation for any of the four countries. Nor does the evidence suggest that adjustment costs caused by changes in the composition of final demand are more severe in energy-intensive sectors. Finally, in contrast with the rigid wages argument, changes in real wages appear to vary negatively with energy intensity in the two shock periods, suggesting that wages were more responsive in labor markets where unemployment has been more serious.

These and other findings suggest that one should look to factors other than energy prices to explain the macroeconomic failures during the 1970s. The alternative hypothesis suggested in Bohi (1989) is that the industrialized countries were already combating inflation when the oil price shocks hit and, except for Japan in 1979, further deflated their respective economies to mitigate increases in their general price levels. Given that Japan was the only industrial country to avoid a recession after the 1979 oil shock, it is plausible that the monetary authorities rather than energy prices are to blame for the recessions.

In empirical analyses of the recessions it is of course difficult to separate the influences of the monetary authorities from those of oil prices, and research to date fails to make a credible distinction.[8] A great deal more study is required before we can begin to understand the nature of energy-economy interactions at the national and regional levels. If nothing definitive can be said about the gross economic costs of energy price shocks, it follows that even less can be said about the magnitude of any embedded externalities.

POLICY IMPLICATIONS

Among the potential externalities associated with the volume of oil imports, only the potential consequences of OPEC market power appear to be significant.

Indirect externalities operating through exchange rates and inflation are neither conceptually nor empirically credible. With regard to variability in the price of energy, there exists a plausible externality associated with institutional and technological constraints on wage and price flexibility, but it is difficult conceptually to identify the extent of any externality and to separate the associated cost from gross adjustment costs. The empirical literature provides no information on the magnitude of the externality and even wide disagreement about the magnitude of the gross adjustment costs.

In short, there is not enough solid empirical information on these externalities to give an informed policy recommendation (other than to invest in economic research that might help resolve some of the ambiguities identified here). However, for the two types of externalities that may be present—market power and adjustment rigidities—the foregoing discussion has useful implications.

Our discussion of the market power issue indicated that, because of threats of retaliation, direct import controls would not be a wise policy choice to address this externality. In principle, a combination of taxes on energy consumption and subsidies for energy production could be devised to achieve the same effect on domestic supply and demand as import controls, but with less visibility as a beggar-thy-neighbor strategy and therefore with less risk of retaliation. However, such alternatives have their own drawbacks. Consumption taxes raise domestic prices to force conservation, which may be inconsistent with concerns about macroeconomic adjustment costs. Subsidies to domestic oil production would have to be very high to overcome the high marginal cost of replacing reserves in the United States.[9] In either case, it is difficult in practice to set taxes or subsidies that balance the clear deadweight losses of resource misallocation against a reduction in the market power problem whose magnitude and timing is uncertain.

The only policy recommendation in this category without a serious drawback is government support of energy R&D that will mitigate OPEC market power. Any R&D that will result in an increase in the price elasticity of world oil supply or demand will serve to reduce OPEC market power. This support for R&D stops short of favoring mandates or inducements to reduce energy use or develop petroleum that otherwise would be noneconomic. Such measures have the same drawback as energy taxes in requiring up-front social costs for uncertain future beliefs. The goal of policy in this area should be confined to developing options until or unless more serious problems of market power emerge in world energy markets.

There are no feasible policy options for directly addressing the causes of adjustment rigidities. For example, it is not feasible to replace collective bargaining or other established labor contract arrangements with an option that allows for greater wage flexibility. Similarly, efforts to make natural gas and electricity prices more responsive to market forces are limited by the recognized need to control the market power of legal monopolies. Thus our attention turns to possible second-best policies.

Taxes may be employed to reduce energy consumption, or to shift consumption away from the most volatile forms of energy, in order to reduce the impact of an energy price shock when it occurs. However, the logic of this option is strained because taxes force the economy to make the same adjustments as external oil price shocks. While self-inflicted pain may be imposed in more manageable doses, the costs are just as real and they are certain and permanent, while the costs of oil market disruptions are uncertain and temporary. Consequently, circumstances are unlikely to weigh in favor of energy consumption taxes.

If it is not possible to mitigate the effects of energy price changes, we are left with policy options that work to dampen fluctuations in energy prices. With respect to oil, two options are available—a Strategic Petroleum Reserve (SPR) and development of new technology—both of which have been undertaken in the United States. Investment in the SPR has been substantial—in excess of $20 billion has been spent to store close to 600 million barrels of oil. The oil can be drawn down at a maximum rate of 3.5 mbd, although to date it has been used sparingly and with questionable effect.

Many policy analysts recommend that the SPR be drawn down at its maximum rate as early as possible to maximize its effect in a crisis (e.g., Horwich and Weimer 1984; and Verleger 1990).[10] Bohi and Toman (1988) and Bohi (1991) suggest a more selective approach where use of the SPR is contingent upon cooperation from other major oil importing countries to limit their demand for imports, either directly through quotas or indirectly through coordinated stock drawdowns of their own. Selectivity and cooperation are recommended because the maximum contribution of the SPR is small relative to the daily oil consumption rate (60 mbd) and the potential increase in private oil storage (several hundred million barrels during the early months of the 1979 crisis, for example). According to this line of reasoning, it would be too costly for the United States to build an SPR that is large enough to dampen oil prices in a crisis without the help of other countries. Cooperation is therefore considered a necessary complement to the SPR to achieve effective control of oil prices.

Investing in R&D will reduce oil price volatility if it results in new technologies that increase energy demand and supply elasticities. This option is the only one that addresses both the problem of OPEC market power and the problem of oil price volatility.

NOTES

1. Apart from this issue, U.S. oil import restrictions will complicate trading relationships with non-OPEC trading partners such as Canada, Norway, and the United Kingdom. This complication, and the overlay of political interests on economic interests (e.g., U.S. support for Saudi Arabia) makes it very difficult to separate friend from foe in designing oil import policy.

2. Margaret Walls (1990) similarly concludes that the direct value of import controls is low.

3. Nevertheless, it is conceivable that some strategic R&D could be subject to scrutiny as a nontariff barrier under the General Agreement on Tariffs and Trade.

4. See Jorgenson, Gollop, and Fraumeni (1987); Jorgenson (1988); and Hogan and Jorgenson (1991).

5. Reports by U.S. Department of Energy (1987, 1988) reinforce this view.

6. U.S. Department of Energy (1988) also estimates large macroeconomic costs due to energy price shocks.

7. Broadman and Hogan (1986, 1988) also calculate a macroeconomic disturbance premium equal to 10–12 percent of the normal-market oil price, though the basis for their calculation is different and they mistakenly attribute the premium to oil imports rather than to total oil consumption.

8. For example, compare Hickman, Huntington, and Sweeney (1987); Sachs (1982); Bruno (1986); and Helliwell (1988).

9. It may be more cost-effective to direct those subsidies to production in other parts of the non-OPEC world where marginal costs are significantly lower, perhaps in a way that mimics Japanese involvement in resource development in Australia and other Pacific Rim countries.

10. Toman (1993) provides an extensive review of previous SPR analyses.

REFERENCES

Adelman, M. A. "The Clumsy Cartel." *Energy Journal* 1 (1) (January 1980): 43–52.

———. "Scarcity and World Oil Prices." *Review of Economics and Statistics* 68 (3) (August 1986): 387–397.

———. "Mineral Depletion, with Special Reference to Petroleum." *Review of Economics and Statistics* 72 (1) (February 1990): 1–10.

Bohi, Douglas R. *Energy Price Shocks and Macroeconomic Performance.* Washington, DC: Resources for the Future, 1989.

———. "On the Macroeconomic Effects of Energy Price Shocks." *Resources and Energy* 13 (2) (June 1991): 145–162.

Bohi, Douglas R. and Michael A. Toman. *Analyzing Nonrenewable Resource Supply.* Washington, DC: Resources for the Future, 1984.

———. "Restructuring the IEA Crisis Management Program to Serve Members' Interests Better." In G. Horwich and D. L. Weimer (eds.), *Responding to International Oil Crises.* Washington, DC: American Enterprise Institute, 1988.

Broadman, Harry G. and W. W. Hogan. "Oil Tariff Policy in an Uncertain Market." Energy and Environmental Policy Center Discussion Paper E–86-11. Cambridge, MA: Harvard University, 1986.

———. "The Numbers Say Yes" (part of a special feature, "Is an Oil Tariff Justified? An American Debate"). *Energy Journal* 9 (3) (July 1988): 7–30.

Bruno, Michael. "Aggregate Supply and Demand Factors in OECD Unemployment." *Economica* 53 (supplement 1986): 535–552.

Energy Modeling Forum. *World Oil*, Summary Report. Stanford, CA: Stanford University, 1982.

Gately, D. "Lessons from the 1986 Oil Price Collapse." *Brookings Papers on Economic Activity* 2 (1986): 237–284.

Griffin, J. M. "OPEC Behavior: A Test of Alternative Hypotheses." *American Economic Review* 75 (5) (December 1985): 954–963.

Hamilton, J. D. "Oil and the Macroeconomy Since World War II." *Journal of Political Economy* 91 (2) (April 1983): 228–248.

Helliwell, John F. "Comparative Macroeconomics of Stagflation." *Journal of Economic Literature* 26 (1) (March 1988): 1–28.

Hickman, B. G., H. G. Huntington, and J. L. Sweeney (eds.). *Macroeconomic Impacts of Energy Shocks.* Amsterdam: North-Holland, 1987.

Hogan, William W. and Dale W. Jorgenson. "Productivity Trends and the Cost of Reducing CO_2 Emissions." *Energy Journal* 12 (1) (1991): 67–85.

Horwich, George and D. L. Weimer. *Oil Price Shocks, Market Response, and Contingency Planning.* Washington, DC: American Enterprise Institute, 1984.

Jones, C. T. "OPEC Behavior Under Falling Prices: Implications for Cartel Stability." *Energy Journal* 2 (4) (Fall 1990): 23–41.

Jorgenson, Dale W. "Productivity and Postwar U.S. Economic Growth." *Journal of Economic Perspectives* 2 (4) (Fall 1988): 23–41.

Jorgenson, Dale W., Frank M. Gollop, and Barbara M. Fraumeni. *Productivity and U.S. Economic Growth.* Harvard Economic Studies, vol. 159. Cambridge, MA: Harvard University Press, 1987.

Krugman, Paul. "Oil Shocks and Exchange Rate Dynamics." In Jacob Frenkel (ed.), *Exchange Rates and International Macroeconomics.* Chicago: University of Chicago Press, 1983.

MacAvoy, P. *Crude Oil Prices as Determined by OPEC and Market Fundamentals.* Cambridge, MA: Ballinger, 1982.

Marion, Nancy Peregrim and Lars E. O. Svensson. "The Terms of Trade Between Oil Importers." *Journal of International Economics* 20 (1/2) (February 1986): 99–113.

Mork, Knut A. "Flexibility in Intercommodity Substitution May Sharpen Price Fluctuation." *Quarterly Journal of Economics* 100 (2) (May 1985): 447–463.

———. "Oil and the Macroeconomy When Prices Go Up and Down: An Extension of Hamilton's Results." *Journal of Political Economy* 97 (3) (June 1989): 740–744.

Sachs, J. "Stabilization Policies in the World Economy: Scope and Skepticism." *American Economic Review* 72 (2) (May 1982): 56–61.

Teece, David J. "OPEC Behavior: An Alternative View." In James M. Griffin and David J. Teece (eds.), *OPEC Behavior and World Oil Prices.* London: George Allen and Unwin, 1982.

Toman, Michael A. "The Economics of Energy Security: Theory, Evidence, Policy." In Allen V. Kneese and James L. Sweeney (eds.), *Handbook of Natural Resource and Energy Economics*, vol. 3: *Economics of Energy and Minerals.* Amsterdam: North-Holland, 1993.

Trehan, Bharat. "Oil Prices, Exchange Rates and the U.S. Economy: An Empirical Investigation." *Federal Reserve Bank of San Francisco Economic Review* No. 4 (Fall 1986): 25–43.

U.S. Department of Energy (DOE). *Energy Security: A Report to the President.* Washington, DC: DOE, 1987.

———. *United States Energy Policy: 1980–1988.* Washington, DC: DOE, 1988.

Verleger, Philip K., Jr. *Oil Markets in Turmoil.* Cambridge, MA: Ballinger, 1990.

Walls, Margaret A. "Welfare Cost of an Oil Import Fee." *Contemporary Policy Issues* 8 (2) (April 1990): 176–189.

Chapter 20

Oil as a Strategic Commodity

Robert R. Copaken

Crude oil is perhaps the world's most strategic commodity. Modern societies, whether industrial or agricultural, cannot function without it. Wars have been fought over access to it. Oil producing countries have used its availability as a political weapon.

Oil is the world's largest cash commodity. In 1992 worldwide crude oil production totaled about 60.3 million barrels a day, which was worth about $370 billion on the free market. In the 20 years since the early 1970s, the oil market's volatility has pushed prices up by as much as 150 percent or pushed them down by 50 percent. Risk management has become a key consideration for the oil industry as well as for commercial and industrial end users. Back in 1978 the New York Mercantile Exchange (NYMEX) established an energy futures trading market in heating oil. In 1981 a gasoline futures contract was added, followed by crude oil futures in 1983, propane futures in 1987, and natural gas futures in 1990. The growth in NYMEX's energy futures trading volume and open interest levels underscores the market's important role in the reduction of the significant price risk inherent in the oil industry today. NYMEX has seen the establishment of other similar commodity exchanges in other trading and financial centers around the world, such as the International Petroleum Exchange (IPE) in London, the Singapore International Monetary Exchange (SIMEX), and even an Oil Exchange in Russia. Thus, the international oil market has become globalized as an element of the world economy, with traders and speculators able to buy and sell at a moment's notice, around the clock as well as around the world.

NYMEX futures prices are widely and rapidly disseminated worldwide, ensuring that the exchange's quotations reflect the real market value of oil—true price transparency. NYMEX ranks as the world's fifth largest futures exchange, allowing companies the world over to use prices generated on the NYMEX trading floor as benchmarks in a multitude of cash markets. Chapter 5 provides a thorough discussion of their derivative products. As one looks at oil's place in world trade one must ask: How has oil come to assume not just economic but strategic value as well? More important: will oil continue to be a strategic commodity in the post–Cold War world? A brief historical survey of oil as an element of national power will help us to address these questions.

OIL AS AN ELEMENT OF NATIONAL POWER

Winston Churchill's conversion of the British Royal Navy fleet of ships from coal to oil as its power source was a critical decision of major strategic significance for later Allied victories during World War I. The navy's traditional fuel, Welsh coal, was safe, secure, and domestically available. Oil, on the other hand, would make the Royal Navy depend upon distant and insecure supplies from Persia, as Iran was then known. But to Churchill, the strategic benefits—greater speed and more efficient use of manpower—made the choice of oil the decisive one for maintaining Britain's naval supremacy (Yergin 1991; 12). In the words of British Lord Curzon in 1918, the Allies "floated to victory on a wave of oil" (Yergin, 1991: 183).

Japan, 1930–41

The Japanese began in the early 1930s to pursue a relentless policy of imperial expansion, to create what they called their "Greater East Asian co-prosperity sphere." Access to petroleum to supply the ships and planes of the Imperial Japanese Navy and Air Force became central to the war aims and planning of the Japanese officers. Those officers who had studied Germany's defeat in World War I attributed its defeat to economic vulnerability, primarily Germany's lack of raw materials. While petroleum amounted to only a small percentage of its total energy consumption, its significance lay in its use by the military and in shipping. Japan imported the vast majority of its oil (about 80 percent) from the United States and another 10 percent from the Dutch East Indies (later known as Indonesia) (Yergin 1991: 307).

The United States pursued an "open door" policy in Asia, which was diametrically opposed to further Japanese expansion of its empire. With conflicting goals, there was bound to be a clash of interests between these two great powers. As Japan's sense of economic vulnerability grew, its military began to focus on its two main sources of oil imports (the United States and the Dutch East Indies) and upon the need to build up Japan's own domestic oil industry, in preparation for possible war against China, a potential rival for power in East and Southeast Asia. Finally, in August 1937, Japan went to war with China. Public opinion in the United States saw China as the victim of Japanese aggression and sought means to limit the export of goods to Japan. Ironically, Japan's apprehension about its dependence upon the United States for most of its oil led it to pursue a policy aimed at expansion in East Asia that ultimately would have to be opposed by the United States. In fact, as has been pointed out by Daniel Yergin (1991: 309), in the late 1930s Japan's supply requirements for its war with China actually increased Japan's trade dependence on the United States.

Eventually, in the summer of 1941, the United States imposed a de facto embargo on the export to Japan of U.S. oil that could be upgraded to aviation gasoline, in retaliation for the Japanese aggression against China in the Manchurian area. The Japanese conceived the daring and provocative attack on the U.S. Pacific fleet stationed at Pearl Harbor, Hawaii, primarily in order to prevent American naval forces from launching interdictory attacks against Japanese oil tankers. These tankers were transporting oil vital to Japan's war efforts from the Dutch East Indies to the home islands of the empire. But for the fact that American aircraft carriers fortuitously happened to be at sea on maneuvers that Sunday, and the fact that the attackers did not go after U.S. oil storage tanks on land, the Japanese surprise attack would have been even more devastating than it was. Although eight battleships and six cruisers and destroyers were sunk or put out of commission and 189 planes were destroyed, the United States retained its ability to wage war in the Pacific (Goralski and Freeburg 1987: 153).

World War II, 1941–45

If oil and access to it was crucial in the Pacific theater during World War II, it was equally important in our conduct of the strategy of the war in Europe. Germany invaded Russia in June 1941, in part to secure the oil resources of Baku and the Caucasus region. Adolf Hitler realized the vital importance of oil to the smooth functioning of his Axis war machine, whether it was gasoline for trucks, diesel fuel for tanks and ships, or aviation fuel for the Luftwaffe. As the battle for Stalingrad graphically demonstrated by outrunning their supply lines, the Germans ran short of their oil supplies and lost their mobility (Yergin 1991: 337). This handicap proved fatal to Germany's making any further advance during the harsh Russian winter months that followed. Hitler also engaged in a costly and systematic effort to develop synthetic oil from coal, in conjunction with the German chemical company I. G. Farben. However, the prohibitive costs involved in this process made it uneconomic to pursue, once other more plentiful oil supplies became available elsewhere.

As World War II dragged on, the critical importance of petroleum to ultimate Allied victory became ever clearer. In the European, North African, and Pacific theaters of the conflict, the American military began to realize the importance of outproducing the enemy in the instruments of war. America's superior economic and industrial strengths were vital to this end. Because of its desperate fuel situation, Japan finally resorted to the kamikaze one-way suicide attacks. The fuel shortage severely limited the amount of training that Japanese pilots could obtain before being sent on operational missions. Thus, suicide attacks became the more effective method of attacking American battleships and carriers because the power of impact of the plane added to that of the bomb. Such attacks also provided spiritual inspiration to the ground units and to the Japanese public at large (Goralski and Freeburg 1987: 313). Japan had lost the power to wage war and finally, after atomic bombs were dropped on two of its major cities in August 1945, Japan surrendered unconditionally, ending the war in the Pacific.

The Middle East, 1945–93

By the close of World War II, the global balance of power had fundamentally shifted and the United States emerged as the most powerful and prosperous country in the world. The immediate postwar period was one of rapid decolonialization and the spread of profound nationalism throughout Asia and Africa. The presence and exploitation of the huge deposits of oil in the Middle East gave this region an economic importance and hence strategic value that it would not otherwise have had. As the biographers of James Forrestal point out, the enormous energy demands generated by World War II had been met almost entirely by American reserves—6 billion barrels out of a total of 7 billion used by the Allied war effort. During the war, the United States produced 75 percent of the world's oil and the Middle East a minuscule 5 percent. By 1947 it was known that the Middle East oil fields were the largest in the world, but they remained relatively undeveloped (Hoopes and Brinkley 1992: 338).

Following the revelations of the atrocities committed by the Nazis against European Jewry during the course of the war, political pressures in the United States began to be brought to bear on both major political parties by American Jewish leaders and others to find a permanent homeland for these displaced Jewish refugees from Hitler's death camps. Although President Harry Truman was sympathetic to the requests being made by American Jewish leaders for unrestricted immigration into Palestine, he was also being heavily lobbied by his own secretaries of State and Defense, as well as several representatives of the American oil industry, not to take a position on this issue that could alienate the key Arab oil states, especially Saudi Arabia's King Ibn Saud.

U.S. Secretary of Defense James Forrestal, who had been secretary of the Navy during the war, was thought by those working closely with him to be sympathetic to the plight of European Jews and their desire for a homeland, but he was "unable to agree that that desire should override every other national consideration" (Hoopes and Brinkley 1992: 390). He was considered by others to be anti-Semitic, and a U.S. press campaign endeavored to portray him as such (p. 398). A more balanced judgment may have been that Forrestal did not understand or fully appreciate the emotionally charged political pressures being exerted on the president by those sympathetic to the cause of a Jewish state.

The pressures exerted by the American oil lobby naturally were pro-Arab and no less intense, since they saw Arabian oil as vital to European economic recovery and consequently to Europe's postwar ability to stand up to the threat of Communism. In addition, the Arabian American Oil Company (Aramco) partners, that were most directly involved in the exploitation of Saudi Arabian oil feared that the Arab world might cut off American access to its oil if the United States supported the Zionists' cause. This fear was, it turned out, an exaggerated one, for a variety of reasons, including the fact that the Arab governments involved were weak and were not disposed to threaten cutting off America's access to their oil. Moreover, the Arab states needed U.S. dollars more, at least in those days, than we needed Arab oil (Cohen 1990: 100).

In the final analysis, despite vocal opposition by both the State and Defense Departments, President Truman went ahead with his decision to recognize the newly created state of Israel on May 14, 1948. Truman's decision, insofar as can be ascertained, was made on both moral and political grounds. He saw the compromise between the rival claims of American Jews and Arab oil interests as one of the most difficult choices he ever had to make. But ultimately it was a moral imperative that he could not ignore combined with the important political calculation not to alienate influential Jewish voters in the forthcoming presidential campaign of 1948 that led Truman to this decision (McCollough 1992: 595).

From that point on, American foreign policy toward the Middle East would be characterized by a distinct bifurcation that sometimes causes U.S. true intentions to be doubted by both sets of policy supporters. One set of considerations points in the direction of maintaining access to Middle Eastern oil by not alienating the Arabs; and a second set of considerations is aimed at resolution of the long-standing Arab-Israeli dispute while not jeopardizing Israel's security as a democratic and strategic ally in this politically unstable region. These two sets of policy considerations rest rather uncomfortably together within our overall policy framework, although less so in recent times because of a number of factors, including the end of the Cold War, the congenital weakness of OPEC, the weakening in Arab solidarity against Israel, the Egyptian peace with Israel, the unprecedented example of military cooperation between Western countries and Arab states against Iraq in the Persian Gulf War of 1990–91, and mutual recognition of Israel and the Palestine Liberation Organization. In the period since 1945, the Cold War came to dominate U.S. strategic thinking and containment of the threat of Soviet expansion became the chosen policy to deal with that threat.

This period was punctuated with a number of energy-related crises, such as the Suez crisis of 1956 and the enunciation of the Carter Doctrine of President Jimmy Carter in his State of the Union address delivered before a joint session of the Congress in January 1980. This statement came in response to the Soviet invasion of Afghanistan in December 1979 and in the wake of the Iranian seizure of U.S. embassy hostages. It made the U.S. position crystal clear. It stated that ''an attempt by any outside force to gain control of the Persian Gulf region will be regarded as an assault on the vital interests of the United States of America, and such an assault will be repelled by any means necessary, including military force'' (Carter 1981: 197).

It was during this period (1979–81) that oil prices went from $13 to $34/barrel, but by 1986 they had collapsed to $10/barrel. OPEC tried to control the market by setting production quotas, but their efforts were ultimately unsuccessful since it was impossible to prevent cheating through overproduction and offering of various forms of price discounts.

Saudi Arabian Oil Minister Sheik Zaki Yamani, who served in this capacity for more than two decades until his dismissal in October 1986, reminded people that oil is not an ordinary commodity like tea or coffee. ''Oil is a strategic commodity,'' the Sheik said (Yergin 1991: 721). Before turning to the future and some final, brief speculations about the strategic quality of oil in future post-Cold War conflicts, it is worthwhile to look back over the energy history of the past two decades, from 1973 to 1993. As most Americans contemplate that period, they are probably struck by how uncertain and unpredictable the worldwide energy situation was over that relatively brief period of time. This period has witnessed the Arab oil embargo of the United States in 1973–74, the Iranian revolution of 1979–80, the Iran-Iraq War that lasted almost a full decade, and finally the Persian Gulf War in which Iraq invaded Kuwait. If this series of conflicts does not serve to underline and emphasize the strategic quality of oil as a commodity, little else would.

In times of emergency or disruption, U.S. policymakers' attentions are focused primarily on dealing with the crisis of the moment. Yet, once that crisis is past or somehow resolved, the general public's perception tends to return to its somewhat parochial and myopic view of energy—namely, what is the price of a gallon of gasoline likely to be when we fill up the car's gas tank at the pump. Surely this here-and-now attitude misses the essential point about oil as a strategic commodity—namely, that it is a scarce, difficult- and expensive-to-find, depletable resource, which we in the West unfortunately must continue to import in larger and larger quantities from a politically unstable part of the world, the Middle East. As we have seen, access to this commodity has been identified as among our vital national interests, for which we are willing to employ the use of military force, if necessary.

The Situation in the 1990s

The United States is the world's largest consumer of energy, using over a quarter of the world's total energy output. That fact is not going to change. The United States is the second largest oil producer in the world, after Russia. However, American oil production is declining and will likely continue to decline gradually, absent major new ''finds'' or initiatives to halt or slow the decline. That is a fact that comes with being a mature oil province. The United States is also the world's largest importer of energy, mainly oil and gas. Oil imports in the future are likely to increase and could amount to 50 percent of our oil consumption by the mid- to late 1990s (Energy Information Administration 1993: 90). Russia's oil production is declining as well, but so is its demand for petroleum due to the anemic state of its economy and the inability of the non-Russian republics to find other sources of imports to replace sharply lower oil exports from the Russian Republic.

The Cold War has ended and with it the dangerous military confrontation between the United States and the Russians. But it does not take a great leap of imagination to wonder what U.S.-Russian relations might be like in the not-too-distant future when both countries are importing ever larger quantities of oil from essentially the same set of sources—the Persian Gulf oil exporting states. Ample evidence of how America's short-term preoccupation with keeping energy prices low makes it difficult to enunciate a coherent energy policy can be found in the recent congressional debate over the president's Deficit Reduction Plan. Specifically under consideration is the element of that plan that had initially begun life as a broad-based energy or Btu tax, but which survived by being reduced to a narrow 4.3 cents/gallon increase in the federal gasoline tax. As the *Washington Post* succinctly put the issue in an August 1, 1993 editorial entitled "Surrender on Energy": "After five months of struggling with energy taxes and the idea of a coherent energy policy, Congress has given up. It has settled for a barely visible increase of 4.3 cents a gallon on the gasoline tax" (p. C6). The problem with a 4.3-cents tax increase is that it is too small to do much good. A one-time increase of 4.3 cents would boost federal tax revenues just $4.3 billion a year.

What does this lengthy and acrimonious debate over the level and type of an energy-based tax say about the U.S. view of the priority of energy in its overall scheme of national security? Surely a growing level of oil imports into the United States should alert it to the strategic dangers inherent in its dependence upon potentially insecure sources of petroleum. In a highly competitive global oil market, it seems unlikely that any single producer or significant group of producers could arbitrarily restrict supplies or raise prices without the market making the necessary adjustments. But so long as Arab Gulf producers continue to try to influence the market, it is not completely competitive, and finding substitutes for imported Arab Gulf oil could be expensive. Perhaps the most striking example of oil's strategic value today is the creation and maintenance of an underground oil stockpile of 575 million barrels in a Strategic Petroleum Reserve, which could compensate for a sudden and complete loss of all Persian Gulf imports into the United States for several months. Other oil consuming countries in Europe and Asia have also stockpiled oil to be used in the event of a supply disruption.

CONCLUSION

The future role of oil as a strategic commodity is not predictable. But the United States must try to react carefully to the new conflicting challenges of the post–Cold War period. If collective security can be used more effectively in the future, then perhaps the United States can rely less on using conventional military force unilaterally to ensure access to oil. In the future, the measure of a nation's security will lie more in economic and less in military terms. International efforts to control global climate change and to protect the environment will also impose limits on what can be done to meet energy needs, vital though they may be. In the final analysis, there will be several constraints upon consuming countries' ability to satisfy their insatiable appetite for oil—an appetite that will continue to be inextricably linked to both economic and military security.

REFERENCES

Carter, Jimmy. *Public Papers of the Presidents, 1980–81.* Book I. Washington, DC: U.S. Government Printing Office, 1981, p. 197.

Cohen, Michael J. *Truman & Israel.* Berkeley: University of California Press, 1990.

Goralski, Robert and Russell W. Freeburg. *Oil and War: How the Deadly Struggle for Fuel in WW II Meant Victory or Defeat.* New York: Morrow, 1987.

Hoopes, Townsend and Douglas Brinkley. *Driven Patriot: The Life and Times of James Forrestal.* New York: Knopf, 1992.

McCollough, David. *Truman.* New York: Simon and Schuster, 1992.

"Surrender on Energy." Editorial, *Washington Post,* August 1, 1993, p. 6C.

U.S. Energy Information Administration. *The Annual Energy Outlook 1993.* Table A8. Washington, DC: U.S. Department of Energy, U.S. Government Printing Office, 1993, p. 90.

Yergin, Daniel. *The Prize: The Epic Quest for Oil, Money, and Power.* New York: Simon and Schuster, 1991.

Chapter 21

Petroleum and National Security

David L. Weimer

Secure access to petroleum has been an important factor in international relations throughout this century (Yergin 1991). The switch of fuel for ships from coal to oil, soon followed by the mechanization of ground forces and the development of airpower, made petroleum an essential military commodity. Indeed, restricted access to petroleum influenced the strategies, and contributed to the eventual defeats, of Japan and Germany in World War II. Of even greater significance today is the widespread use of petroleum as an input in transportation, electricity generation, space heating, and the petrochemical industry. Because petroleum is such an important input to modern industrialized economies, large and sudden rises in crude oil prices can have negative economic effects: reduced domestic product, increased unemployment, and greater price inflation. It is the vulnerability of economies to such oil price shocks, rather than access to crude oil per se, that today lies at the heart of the energy security problem for the United States and other net importers of petroleum.

This chapter focuses on the energy security of the United States. While most of the discussion applies to other net importers of petroleum, two factors distinguish the circumstances of U.S. energy security policy from that of most other countries. First, because the United States accounts for a large fraction of the world demand for crude oil (26 percent in 1992; 15.9 million barrels/day of petroleum consumption versus world crude oil production of 60.4 million barrels/day), its energy security policies have potential for affecting the world price of oil. Second, because the United States has substantial domestic production (8.98 million barrels/day of crude oil and natural gas plant production in 1992), its energy security policies involve substantial distributional effects of political significance. These points have relevance to both the effectiveness and political feasibility of alternative U.S. energy security policies.

The discussion of energy security in this chapter proceeds as follows: First, it begins by making the distinction between dependence on imported oil and vulnerability to oil price shocks. Second, it emphasizes the importance of thinking about energy security in terms of a world oil market that distributes available supplies to their most valued uses. Third, it provides a framework for understanding the costs of oil price shocks. Finally, it considers the advantages and disadvantages of the two most prominent energy security policies: oil import fees and oil stockpiling.

DEPENDENCE VERSUS VULNERABILITY

The United States relies on petroleum for about 40 percent of its energy. It currently imports over 40 percent of the petroleum it uses.[1] Thus, the United States depends on foreign supplies of petroleum for an important fraction of its energy. Nevertheless, U.S. dependence on petroleum imports by itself does not necessarily pose a serious public policy problem. One of the simplest but most important insights from economics is that both buyers and sellers enjoy gains from trade. In the case of petroleum trade, the U.S. economy benefits greatly from the availability of petroleum imports that provide energy at less cost than do domestic sources.

The public policy concern about petroleum import dependence arises because the world oil market is vulnerable to price shocks. Large and sudden increases in the price of oil inflict large economic costs on the U.S. economy. An important component of these costs is the dollars, which represent claims on goods and services, that flow from U.S. consumers to foreign oil producers. For any particular price shock, higher levels of postshock imports result in greater transfers of wealth out of the U.S. economy. Because they are the starting point for postshock adjustments, higher preshock import levels generally result in greater economic costs, other things equal.

The major source of the vulnerability of the world oil market to price shocks is the concentration of production and reserves in the Persian Gulf, a politically unstable region of the world with high risks of conflicts that can interfere with the supply of oil to the world market. In 1992 the Persian Gulf countries accounted for about 27 percent (16.1 mbd) of the total world production of crude oil. Saudi Arabia alone accounts for over one-half of this production. Events, such as the closing of the Persian Gulf to shipping or the loss of Saudi production because of invasion or insurrection, could remove sufficient quantities of crude oil from the world market to cause economically significant price shocks.

Oil price shocks during the last 20 years have had their origins in the Persian Gulf. The 1973–74 quadrupling of prices resulted from production reductions orchestrated by the Organization of Arab Petroleum Exporting Countries (OAPEC) in retaliation for U.S. support of Israel in the October War. The 1979–80 doubling of prices followed reductions in Iranian production during the revolution against the shah. More modest price rises caused by attacks on shipping during the war between Iran and Iraq and the recent Gulf War following the Iraqi invasion of Kuwait remind us of the region's continuing potential for conflict.

The importance of the Persian Gulf to the world oil market is likely to grow in the future. It currently contains approximately half the world's proven reserves of crude oil with excellent prospects for further additions. With oil production already falling in the United States and the former Soviet Union, the countries that until recently produced the most crude oil, it is likely that the Persian Gulf will account for an even larger share of world supply in the future. Thus, unless political circumstances change to reduce the risks of the loss of supply from the Persian Gulf, it is likely to remain the major source of the vulnerability of the world oil market to price shocks.

Note that the energy security problem is not that the world is about to run out of crude oil. Proven reserves are at an all-time high and likely to grow before declining. As reserves become depleted sometime in the future, market forces will lead to gradual, and easily accommodated, energy price increases. The expectation of higher prices will elicit investments in a large variety of alternative energy sources that will substitute for crude oil. Unlike many other areas of public policy, energy security should be viewed as a short-run rather than long-run problem.

THE WORLD OIL MARKET

Oil is a highly fungible commodity that is traded in a world market. Traders can profit by moving crude oil and petroleum products among regions until prices differ only by transportation costs. Their efforts tend to equalize prices across regions so that all importers and exporters effectively trade in the same market. That market is governed by the law of supply and demand, which national policies cannot repeal.

Much confusion about energy security policy has resulted from the failure to understand the world oil market. Several misconceptions are worth considering. The first is that oil producing countries can effectively target an embargo against specific importing countries. The ease with which oil can be transshipped from one destination to another, however, renders targeted embargoes ineffective. Despite the fact that the OAPEC embargo against the United States and the Netherlands in 1973 failed to reduce supply or raise prices disproportionately in these countries, the framers of the International Energy Agency (IEA) included among its powers the imposition of an emergency sharing plan to administratively counter targeted embargoes (Smith 1988). Analysis suggests that if it were to be implemented, an extremely difficult task because of limitations of information, the sharing agreement would substantially raise the aggregate costs of the price shock to IEA members (Horwich, Jenkins-Smith, and Weimer 1988; Horwich and Weimer 1988a&b). To the extent that any policy is needed to resist targeted embargoes, it is simple for IEA members to facilitate easy transshipment by agreeing not to restrict the export of crude oil and petroleum products.

The second misconception is that the energy security of a country depends on the vulnerability of its sources of supply. Because traders will move supplies to exploit price differences, the instantaneous loss of supply to any one country will soon be spread among all countries. Thus, the percentage of U.S. imports from the Persian Gulf is not the relevant consideration for assessing U.S. vulnerability. Rather, the percentage of world supply from the Persian Gulf is the relevant consideration.

The third misconception is that the oligopolistic power exercised by OPEC renders the analysis of oil price shocks in terms of supply and demand invalid. The willingness of OPEC, especially Saudi Arabia, to restrict production has enabled it to keep the world price of oil above what it would be in a perfectly competitive market. Though directly costly to importers, the higher prices have had the effect of reducing the vulnerability of the world market to price shocks by encouraging production outside of OPEC (and the Persian Gulf). In terms of analyzing oil price shocks, the important consideration is the competitiveness of the distribution system for crude oil and petroleum products. The presence of many traders makes the distribution system highly competitive so that, given any supply reduction, market forces will allocate the remaining supply to its most valued uses. It does not matter whether the reductions are due to an unintentional loss of production or a purposeful reduction in supply to raise price.

The possibility of purposeful reductions, however, may be relevant to the evaluation of some energy security policies. For example, import quotas that affect the shape of the world demand schedule for crude oil may create strong incentives for oligopolistic behavior (Horwich and Miller 1988). Thus, while the presence of OPEC does not render basic analysis of price shocks in terms of supply and demand inappropriate, it does call for some caution in the evaluation of policy alternatives.

THE COSTS OF AN OIL PRICE SHOCK TO THE U.S. ECONOMY

The evaluation of energy security policies requires a framework for measuring the costs of an oil price shock to the U.S. economy. Changes in social surplus provide a measure of the direct costs of an oil price shock. The full costs also include the indirect costs associated with macroeconomic adjustments to the direct costs.

Figure 21.1 provides the framework for measuring the direct costs of an oil price shock. The left-hand panel represents the world oil markets and the right-hand panel the U.S. oil market. The preshock price of oil is determined in the world market by the intersection of the demand schedule for crude oil, D_W, and the preshock supply schedule, S_W. In this illustration the intersection occurs at a price of $18/barrel and a quantity of 60 mbd. The quantity supplied by U.S.

Figure 21.1
Direct Costs of an Oil Price Shock

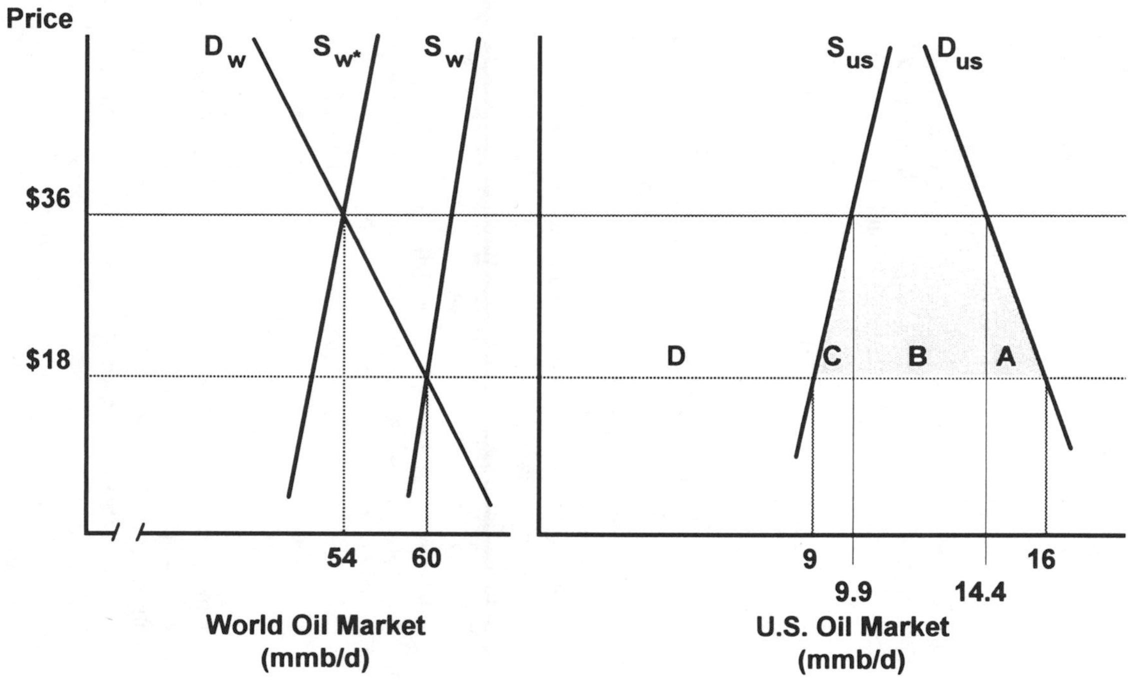

oil producers is determined by the intersection of the world price with the U.S. supply schedule, S_{US}, and the quantity demanded by U.S. consumers is determined by the intersection of the world price with the U.S. demand schedule, D_{US}. The quantity demanded is 16 mbd and the quantity supplied domestically is 9 mbd so that net imports are 7 mbd.

A price shock results when a quantity of oil is removed from the market. This is represented by a shift to the left of the world supply schedule to S_{w*}. Figure 21.1 shows a reduction in supply of 6 mbd and a doubling of world price from $18/barrel to $36/barrel. Because the supply schedule, S_w, is not perfectly inelastic, the final loss of 6 mbd implies a somewhat larger initial loss. This illustrative scenario can be thought of as involving, say, a loss of about 7 mbd of oil from the Persian Gulf, which is offset by 1 mbd of additional production elsewhere in the world. Note that expectations of future rises in prices may create a short-run demand for additional stocks, which could be modeled in this framework as a temporary shift to the right in the demand schedule that would further increase price (Verleger 1982, 1990). As the additional desired stocks were accumulated, the demands schedule would shift back toward its original position.

In this example, the increase in price to $36/barrel causes demand to fall to 14.4 mbd and domestic supply to increase to 9.9 mbd in the U.S. market so that imports fall to 4.5 mbd from the preshock level of 7 mbd.

The change in social surplus, the yardstick economists use for placing a dollar value on changes in social welfare, is represented by the shaded trapezoid in the U.S. market. It consists of the components labeled A, B, and C. Triangle A represents the consumer surplus loss from reductions in consumption. Rectangle B represents the increased payments to foreign oil producers for the oil that continues to be imported. Triangle C represents the increase in real resource costs used to expand domestic production that is not offset by savings from displaced imports. In this illustration, these direct costs would be approximately $37.8 billion for a shock lasting one year.

Indirect costs arise from a number of factors. The ''comparative statics'' for measuring the direct costs assumes that the economy can costlessly adjust from the equilibrium at $18/barrel to the one at $36/barrel. But in the real world the adjustment is not costless. One important reason is that not all prices are fully flexible. In the short run, for example, nominal wages are unlikely to be cut so that sectors that experience a reduction in demand for their products are likely to experience unemployment rather than wage reductions. Wealth transfers away from consumers create uncertainty about the new composition of aggregate demand that depresses investment. Oil price rises contribute to a higher rate of price inflation that, while speeding the adjustment to real (inflation adjusted) prices consistent with the new equilibrium, may also distort investment. The sum of direct and indirect costs can be measured through macroeconomic models (Horwich and Weimer 1984). Macroeconomic models based on experience with the price shocks of the 1970s suggest that a doubling of the price of oil may involve indirect costs several times larger than the direct costs (Hickman, Huntington, and Sweeney 1987). These models also suggest that indirect costs grow more than proportionally with direct costs. That is, for small price rises the direct costs measure almost all of the total costs, but for large price rises they grossly underestimate total costs. Some researchers, however, believe that these models grossly overestimate the macroeconomic costs of oil price shocks (Bohi 1989). Therefore, caution is warranted in analyzing energy policy using other than the direct economic costs of oil price shocks.

The unshaded trapezoid D in Figure 21.1 represents increased payments to domestic oil producers. Unlike the increased payments to foreign oil producers, they are transfers of wealth within the U.S. economy and therefore are not a component of the direct costs of the price shock to the United States. These domestic transfers are significant in two important ways, however. First, they may contribute to the indirect costs described above by increasing uncertainty about the composition of demand within the economy. Second, they create political pressure for policies intended to redistribute wealth from domestic oil producers to consumers.

The redistributive policies imposed during the 1970s greatly increased the costs of 1973–74 and 1979–80 oil price shocks (Horwich and Weimer 1984). Petroleum product price controls and administrative allocations increased the direct and indirect costs of the price shocks by interfering with the movement of available supplies to their most valued uses. Wellhead price controls on domestic oil depressed domestic production. The entitlements program, which gave refiners access to price-controlled domestic oil in proportion to their imports, was in effect a subsidy for imports that shifted the demand schedule in the world market to the right and thus increased the world price above what it otherwise would have been (Kalt 1981). Figure 21.1 provides a framework for evaluating energy security policies. Consider, for example, policies to encourage petroleum users to develop capacity to switch to alternative fuels such as natural gas during oil price shocks. Two beneficial effects would result. First, the U.S. demand would be more price elastic (less steep), so that for any price rise the reduction in imports would be larger, and the size of the trapezoid representing the direct cost of the price shock would be smaller. Second, because U.S. demand makes up a large fraction of the world demand, the latter would also be more elastic so that for any given reduction in supply to the world market, the size of any price shock would be smaller. These reductions in the direct costs of price shocks, averaged using their probabilities of occurrence, provide a measure of the expected benefits of the fuel switching policy that could be compared to its costs.

Policies to promote conservation could be evaluated in a similar way. They provide energy security benefits by reducing the preshock and postshock levels of imports. Ironically, however, they may contribute to less price elasticity of demand in the U.S. and world markets by eliminating routine energy uses that could otherwise be easily reduced during price shocks. The less elastic demand would mean larger price shocks for any given reduction in supply to the world market.

THE OIL IMPORT PREMIUM AND OIL IMPORT FEES

Does the world market price represent the true social marginal cost of oil imported into the United States? If the answer is no, then there is a market failure with respect to imports in the form of an externality. This externality is referred to as the "oil import premium." A direct way to correct the market failure, and thereby increase economic efficiency, is to impose a tariff on imported oil equal in size to the oil import premium.

The oil import premium consists of two major components: the monopsony premium and the security premium (Hogan 1981). The monopsony premium arises because the United States imports large quantities of oil. By importing more oil, the United States shifts the demand schedule for oil in the world market to the right in Figure 21.1, which in turn increases the world price. But this world price is paid for all barrels of imported oil. If, for example, a one-barrel increase in imports raised the world price by only one millionth of a dollar, the U.S. import bill on inframarginal barrels would increase by $7 (7 million barrels/day times one millionth dollar/barrel). Thus, while the private marginal cost of the barrel is just its price of $18, its social marginal cost is $25, the sum of the private marginal cost to the purchaser and the cost increase to all other oil importers. In other words, the monopsony premium in this example is $7.

The security premium arises because larger import levels contribute to larger costs of oil price shocks. Shifting the U.S. demand schedule to the right in Figure 21.1 increases the size of the shaded trapezoid, which measures the direct costs of the price shock. The larger direct costs in turn contribute to larger indirect costs. Thus, the marginal barrel of imported oil has associated with it larger costs of price shocks, which, when averaged using their probabilities of occurrence, provide a measure of the security premium.

Advocates of oil import fees (petroleum tariffs) justify their positions with estimates of oil import premiums of comparable magnitude. For example, Harry Broadman and William Hogan (1988) estimate the monopsony premium to be between $3.25 and $5.48/barrel and the security premium to be between zero and $7.78/barrel in support of an oil import fee of approximately $10/barrel. Critics, however, argue that these premium estimates are unrealistically high so that an oil import fee of this size would actually involve net economic costs (Nesbitt and Choi 1988).

Some of the debate centers around whether the oil import fee should be viewed as if it were a price shock. It raises the price of oil to domestic consumers, though not necessarily by the amount of the fee because of the monopsony effect. Much of the direct costs of the price rise are offset by government revenue (area B in Figure 21.1, interpreting the price rise as due to the import fee).

Nevertheless, the indirect costs could be large. The fact that the import fee could be implemented in a gradual and predictable way, however, suggests that these indirect costs would not be as large as they would be for a price shock of comparable size (Huntington 1988).

A number of practical problems probably swing the balance against the oil import fee. First, there is danger that policy concerning the level of the fee would be influenced by the relative political resources of domestic oil producers versus oil consumers rather than on economic grounds (Bradley 1989). Second, adjustments in the fee to favor certain trading partners can radically shift patterns of oil trade. For example, if oil imports from Canada were exempted, as they were under previous tariff and quota programs, then they would be drawn to the U.S. market, where they would fetch a price higher than that in the world market. Canada would thus export more oil to the United States and import more oil from the world market, reducing the net effect of the tariff in the world market. Third, fees would have to be imposed on imported petroleum products at levels at least as large as crude oil fees or there would be an incentive for refiners to locate offshore. The fact that a barrel of oil can produce various fractions of petroleum products makes it difficult to determine the appropriate equivalent fees. Further, domestic refiners would have an incentive to seek larger-than-equivalent fees as a barrier to competition in the petroleum product markets.

In view of these practical considerations, concerns about macroeconomic effects, and disagreement over the size of the oil import premium, the case for an oil import fee is far from overwhelming.

STRATEGIC STOCKPILING

The most direct response to an oil price shock is the addition of new supplies to the world market. An addition to supply causes a parallel shift to the right of the postshock supply schedule in Figure 21.1. This shift reduces the postshock price. The direct benefits to the United States from the addition to supply would be measured as the reduction in the size of the shaded trapezoid. If indirect costs do indeed grow more than proportionally with direct costs, then even small reductions in price could produce large benefits in terms of avoided indirect costs.

''Surge capacity'' from existing oil wells is one possible source of additions to supply during price shocks. The upward slope of the supply schedule represents the response of existing oil producers to higher prices. Surge capacity would require wells to be shut-in during normal times so that they could be activated during price shocks. Such in situ storage of oil turns out to be extremely expensive relative to storage of extracted oil in stockpiles (Weimer 1982).[2]

The United States and other members of the IEA have agreed to build stockpiles of oil for release during oil price shocks. By the end of 1992 the U.S.

stockpiling program, the Strategic Petroleum Reserve, had 575 million barrels of crude oil stored in salt formations in Louisiana and Texas that could be drawn down at an initial rate of 3.5 million barrels/day for the first three months, followed by a gradually declining rate as reservoirs empty.

Oil refiners hold stocks of crude oil to smooth deliveries. Users of petroleum typically hold stocks to take advantage of seasonal price differences. Why doesn't the anticipation of profits during oil price shocks lead these private-sector actors to stockpile at the economically efficient levels? There are three reasons why private actors are likely to stockpile too little from the social perspective (Horwich and Weimer 1984). First, private actors do not capture the full benefits from drawdowns, which lower prices to all oil consumers. In other words, there is an externality of the sort considered in the discussion of oil import fees. Second, in view of the past history of domestic price controls and allocations, stockpilers must anticipate the risk that the government will prevent them from realizing the full profits from drawdowns during price shocks. Third, because stockpiling is profitable only in the event of an oil price shock, a relatively low probability event in any given time period, if private actors are risk averse, they will stockpile too little from the social perspective of either risk neutrality or risk aversion. In other words, for individuals stockpiling is a form of gambling (low probability of big gains) while for society as a whole it is a form of insurance (low probability of avoiding large losses).

The determination of the optimal size of the public stockpile involves a comparison of benefits and costs. The quantifiable economic benefits result from drawdowns during oil price shocks: the reduction in the direct and indirect costs of the shock and the revenue realized from sale of the oil on the world market. Other benefits include the possible deterrence of purposeful price shocks by foreign governments, greater foreign policy flexibility during conflicts in the Middle East, and the reduction in political pressure to return to the counterproductive petroleum price controls and allocations that raised the costs of oil price shocks during the 1970s. The quantifiable economic costs include those associated with storage, purchasing oil, and price increases caused by the purchases. The latter can be measured by the same procedure as price shocks in the framework of Figure 21.1. Other costs include the possible displacement of private and foreign government stockpiling.

The best analytical efforts to calculate the present value of expected net benefits of stockpiling employ some form of stochastic dynamic programming to take account of the uncertainty about the likelihood, timing, magnitude, and duration of oil price shocks (Teisberg 1981; Sweetnam 1982; Chao and Manne 1983; Hogan 1983; and Murphy, Toman, and Weiss 1986). These studies generally find optimal stockpile sizes of greater than 1 billion barrels, a quantity much larger than the current size of the SPR or its storage capacity of 750 million barrels.

These analyses assume that the stockpile will be used effectively—that is, that oil will be released from the stockpile without delay at the onset of price shocks. Under the current program structure, however, drawdowns are political decisions subject to noneconomic as well as economic considerations. For example, the negative economic effects of the oil price rise at the onset of the Gulf War could have been reduced by an earlier decision to draw down the SPR; the delay may have been the result of a political decision to build support for the war by allowing consumers to see higher petroleum prices (Horwich 1992).

Several proposals have been made with an eye toward making the early use of the SPR more likely (Horwich and Weimer 1984). One approach is political: create a constituency for early drawdowns by earmarking revenue from sale of oil for distribution to the states for emergency relief to localities that must legally operate under balanced budgets. Another approach is to enable private actors to initiate drawdowns through an options system. Options, conferring the right to purchase oil within some period from the SPR at some price higher than the current market price, would be continually auctioned. If the market price were to rise above the price specified in the option, then holders of options would exercise them and drawdown would commence. Creating mechanisms like these to increase the likelihood that the existing SPR will be used at the onset of disruptions may be more valuable than simply expanding its size.

CONCLUSION

The energy security problem facing the United States results from the vulnerability of the world oil market to sudden losses of oil supply from the Persian Gulf. It is clear that the United States should not respond to oil price shocks by repeating the mistaken price controls and administrative allocations that were so economically costly in the 1970s. Most debate about policies for increasing energy security has focused on oil import fees and oil stockpiles. Sufficient questions remain about the effects of oil import fees to raise serious doubts about their desirability; a much less equivocal body of analysis supports an oil stockpile at least as large as the current Strategic Petroleum Reserve.

NOTES

1. The ratio of net petroleum imports (crude oil and petroleum products) to total petroleum products supplied (including exports) was 40.5 percent. The ratio of net petroleum imports (6.895 mbd) to the sum of net petroleum imports and domestic production (7.153 mbd crude oil and 1.696 mbd natural gas plant production) is 43.4 percent (Energy Information Administration 1993).

2. A surge capacity of 1 billion barrels/year would require that about 7 billion barrels of reserves, a substantial fraction of total U.S. proven reserves, be developed and then shut-in. If the reserves were in northern Alaska, then a second pipeline to handle the surge would have to be built.

REFERENCES

Bohi, Douglas R. *Energy Price Shocks and Macroeconomic Performance*. Washington, DC: Resources for the Future, 1989.

Bradley, Robert L., Jr. *The Mirage of Oil Protection*. New York: University Press of America, 1989.

Broadman, Harry G. and William W. Hogan. "Is an Oil Tariff Justified? II. The Numbers Say Yes." *Energy Journal* 9 (3) (1988): 7–29.

Chao, Hung-po and Alan Manne. "An Integrated Analysis of U.S. Stockpiling Policies." In James L. Plummer (ed.), *Energy Vulnerability*. Cambridge, MA: Ballinger, 1983, pp. 59–82.

Energy Information Administration. *Monthly Energy Review*. Washington, DC: U.S. Government Printing Office, April 1993.

Hickman, Bert G., Hillard G. Huntington, and James L. Sweeney (eds.). *Macroeconomic Impacts of Energy Shocks*. Amsterdam: North-Holland, 1987.

Hogan, William W. "Import Management and Oil Emergencies." In David A. Deese and Joseph S. Nye (eds.), *Energy and Security*. Cambridge, MA: Ballinger, 1981, pp. 261–301.

———. "Oil Stockpiling: Help Thy Neighbor." *Energy Journal* 4 (3) (July 1983): 49–72.

Horwich, George. "Energy Policy, Oil Markets, and the Middle East War: Did We Learn the Lessons of the 1970s?" In James P. Dorian and Fereidun Fesharaki (eds.), *International Issues in Energy Policy, Development, and Economics*. Boulder, CO: Westview Press, 1992, pp. 25–39.

Horwich, George, Hank Jenkins-Smith, and David L. Weimer. "The International Energy Agency's Mandatory Oil-Sharing Agreement: Tests of Efficiency, Equity, and Practicality." In George Horwich and David L. Weimer (eds.), *Responding to International Oil Crises*. Washington, DC: American Enterprise Institute for Public Policy Research, 1988, pp. 104–133.

Horwich, George and Bradley A. Miller. "Oil Import Quotas in the Context of the International Energy Agency Sharing Agreement." In George Horwich and David L. Weimer (eds.), *Responding to International Oil Crises*. Washington, DC: American Enterprise Institute for Public Policy Research, 1988, pp. 134–178.

Horwich, George and David L. Weimer. "The Economics of International Oil Sharing." *Energy Journal* 9 (4) (1988a): 17–33.

——— (eds.). *Responding to the International Oil Crisis*. Washington, DC: American Enterprise Institute, 1988b.

———. *Oil Price Shocks, Market Response, and Contingency Planning*. Washington, DC: American Enterprise Institute, 1984.

Huntington, Hillard G. "Should GNP Impacts Preclude Oil Tariffs?" *The Energy Journal* 9 (2) (1988): 31–44.

Kalt, Joseph P. *The Economics and Politics of Oil Price Regulation*. Cambridge, MA: MIT Press, 1981.

Murphy, Frederic H., Michael A. Toman, and Howard J. Weiss. "An Integrated Analysis of U.S. Oil Security Policies." *The Energy Journal* 7 (3) (1986): 67–82.

Nesbitt, Dale M. and Thomas Y. Choi. "Is an Oil Tariff Justified? III. The Numbers Say No." *Energy Journal* 9 (3) (1988), pp. 31–59.

Smith, Rodney T. "International Energy Cooperation: The Mismatch between IEA Policy Actions and Policy Goals." In George Horwich and David L. Weimer (eds.), *Responding to International Oil Crises*. Washington, DC: American Enterprise Institute for Public Policy Research, 1988, pp. 17–103.

Sweetnam, Glen. "Stockpile Policies for Dealing with Oil Supply Disruptions." In George Horwich and Edward J. Mitchell (eds.), *Policies for Coping with Oil-Supply Disruptions*. Washington, DC: American Enterprise Institute for Public Policy Research, 1982, pp. 82–96.

Teisberg, Thomas J. "A Dynamic Programming Model of the U.S. Strategic Petroleum Reserve." *Bell Journal of Economics* 12 (2) (Autumn 1981): 526–546.

Verleger, Philip K. Jr. *Oil Markets in Turmoil*. Cambridge, MA: Ballinger, 1982.

———. "Understanding the 1990 Oil Crisis." *Energy Journal* 11 (4) (1990): 15–33.

Weimer, David L. *The Strategic Petroleum Reserve: Planning, Implementation, and Analysis*. Westport, CT: Greenwood Press, 1982.

Yergin, Daniel. *The Prize: The Epic Quest for Oil, Money, and Power*. New York: Simon and Schuster, 1991.

Chapter 22

Sources of Information on the Oil Industry

Harry E. Welsh and John C. Gormley

Selecting the sources of information about an industry as complex and controversial as oil could in the broadest sense involve areas of technology and engineering, economics and public policy, and even culture and history. Every attempt, therefore, has been made in this effort to concentrate narrowly the focus of this guide. The sources of information included here are intended primarily for those engaged in the study of the financial and commercial aspects of the production and distribution of oil, and for the practitioner working in the industry who is seeking primarily economic activity information about the oil business. Accordingly geologic materials such as maps or manuals about petroleum technology or about commercial practices that may have limited implications for the petroleum industry have been deliberately excluded. Titles have been chosen with their availability in mind and should be found in most metropolitan public libraries and in medium-sized academic and corporate libraries. Obscure works that could be found only in a few research libraries have been excluded.

Because of the international dimensions of the oil business, many publications and relevant sources of information are in numerous languages and including them would expand the focus and length of this guide beyond its original intention. Primarily titles published in English and deemed of interest to American companies operating abroad or engaged in the international marketing of oil have been selected. So that the titles listed are as accessible to the reader as possible, most date from 1985 and ought to be found in libraries or still in print. The serials or continuations included are being updated regularly unless otherwise noted. Annotations will elaborate on the scope of number of titles to help define more clearly their usefulness.

This guide is organized to provide initially some background sources where one can locate economic information about companies and some of the main players in the oil business. It will then follow the format familiar to most literature guides listing bibliographies of references, followed by a section of current awareness indexing and abstracting services both in print and online. Next are special reference sources such as encyclopedias, manuals, and handbooks that render in-depth treatment of the topic or give the information seeker statistical and factual information. A final comment on the evolving Internet and its potential for global information will conclude the guide.

SOURCES FOR BACKGROUND INFORMATION ABOUT CORPORATIONS

The comprehensive investment advisory services are good sources for background information about the economic activities and performance of major corporations, including a representation of oil companies. These services can provide financial statements and industry analyses and are listed below with some recently published handbooks of company historical information.

Investment Services

Moody's Investors Service. New York: Moody's, 1954–. [*Industrial Manual.* 1954–. ISSN 0545–0217; *International Manual.* 1981–. ISSN 0278–3509; *Public Utility Manual.* 1954–. ISSN 0545–0241; *Transportation Manual.* 1954–. ISSN 0545–025x; *OTC Manual.* 1970–. ISSN 0027–0865; *OTC Unlisted Manual.* 1986–. ISSN 0890–5282. All manuals are published annually with weekly supplements.]

Standard & Poor's. *Standard Corporation Descriptions.* New York: S&P, 1915–. ISSN 0277–500x (daily supplements).

Value Line Investment Survey. Weekly. New York: Value Line, 1936–. ISSN 0042–2401.

Industry Analysis

Center for International Financial Analysis and Research (CIFAR). *Global Company Handbook.* Princeton, NJ: CIFA Res., Inc., 1992. ISBN 1–8775887–04–4.
[An analysis of the financial performance of the world's leading 7,500 companies.]

Standard & Poor's. *Industry Surveys.* New York: S&P, 1973– (weekly updates).
[Of the approximately 25 industry categories surveyed, "Oil, including drilling and services" is one of the *Basic Analysis* updates.]

Standard & Poor's. *Analyst's Handbook.* Annual. New York: S&P, 1964–. ISSN 0884–6936 (monthly updates).
[Historical financial information for the past 30 years for S&P 500 industries.]

Selected Corporate Directories

Directory of Multinationals. 4th edition. 4 volumes. New York: Stockton Press, 1992. ISBN 0–333–57756–3.

Hoover's Handbook of American Business. Annual. Austin, TX: Reference Press, 1991–. ISSN 1055–7202.

Hoover's Handbook: Profiles of Over 500 Major Corporations. Irregular. Austin, TX: Reference Press, 1991. ISBN 1–878753–00–2.

Hoover's Handbook of World Business. Annual. Austin, TX: Reference Press, 1992–. ISSN 1055–7199.

International Directory of Company Histories. 7 volumes. Chicago: St. James Press, 1988–1993. ISBN 1–55862–322. [Volume 4: Mining and minerals.]

BIBLIOGRAPHIES AND GUIDES

Anyone beginning a study of the oil industry or gathering information about one of its facets should start by trying to locate a published bibliography or guide to the literature that can provide a broad listing of books, articles, and special reference materials on the subject or on an aspect of particular interest. Bibliographies and guides generally vary in length, comprehensiveness, and selectivity of the types of resources included. They can be extremely useful as the initial basis for study and research.

Barbara Pearson and Katherine Ellwood's *Guide to the Petroleum Reference Literature* (1987) is the most comprehensive review of the oil and oil-related references covering all aspects of the industry with comprehensive descriptive annotation for each title or service listed. It is an indispensable source and should be consulted by anyone doing research or seeking extensive information. Because of the proliferation of text and data base publishing that has continued about the oil business since 1986, the guide is now dated and, unfortunately, out-of-print. This bibliography attempts to provide the student and practitioner with the supplementation and updating of sources that will be useful to them.

In the case of the oil industry one may want to look as well at some general guides about businesses and corporations that will include a representation of oil. Some of the more notable and more widely available of these are included in this section. The general guides to business literature that will incorporate information about oil companies are listed first; followed by the sources of information that concentrate on the oil and energy industry. More recent publications or series of greater frequency that can update and supplement the basic guides will be presented in a following section, Indexing and Abstracting services.

Basic Sources for Business Information

Ball, Sarah. *The Directory of International Sources of Business Information.* London: Pitman, 1989. ISBN 0–273–03047–7.

Daniells, Lorna. *Business Information Sources*, 3rd ed. Berkeley: University of California Press, 1993. ISBN 0–520–08348–2.

European Markets: A Guide to Company and Industry Information Sources, 4th ed. Washington, DC: Washington Researchers, 1992. ISBN 1–56365–012–6.

How to Find Information about Companies: The Corporate Intelligence Sourcebook, 7th ed. Washington, DC: Washington Researchers, 1991. ISBN 0–685–49323–7.

Lavin, Michael R. *Business Information, How to Find It, How to Use It,* 2nd ed. Phoenix: Oryx, 1992. ISBN 0–89774–566–6.

Sources of Oil and Energy Information

Anthony, L. J., ed. *Information Sources in Energy Technology.* Stoneham, MA: Butterworths, 1988. ISBN 0–408–03050–x.

Cambridge Information and Research Services, Ltd. *World Directory of Energy Information.* Compiled by Christopher Swain. New York: Facts on File, 1984. ISBN 0–87196–483–x.

Evans, John. *OPEC and the World Energy Market: A Comprehensive Reference Guide,* 2nd ed. London: Longman Current Affairs, 1991. ISBN 0–58208–527–6.

Guide to Petroleum Statistical Information. Annual. New York: American Petroleum Institute (API), 1987–. ISSN 0742–8464.

Pearson, Barbara C. and Katherine B. Ellwood. *Guide to the Petroleum Reference Literature.* Littleton, CO: Libraries Unlimited, 1987. ISBN 0–87287–473–7.

U.S. Library of Congress. *Arab Oil: A Bibliography of Materials in the Library of Congress.* Compiled by George D. Selim. Washington, DC: Government Printing Office, 1982. SuDocs: LC41.9:Arl.

Weber, R. David. *Energy Update: A Guide to Current Reference Literature.* San Carlos, CA: Energy Information Press, 1991. ISBN 0–9628518–5–x.

CURRENT AWARENESS SOURCES

Indexing and Abstracting Services

The hundreds of articles published in one year about the oil industry can present a daunting task for anyone trying to keep abreast of current developments. Abstracts and indexes that are characterized as current awareness services can provide a means of systematic subject access to the latest publications of topical interest, and can also be helpful in locating a current specific reference. These services vary in the scope of the types of publications regularly indexed and could include books, journal articles, government reports, patents, conferences and proceedings, dissertations, and other special reports. Because of the breadth of the publications regularly analyzed in these services, they are useful supplements to business bibliographies and guides presented in the previous section.

Indexes usually appear monthly or more frequently and cite the author, title, and other important identifiers needed for procuring the document. Abstracts are issued as frequently but provide in addition to the subject analysis a synopsis of the contents of the publication.

Today all indexing and abstracting services have their computerized complement and are available to the user online or on CD-ROM. A number of these services will be noted in the next subsection, Online and CD-ROM Services.

General Business Abstracting and Indexing Services

Business Index. Monthly. Belmont, CA: Information Access, 1979–. [Microfilm service also available on CD-ROM.]

Business Periodicals Index. Monthly. New York: H. W. Wilson. 1958–. ISSN 0007–6961.
    [Basic and most widely available business index.]

Predicasts F&S Index International. Quarterly. Cleveland: Predicasts. 1980–. ISSN 0014–5661.

Predicasts F&S Index United States. Weekly. Cleveland: Predicasts, 1979–. ISSN 0270–4560.

Oil and Energy Abstracting and Indexing Services

Energy Abstracts for Policy Analysis. Monthly. Oak Ridge, TN: U.S. Department of Energy, 1975–1989. ISSN 0098–5104.
    [Concentrates primarily on government reports and matters of public policy.]

Energy Information Abstracts. Monthly. New York: Energy Information Center (EIC), 1976–. ISSN 0147–6521.
    [Monthly service of EIC abstracts, journals, government conferences, and research reports. Focus is often but not exclusively public policy issues. *Energy Index* is the annual cumulation. Energyline is the online service.]

Energy Research Abstracts. Semimonthly. Oak Ridge, TN: U.S. Department of Energy, 1965–. ISSN 0160–3604.

Fuel and Energy Abstracts. Bimonthly. Oxford: Butterworth-Heinmann, 1960–. ISSN 0140–6701.
    [Formerly: *Fuel Abstracts and Current Titles.*]

International Petroleum Abstracts. Quarterly. Sussex, UK: John Wiley, 1973–. ISSN 0309–4944.

Literature Abstracts. Monthly. New York: American Petroleum Institute, 1954–. ISSN 1065–0504.

New Publications of the Geological Survey. Monthly. Washington, DC: U.S. Geological Survey, 1984–.
    [Numerous publications of the U.S. Geological Survey including the map series listed and indexed. Continues *Publications of the Geological Survey* (1879–1983).]

Petroleum Abstracts. Weekly. Tulsa: University of Tulsa, 1961–. ISSN 0031–6423.

Petroleum/Energy Business News Index. Monthly. New York: American Petroleum Institute, 1975–. ISSN 0098–7743.

Online and CD-ROM Services

Today practically all the publishers of business and technical information are also database producers and have their services available to users online or as

CD-ROM products. Publishers use computers and magnetic tape in the production of printed texts and can therefore easily produce a database and make it accessible to anyone who has a computer with a modem or CD-ROM drive. There are a number of database producers whose products may not have a print counterpart or whose electronic counterpart varies substantially from the hard copy text in frequency, coverage, and indexing depth. Print sources are generally more inclusive of retrospective and historical information, while the computer-based products are more current and allow the user greater subject searching flexibility.

Publishers who are database producers may also be database vendors and market their service directly to the public through major utilities such as CompuServe and BT Inc. Most, however, engage database vendors who develop software for standard search strategies and provide other services such as documentation, training, and some document (full-text) delivery for the databases they offer. The most familiar vendors today are BRS, DIALOG, NEXIS, ORBIT (SDC), and H. W. Wilson (Wilsonline). Increasingly these vendors are developing CD-ROM products to parallel their online resources: DIALOG OnDisc and WILSONDISC are examples. Although the CDs may not be updated as frequently as the online versions, they often provide more searching ease for the end user and have particular merit for graphic and illustrative matter. Their storage capacity lends itself to full-text delivery as well.

Within the last few years the online database vendors have been targeting the end user with "friendlier" menu-driven protocol interfaces. DIALOG has developed DIALOG Business Connection, focusing chiefly on business resources and providing much statistical and numerical information; BRS After Dark and Knowledge Index are end user discount packages intended for the home computer access. Those interested in the online and CD-ROM products and their latest developments should consult the current edition of the *Information Industry Directory*.

General Sources for Online and CD-ROM Products

Business and Legal CD-ROMs in Print. Annual. Westport, CT: Meckler, 1993–. ISBN 0–88736–912–x.

CD-ROM Finder. Annual. Medford, NJ: Learned Information, Inc. 1993–.
　　[Formerly *Optical Publishing Directory*, 1987–92.]

CD-ROMS in Print: An International Guide to CD-ROM, CD-I, CDTV, Multimedia and Electronic Book Products. Annual. Westport, CT: Meckler, 1987–. ISSN 0891–8198.

Computer-Readable Data Bases. Annual. Compiled by Martha E. Williams. White Plains, NY: Knowledge Industry Publications, 1979–. ISSN 0271–4477.
　　[Continues earlier *Computer-Readable Bibliographic Data Bases* with broader scope including numerical data bases.]

Information Industry Directory. Annual. Detroit: Gale, 1991–. ISSN 1051–6239.
　　[Continues *Encyclopedia of Information Systems and Service*, 1971–90 and

is the most comprehensive listing of both online and optical services and software products.]

Major Business and Corporate Online and CD-ROM Services

The well-known investment and financial services that report on the earnings and economic performance of domestic and international corporations, including the oil companies, have been generally available online to subscribers through major database vendors since the late 1970s. Online access permits more frequent updating—permitting the user to keep current. A number of these are listed below together with other sources of technical and public affairs information that could prove useful to the oil industry investigator. As more and more databases become available it becomes harder to keep track of them. The listing below has been composed to represent the kinds and types of information available online and as a CD-ROM product.

ABI/INFORM. Weekly. Louisville: Data Courier, 1971–.
> [No hard copy counterpart, indexes about 600 business journals. Available online and as CD-ROM. Full-text service for selected journals.]

Business Index. Monthly. Belmont, CA: Information Access, 1986–.
> [Service available as INFOTRAC on CD-ROM. Coverage from 1986 to date.]

Business Periodicals Index. Semiweekly. New York: H. W. Wilson, 1982–.
> [Probably best-known and most widely available periodicals indexing service accessible through Wilsonline since 1982.]

CENDATA. Daily. Washington, DC: U.S. Bureau of the Census, 1984–.
> [A textual-numeric file available from the Census Bureau based on census publications and services, including *Census of Manufacturing, Census of Mineral Industries*, foreign trade statistics, and press releases.]

Disclosure. Quarterly/Weekly Supplements. Bethesda, MD: Disclosure Information, 1978–.
> [Extensive public information about corporations gathered from annual reports and data submitted to Securities and Exchange Commission. Full-text service.]

Federal Research in Progress (FEDRIP). Weekly. Springfield, VA: U.S. National Technical Information Service, 1983–.
> [Summaries of U.S. government research projects, including Department of Energy and Geological Survey.]

Financial Times. Weekly. London: Financial Times Business Information, 1981–.
> [Company abstracts and full text with particular strong coverage of European companies.]

Global Report. Daily. New York: Citibank, 1986–.
> [Citibank's online integrated information service incorporates textual and numeric data from a dozen information providers for four topic areas: industry news, companies and industries, countries, and markets available through CompuServe.]

Industry Data Sources. Monthly. Belmont, CA: Information Access, 1979–.

[Regular update of *Directory of Industry Data Sources* contains summaries of financial and marketing data for major industries including energy.]

McGraw-Hill News. Daily. New York: McGraw-Hill News, 1982–.
[Up-to-the-minute company and industry news from the publisher of *Business Week.*]

Moody's. Weekly. New York: Moody's Investor Services, 1983–.
[Online complements of *Moody's Manuals* and investment advisory services provides corporate news–U.S., corporate news–International, and corporate profiles.]

Predicasts/F&S Indexes. Monthly. Cleveland: Predicasts, 1971–. (Weekly updates.)
[Full range Predicasts services available from major online vendors include: annual reports abstracts, time series and economic forecasts for U.S. and international industries and companies, new products announcements, and indexes of articles. Predicasts PROMT services online provide daily updates.]

Standard and Poor's. Semiweekly. New York: Standard and Poor's, 1979–. (Daily updates.)
[*Standard and Poor's Corporation Records* with greater frequency online from DIALOG and CompuServe.]

Value Line Data Base II. Weekly. New York: Value Line, 1981–.
[Online counterpart of the popular *Value Line Investment Survey.*]

Major Oil and Energy Online and CD-ROM Services

APILIT. New York: American Petroleum Institute (API), 1964–.
[Machine-readable index originated in 1964, abstracts added in 1978. Covers all types of publications from technical journals to trade magazines and newspaper accounts relating to all aspects of the petroleum and oil industry. API-PAT is the Patent file.]

DRI/Platt's Oil Prices. New York: McGraw-Hill.
[Compiled from Platt's Oilgram Price Report and available in print as *Platt's Oil Price Handbook and Oilmanac.*]

Energyline. New York: EIC, 1971–.
[Indexes about 200 core journals, and some selected reports and monographs.]

P/E News. Weekly. New York: American Petroleum Institute, 1975–.
[*APILIT* subset covers major oil industry publications.]

TULSA. Weekly. Norman, OK: University of Tulsa, 1965–.
[*Petroleum Abstracts* online. Concentrates on exploration, development, and production.]

REFERENCE SOURCES

Encyclopedias, Handbooks, Annuals/Yearbooks

Encyclopedias have articles written by authorities and are useful for quickly informing the reader of essential background information and providing some depth on the subject, and they often include bibliographic references or a list of core readings to guide the reader in further inquiry. Business and economics encyclopedias are not the large comprehensive multivolume tomes familiar to many people, but are generally single compact book sources resembling a handbook or manual. The *International Petroleum Encyclopedia* is a good example of useful background reading and concise presentation.

Handbooks are special encyclopedias and are generally compilations or compendia of facts and data packaged for convenience and quick consultation and may be richer in graphics, tables, formulas, illustrations, and useful "how to" instructions. Unlike encyclopedias they may assume that the reader has some previous knowledge of the subject.

Yearbooks or annual reviews are useful for apprising the reader of new developments and events and supplement encyclopedias with the latest information. Annuals, handbooks, and yearbooks that primarily publish statistics because of the significance of this information to the oil industry are listed separately under a later subsection, Statistical Sources.

Encyclopedias/Handbooks

International Petroleum Encyclopedia. Annual. Jim West, ed. Tulsa: PennWell, 1980–. ISSN 0148–0375.

Landman's Encyclopedia, 3rd edition. R. L. Hankinson, ed. Houston: Gulf Publishing Co., 1988. ISBN 0872–0142x.

Oil Economists' Handbook, 5th edition. 2 vols. New York: Elsevier Applied Science, 1989. ISBN 1–85166–345–2.

Annuals/Yearbooks

Annual Review of Energy and the Environment. Jack Hollander, ed. Palo Alto, CA: Annual Reviews, Inc., 1976–. ISSN 1056–3466.

Financial Times International Yearbooks: Oil and Gas. Annual. Essex, UK: Longman Group, 1910–. ISSN 0141–3228.

Political Risk Yearbook. Annual. 7 vols. New York: Sullivan and Frost, 1987–. ISSN 0889–2725.
> [Volumes for North and Central America; Middle East and North Africa; South America; Sub-Sahara Africa; Asia and the Pacific; Europe—Countries of the EC; Europe—Outside the EC.]

Dictionaries

The oil industry appears to have more than its fair share of dictionaries. Like most dictionaries in specialized fields, these are usually consulted by someone seeking the definition of a technical term or attempting to understand some aspect of the industry's literature. Because of the international dimension of the industry, one is not surprised to find a number of multilingual and illustrative dictionaries that could be useful.

Energy

Dictionary of Energy, 2nd ed. Malcolm Slesser, comp. New York: Nichols/GP Publishing, 1988. ISBN 0–89397–320–3.

Godman, Arthur. *Energy Supply A-Z.* Hillside, NJ: Enslow, 1991. ISBN 0–89490–262–8.

Petroleum

Handbook of Oil Industry Terms and Phrases, 4th ed. R. D. Langenkamp, comp. Tulsa: PennWell, 1984. ISBN 0–87814–258–4.

The Illustrated Petroleum Reference Dictionary, 3rd ed. R. D. Langenkamp, comp. Tulsa: PennWell, 1985. ISBN 0–87814–272–x.

Oil and Gas Dictionary. Paul Stevens, ed. New York: Nichols/GP Publishing, 1988. ISBN 0–89397–325–4.

Petroleum Extension Service. *A Dictionary for the Petroleum Industry.* Austin: University of Texas, 1991. ISBN 0–88698–152–2.

Petroleum Extension Service. *Petroleum Fundamentals Glossary.* Austin: University of Texas, 1990. ISBN 0–88698–149–2.

Multilingual

Russian-English Oilfield Dictionary. D. E. Stoliarov, ed. New York: Pergamon Press, 1983. ISBN 0–08–028169–9.

World Energy Conference Staff, ed. *Energy Terminology: A Multi-Lingual Glossary.* New York: Pergamon Press, 1986. ISBN 0–08–034071–7.

Industry Directories

Directories may be published by a commercial publisher, a government agency, or a trade or research association. Often more than just an address book, they can provide information about industry capacity and products as well and are particularly useful in the oil business that has many facets, including exploration, drilling, refining, transportation, storage, marketing, and management. One should always be aware that the scope of a source may be limited to a particular aspect of the business. *The Whole World Oil Directory*, for example, attempts to be comprehensive in its coverage, ranging from exploration to sales, while the name of the *Worldwide Offshore Contractors and Equipment Directory* itself implies a more limited kind of exploration focus and interest. In addition to the directories published separately with regular frequency, a number of journals—most notably the *Oil and Gas Journal*—will provide this kind of information as part of a special issue or supplement.

United States

Oil and Gas Directory. Houston: Geophysical Directory, Inc., 1970–. ISSN 0471–380x.

U.S.A. Gulf Coast Oil & Gas Industry Directory. Tulsa: PennWell, 1992. ISSN 1056–795–x.

Foreign and International

Arab Oil and Gas Directory. Annual. Paris: Arab Petroleum Research Center, 1974–. ISSN 0304–8551.

Whole World Oil Directory. Wilmette, IL: National Register Publishing, 1979–. ISSN 0148–3609.

World Energy Industry. Quarterly. San Diego: Business Information Display, 1979–. ISSN 0886–5000.

Worldwide Natural Gas Industry Directory. Annual. Tulsa: PennWell, 1991–. ISSN 1051–3973.

Worldwide Petrochemical Directory. Annual. Tulsa: PennWell, 1962–. ISSN 0084–2583.

Worldwide Refining and Gas Processing Directory. Annual. Tulsa: PennWell, 1942–. ISSN 0277–0962.

Personnel

Financial Times Who's Who in World Oil and Gas, 11th ed. Harlow, UK: Longman Publishing Group, 1993. ISSN 0141–3236.

U.S.A. Oil Industry Directory. Annual. Tulsa: PennWell, 1970–. ISSN 0082–8599. [Continues *Personnel Directory of U.S.A. Oil Industry.*]

Products and Services

Offshore Contractors and Equipment Worldwide Directory. Tulsa: PennWell, 1969–. ISSN 0475–1310.

Petroleum Software Directory. Annual. Tulsa: PennWell, 1983–. ISSN 0743–6750.

Petroleum Software Sourcebook for PCs, 3rd ed. Houston: Stalby–Wilson, 1990. ISBN 0–911299–39–4.

U.S.A. Oilfield Service, Supply and Manufacturers Directory. Annual. Tulsa: PennWell, 1985–. ISSN 0736–038x.

Worldwide Offshore Contractors and Equipment Directory, 22nd ed. Tulsa: PennWell, 1990. ISBN 0475–1310.

Trading Organizations

World Trade Resources Guide. Irregular. Detroit: Gale, 1992. ISSN 1058–1618. [Addresses of major banks and financial institutions, chambers of commerce, government agencies, transportation and shipping contacts for each country of the world.]

Statistical Sources

Statistics take on a great importance to those in the oil industry. Economic decisions, particularly in the global environment, can rely heavily on timely statistical data involving production, reserves, trade, pricing, supply, and balances. Government agencies, international organizations, and trade associations collect and publish statistics on all of these aspects of the energy industry. The most complete statistical information on the oil industry is compiled in the United States by the Energy Information Center of the Department of Energy, and worldwide by a number of international organizations, most notably the Organization for Economic Cooperation and Development and the Organization of Petroleum Exporting Countries. The numbers collected and issued by these organizations are macro-indicators at national and regional levels. Figures for a firm or specific companies will most likely be found in the investment and company sources. A critical concern for those needing statistical information is obtaining the data as soon as it is released—increasingly the figures are available online in some of the sources listed in the previous Online and CD-ROM Services subsection.

U.S. Government

U.S. Central Intelligence Agency. *International Energy Statistical Review*. Monthly. Springfield, VA: National Technical Information Center (NTIS), 1978–. ISSN 0163–3724.

U.S. Energy Information Administration. Publications. Washington, DC: Department of Energy (DOE).
>[Major annual statistical series include: *Annual Outlook for Oil and Gas*, 1991–. *Annual Report to Congress*, 1987–. *Annual Energy Review*, 1983–. *Performance Profiles of Major Energy Producers*, 1980–. *Petroleum Supply Annual*, 1982–. *International Energy Outlook*, 1986–.]

International Organizations

Organization for Economic Cooperation and Development (OECD). Publications. Paris: OECD Publication Information Center.
>[Major statistical series include: *OECD Annual Oil Market Report*, Annual, 1977–. *Energy Balances of OECD Countries*, Irregular, 1973–. *Energy Statistics of OECD Countries*, Annual, 1990–. *Oil Statistics and Energy Balances*, Quarterly, 1988–.]

Organization of Petroleum Exporting Countries (OPEC). *Annual Statistical Bulletin*. Vienna: OPEC, 1979–. ISSN 0475–0608.

United Nations. Statistical Office. *Energy Statistics Yearbook*. Annual. 1982–. ISSN 0256–6400.
>[Continues *Yearbook of World Energy Statistics*, 1979–81.]

Industry and Trade Associations

Basic Petroleum Data Book. Triannual. New York: API, 1982–. ISSN 0730–5621.

BP Statistical Review of World Energy. Annual. London: British Petroleum (BP) Ltd., 1981–. ISSN 0263–9815.
>[Formerly *BP Statistical Review of World Oil Industry*, 1969–80.]

Energy Statistics Sourcebook. Annual. Tulsa: PennWell, 1986–. ISSN 089–5260.
>[Statistics selected from *Oil and Gas Journal* energy database.]

Oil and Energy Trends: Annual Statistical Review. Annual. Oxford: Basil Blackwell, 1975–. ISSN 0953–1033.

Oil Industry Outlook for the U.S.A. Annual. Tulsa: PennWell, 1984–. ISSN 1056–3466.

A GLOBAL INFORMATION NETWORK

Since the late 1980s a super network of global information has evolved in the United States that reaches out to the world and will permit anyone with a computer and a long-distance modem to enter an information highway commonly called Internet and gain access through modern telecommunications to informal collegial contacts as well as some of the traditional sources of information featured in this guide. Defining the Internet itself is a difficult task since it is not a physical entity, but a network of networks or a series of interconnections. This is an amalgam of computers and communications systems owned and operated by governments, universities, corporations, and research organizations and available to information professionals, librarians, executives, and researchers through protocols and proper authorizations. It can deliver information in virtually every discipline and field of interest.

The varieties of information activities and resources on the Internet are:

- Exchange of electronic mail and data files in a wide-area environment (WAIS).
- Online "real-time" interactions with other network users.
- Participation in electronic mailing lists and conferences in ever-expanding areas of interest.
- Use of file transfer protocol (FTP) to access remote archives of text file, software, and graphics, and retrieve them for one's own use.
- Receipt of electronic publications—electronic bulletins, newsletters, and journals.
- Use of telnet to access data stored on remote computers including library catalogs and proprietary databases.
- Access to a wide selection of public domain software.

Some useful titles published in recent years can provide the potential user roadmaps to navigate the Internet and locate needed information. For background, John Quartermain's *The Matrix: Computer Networks and Conferencing Systems Worldwide* (Bedford, MA: Digital Press, 1990) will supply the information seeker with a comprehensive history of Internet and its complex organization. Tracy LaQuey's *The Internet Companion: A Beginner's Guide to Global Networking* (Reading, MA: Addison-Wesley, 1992) provides a simpler approach to what Internet is and what it can do for someone about to sign up and log on. Gaining access is covered competently in April Marine et al., *Internet: Getting Started* (Englewood Cliffs, NJ: Prentice-Hall, 1992); while Richard Smith and Mark Gibbs present the Internet navigator with a "user-friendly" subject listing of resources in *Navigating the Internet* (Carmel, IN: SAMS, 1993). Computer scientists, librarians, and other information professionals will find Elizabeth Lane and Graig Summerhill, *Internet Primer for Information Professionals* (Westport, CT: Meckler, 1993) particularly to their liking, not only for its review of network resources but also for its proficient discussion of special Internet technical applications.

Index

About the Editor and Contributors

SIAMACK SHOJAI is Associate Professor and Chairman of the Economics and Finance Department at Manhattan College. His articles have appeared in the *Journal of Energy and Development* and the *Journal of Economic Development.* He is the Senior Editor of a recent volume in the area of oil markets entitled *The Oil Market in the 1980s: A Decade of Decline.* Dr. Shojai has been interviewed on many occasions by the Voice of America on the U.S. economy, the Iranian economy, and on global economic issues. He is a regular commentator and economic consultant to Radio Sedaye Iran (Voice of Iran) in Los Angeles.

ROBERT A. BIOLSI has taught various courses in economics and finance at St. John's University and at Manhattan College, where he served as Assistant Professor of Economics and Finance. Dr. Biolsi is currently Manager of Options and Risk Analysis with the New York Mercantile Exchange.

JOHN T. BOEPPLE is a Senior Consultant in the Energy and Refining Practice of Chem Systems, Inc., a management consulting company serving the refining and petrochemical industries. Prior to joining Chem Systems in 1992, he gained over 20 years of refining industry experience while working for Caltex Petroleum Corporation and Phibro Energy Inc.

DOUGLAS R. BOHI is the Director of Energy and Natural Resources for the Future in Washington, DC. He previously served as Chief Economist and Director in the Office of Economic Policy of the Federal Energy Regulatory Commission. Dr. Bohi was a member of the National Research Council Committee on the National Energy Modeling system in 1991–92. He has published numerous journal articles in addition to authoring various books and monographs.

GENEVIEVE BRIAND is completing her doctoral studies in economics at the University of Wyoming, specializing in resource and environmental economics.

J. CALE CASE is Vice President of the Palmer Bellevue Corporation, a Chicago-based consulting firm specializing in energy resources, electric and gas utilities, telecommunications, and financial services. He has contracted or subcontracted for the Bonneville Power Administration, the U.S. Department of Energy, and the Swedish National Energy Administration. He has written numerous reports and publications for various commissions and journals.

ROBERT R. COPAKEN serves as the senior political economist in the Office of Energy Assessments, Office of Policy, in the U.S. Department of Energy. During his more than two-decade career with the federal government, Dr. Copaken has worked in policy analysis primarily related to the activity of the domestic and international energy industry, particularly petroleum and natural gas. He has served in the Departments of Energy, Commerce, Treasury, State, and in the White House.

THOMAS D. CROCKER is Professor of Economics and Director of the School of Environment and Natural Resources at the University of Wyoming. He is author or coauthor of more than 120 refereed publications in resource and environmental economics.

DIANA DENISON is a doctoral student in economics at the University of Wyoming, where she is specializing in resource and environmental economics.

EDWARD T. DOWLING serves as Chairperson of the Department of Economics and Director of the Soviet Studies Program at Fordham University. He is affiliated with the American Economic Association, the Allied Social Science Association, and the Atlantic Economic Association. Fr. Dowling has authored various books and articles in the field of economics.

CARLOS G. ELÍAS is Assistant Professor of Economics and Finance at Manhattan College. His previous positions include Assistant Professor at the University of Massachusetts-Dartmouth in 1989–90 and the Research Department of the Federal Reserve Bank of New York in the summer of 1988.

LOWELL S. FELD is an International Economist/Energy Analyst with the U.S. Energy Information Administration in Washington DC. He has contributed extensively to the writing, editing, and graphic presentation of the 1989–92 *International Energy Outlooks* in addition to authoring or coauthoring five articles published in *Geopolitics of Energy*.

JOHN C. GORMLEY is a Reference Librarian, assigned to the Engineering

Library at Manhattan College. Prior to his current position, he was an Assistant Branch Manager in the Queens Borough Public Library in New York.

FRANCIS G. HILTON is a researcher and analyst in the area of international oil markets. He has served as project manager for World Oil Trend and the Future Pacific Rim Oil Market. Currently, he is a research associate at Cambridge Energy Research Associates, in Cambridge, Massachusetts. He is the editor of the *New World of Natural Gas and Electric Power*, and a coauthor of *Oil in the 1980s: An OECD Perspective*. He has taught economics at Fordham University, Canisius College, and Boston College.

KUSUM W. KETKAR is Associate Professor in the Department of Economics at Seton Hall University. She has worked for the 1990 Oil Production Act Staff and the U.S. Department of Transportation. She currently is a consultant for the United Nations Development Program and the U.S. Coast Guard. She has written extensively for numerous publications, papers, and book reviews.

FRANK W. MILLERD is Associate Professor and Chairperson of the Department of Economics at Wilfrid Laurier University, where he has taught various courses in the field. His work has been published widely in various academic journals. He completed the research for his chapters in this book while he was a visiting professor at the Centre for the Economics and Management of Aquatic Resources, University of Portsmouth, United Kingdom.

CAROLYN E. PREDMORE is an Assistant Professor of Marketing at Manhattan College. Her research work, funded by a Capalbo grant, has been published in *The Journal of Personal Selling and Sales Management.*

DOMINICK SALVATORE is professor of Economics and Director of Graduate Studies in Economics at Fordham University. He is the author of numerous articles published in international journals as well as the author of many internationally recognized economics textbooks. He is also a consultant to the United Nations.

MASSOOD V. SAMII has served as Associate Professor of International Business and Policy with the Graduate School of New Hampshire College since 1988, where he is also coordinator of the International Business Program. Prior to joining New Hampshire College, Dr. Samii was with the Energy Environment Center of Harvard University. He served the OPEC secretariat in Vienna for eight years as Senior Economist and head of the Finance Section. He is the author of numerous publications in the area of international oil markets.

SALAH EL SERAFY has been an economist with the World Bank in Washington, DC for 20 years. Previously he had been Project Director, The Economist

Intelligence Unit, London; Research Fellow in economics, Harvard University; postdoctoral Fulbright Scholar; United Nations economic advisor to the Kingdom of Libya; and Associate Professor of Economics, Alexandria University. He has written extensively on the subject of environmental accounting.

CLIVE L. SPASH teaches environmental economics in the Economics Department and is Assistant Director of the Environmental Economics Research Group at Stirling University. He is coauthor, with N. Hanley, of *Cost-Benefit Analysis and the Environment* (1993), and coordinator of the Scottish Environmental Economics Discussion Group. He has published widely in academic journals, including *Energy Policy*, *Journal of Environmental Management*, and *Ecological Economics*.

MICHAEL A. TOMAN is a Senior Fellow of the Energy and Natural Resources Division, Resources for the Future. Dr. Toman is also a Professional Lecturer at Johns Hopkins School of Advanced International Studies and serves as a consultant for the U.S. Department of Justice, INF Inc., Energy Information Administration, MathTech Inc., and the National Aeronautical and Space Administration, as well as a reviewer for various publications. Dr. Toman is the author of refereed journal articles, books, and edited volumes.

ASBJORN TORVANGER is a Senior Research Fellow at the Center for International Climate and Energy Research in Oslo, Norway, where he is working on climate policy related to intergenerational efficiency and equity in energy use. His work has been published in UNESCO Yearbook, and *Energy Economics*, among others.

WALLACE E. TYNER is Professor and Head of the Department of Agriculture Economics at Purdue University. He serves as consultant for various governmental agencies, private corporations, and universities, including the U.S. Department of Energy, U.S. Agency for International Development, U.S. Department of the Interior, International Baltic Economic Commission, and the World Bank. Dr. Tyner has published an abundance of books, book chapters, journal articles, station bulletins, research bulletins, and research abstracts.

DAVID L. WEIMER is Professor of Policy Analysis at the University of Rochester and serves on the editorial board of the *Journal of Political Analysis and Management*. Dr. Weimer served on the Policy Council of the Association for Policy Analysis and Management and was a member of the Committee on State and Federal Roles in Energy Emergency Preparedness for the National Research Council. He has published many books, articles, book chapters, and book reviews on the subject of public policy.

HARRY E. WELSH is the Director of Libraries, Manhattan College. From 1979 to 1983 he was Library Director, South Dakota School of Mines and Technology, and from 1975 to 1979 served as Head of Government Publications Center, University of Washington Libraries. He is an editorial advisor to the *Digests of Environmental Impact Statements*.

ANDREW YOUNG is a research fellow of the Environmental Economics Research Group at Stirling University. He has specialized in the study of interactions between economic systems and environmental studies. His recent research has included the viability of inshore wave power in Scotland and externalities related to nonconventional energy sources.

ISBN 0-275-94583-9

90000>

EAN

9 780275 945831

HARDCOVER BAR CODE